DAYS THAT SHOOK
THE WORLD

DAYS THAT SHOOK THE WORLD

BRIDGES ACROSS TIME:
DAYS THAT SHAPED OUR DESTINY

 BBC

Hugo Davenport

HYLAS
PUBLISHING

Hylas Publishing
Publisher: Sean Moore
Creative Director: Karen Prince

This book is published to accompany the television series *Days that Shook the World*
produced by Lion Television and first broadcast on BBC2 in 2003.
Executive Producer: Richard Bradley

First American Edition published in 2003
02 03 04 05 10 9 8 7 6 5 4 3 2 1

ISBN: 1-592558-050-5

Published by BBC Worldwide Ltd, Woodlands,
80 Wood Lane, London W12 0TT

Designers: Paul Vater and Grade Design
Set in Foundry Sans by BBC Worldwide Ltd

This book was produced for BBC Worldwide by designsection, Frome, Somerset
Project Editor: Emma Clegg
Designer: Carole McDonald

Printed and bound in Great Britain by Butler and Tanner Limited, Frome and London
Colour separations by Radstock Reproductions Limited, Midsomer Norton, Somerset

Distributed by St. Martin's Press

CONTENTS

FOREWORD
by Richard Bradley

Above: Firefighters at the World Trade Center, 2001
Below: Apollo 11 astronauts during a parade, 1969

On 11 September 2001 millions upon millions of us throughout the world crowded around our television screens to watch the chilling sight of the Twin Towers collapsing in flames in New York. As the horror unfolded, we all knew we were witnessing a day of immense historical magnitude. One of those days that would be etched into the individual memory, one of those rare events that would define a generation and prompt the question 'Where were you when you heard the news?'

Every generation has its own such days: the sinking of the *Titanic*; the Wall Street Crash; Pearl Harbour; Hiroshima; 'Freedom at Midnight' for India and Pakistan; the launch of Sputnik, the world's first artificial satellite; the assassination of JFK; or the Apollo 11 moon landings. History distils these days – some become turning points, some shock or amaze for a while but change little. Then there are other kinds of historic days: those that mark the culmination of years of process and those, often relating to scientific and technological breakthroughs, that pass almost unnoticed at the time but come to be seen as utterly transforming.

Days that Shook the World grew out of a simple idea – to rescue pivotal moments from the history books. To reinvest them with the power and drama with which they occurred. To peel back the years of retrospective analysis and immerse ourselves in the drama and tension of events as they unfolded minute by minute, hour by hour. To recreate these days in the present tense in which flesh-and-blood individuals got up, had their breakfast, then took courses of action, accomplished deeds and achieved breakthroughs that would become historic events.

It is powerful and revealing to do this, because once written down or recorded in photographs and archive film, it becomes hard to believe events could have happened any other way. By immersing yourself in first-hand accounts, diaries and recollections you realize just how differently things could have turned out.

Had Archduke Ferdinand's driver had not taken a wrong turn in the streets of Sarajevo, his assassin would not have had the opportunity to shoot him and trigger the events that led to World War I. Had the NASA guidance officer, Steve Bayles, reacted differently to a last-minute computer alarm from the lunar module, Neil Armstrong would not have been the first man to walk on the moon. Had a lifeboatman not been passing, there would have been no photographic proof of the Wright brothers' first powered flight at Kitty Hawk. Had there been clouds over

Hiroshima on the morning of 6 August 1945, the name of a different city would be forever synonymous with nuclear obliteration.

So much of our fascination with history is in the details. It is these details that humanize and make distant events seem immediate. Afrikaans prison officer James Gregory cried as he released Nelson Mandela, who had become his friend over 20 years in prison. Mandela left his reading glasses on his release and had to borrow Winnie's to read his first public speech for 30 years. Martin Luther King had remained safely in his motel room all day, but was shot on his balcony at 6 p.m. when he and his friends decided to grab some dinner. It was a 26-year-old bombardier, Thomas Ferebee, whose dream was to play baseball for the Boston Red Socks, who released the bomb on Hiroshima that killed more than 100,000 people.

Although it offers context, this book makes no attempt to be definitive. History is shot through with momentous days – and most events have a different historic importance depending on where in the world we are born. But there are days that have reverberated around much of the world – and to look at those in detail is, we hope, a fresh and exciting way to revisit the past.

We chose to pair up two days in history by each chapter's theme, not because we want to make glib or spurious links of cause and effect, but because it adds a richness to the story of one historic day to think about its links to another. Some of these days are linked tangibly – Jesse Jackson handled the press in the emotional aftermath of Martin Luther King's assassination in 1968, and was in South Africa to greet Nelson Mandela on his release from prison. Others have thematic links: the bloody execution of the Romanovs ushered in the era of Soviet communism and the events around Checkpoint Charlie at the Berlin Wall in 1989 heralded its collapse. A single bullet killed Archduke Ferdinand to help precipitate World War I and it was a bullet with which Hitler killed himself in his bunker that brought World War II to a close. We hope that in interesting ways these days 'speak to each other' across time.

In a period of unpredictability and international conflict, this book is a reminder, if one were needed, that what becomes history was once the unfolding reality of a group of human beings. It is clear that with the imperative of an ever-present global media – television and live 24-hour news, the internet, satellite transmission – more and more events will reverberate around the world. For better or worse, there will be many more 'Days that Shook the World'.

**Above: East Germans tearing down the Berlin Wall, 1989
Below: Marchers cheering King's 'Dream' speech, 1963**

The shifting fortunes of British monarchs through the centuries have veered from triumphant affirmation to dynastic despair. In the twentieth century the coronation of Elizabeth II and the funeral of Diana, Princess of Wales, were two days when the British public's attention was irresistibly captured.

[1042] : [2003]

THE BRITISH MONARCHY: CRISIS AND SURVIVAL

At 2 p.m. on 30 January 1649, Charles I stepped on to the black-draped scaffold to face his executioner. The scene was in Whitehall outside the Banqueting House, a grand stone building commissioned by Charles's father, James I, where extravagant royal masques had been mounted by Inigo Jones and Ben Jonson to illustrate Stuart notions of the duties, powers and privileges of kingship.

Now, in the bleak depths of winter, this stage of past royal revelries was to be the backdrop for a far more traumatic occasion. Ancient beliefs in the king's inviolability were about to be tested by the keen edge of the executioner's axe.

It was, says one account, a cold, dark day, 'melancholy and dismal beyond any that England had ever beheld'. Among the waiting crowd there were already signs of grief and distress. Even

after the bloody civil wars of Charles's reign, which had shattered the peace of England from 1642, setting father against son and brother against brother, the beheading of a king was an event that, to many, seemed an unnatural violation of the revered tradition of monarchy and a threat to all forms of settled order.

Around the execution block had been arranged a selection of 'hooks and staples' that would be used to drag the king to

The history of the monarchy

1066–87
William I takes the English throne after defeating the Anglo-Saxons at the Battle of Hastings. He establishes the feudal system with large gifts of land to his barons.

1199–1216
King John is in constant need of money to refill the treasury; in 1215 he is forced to concede some power by the barons, signing the Magna Carta at Runnymede.

1272–1307
Edward I is astute in his early reforms of English law, but his battles to subdue the Welsh and Scots, led by William Wallace, leave a legacy of bitterness.

his knees should he show any signs of resistance, but Charles gave no sign of wishing to sacrifice his dignity on such futile gestures. The *ars moriendi*, or the art of dying well, was then still seen as a key test of character, and Charles did not regard himself as in any sense an ordinary man. He was, after all, a king. Dressed in two undershirts to stop him shivering and thus seeming fearful of his fate, he inquired of the masked

Above left: With orb and crown resting at the foot of a pillar, Charles I is the proud icon of sovereignty.

Above right: An illustration of Charles I's execution in 1649 ... and a far cry from the dignified monarchical figure shown to the left.

1483–5
Richard III is blamed for the murder of the Princes in the Tower and finishes up as the last ruler in the House of York. As 'Crookback Dick', he makes a great Shakespearean villain.

1509–47
Henry VIII's quest for an heir leads to six marriages, the beheading of two wives and two divorces, as well as a decisive schism with the Church of Rome.

1558–1603
Elizabeth I survives early dangers at court to lead England to victory against the Armada: fear of Catholic plots persuades her to sanction the execution of Mary, Queen of Scots.

axeman, 'Is my hair well?': a flicker of all-too-human vanity, perhaps? Or, just as likely, a deep desire to meet his death looking like a king to the last.

Then he stripped off his cloak, handed over his Order of St George to the attendant bishop with just a single word, 'Remember', and removed his doublet. He glanced at the block and told the executioner, 'You must set it fast', adding: 'when I put out my hands, then.' As the executioner tucked his hair into his cap, the king mistook the gesture and asked the man to wait for his signal. 'Yes, I will and it please your Majesty,' the axeman replied. At last the king stretched out his hands and the executioner swung the axe, severing Charles's head at a single blow.

According to Laurence Echard's *The History of England*, Archbishop Usher fell down in a dead faint at the window from where he was watching. And despite cheers from some soldiers who had pressed the case against the king to the very end, a deep groan rose from the crowd as the king's head was held aloft. An explosion of protest burst forth from leading royalists and Presbyterian ministers soon after. The shock and indignation were widely shared among the people, too. 'As the Rumour of his Death spread throughout the Kingdom,' Echard wrote later, 'women miscarry'd, many of both Sexes fell into Palpitations, Swoonings and Melancholy and some, with sudden Consternations, expired.' One member of the Rump Parliament that had condemned the king, Thomas Hoyle, killed himself on the first anniversary of Charles's death, while the death in the same year of a second member, Rowland Wilson, was widely attributed to guilt-induced melancholia.

How had it come to this? Was Charles I truly the wronged monarch portrayed by writers such as David Hume or Lord Clarendon, who in the early nineteenth century described the king's decapitation as 'the most execrable murder that was ever committed since that of our blessed Saviour', extolling Charles as 'the worthiest gentleman, the best master, the best friend, the best husband, the best father, and the best Christian, that the age in which he lived produced'? Or was he the 'wicked king' portrayed by the poet John Milton in his *Tracts on Regicide*, of the type whom it had always been lawful to depose and put to death if magistrates had neglected or refused to do so?

The fate of Charles I may have been a profound shock to the nation, but in one simple respect it was true to form. When he lost his head, kingship had for centuries been a high-risk occupation. There may even be a distant echo of the pagan goddess-worship that once held sway in the British Isles, long before Christianity, in the old belief that the British nation invariably prospers under a queen. Elizabeth I (1533–1603) and Victoria (1819–1901) are the obvious examples; there are others. Under the ancient fertility cults, in contrast, a king's fate was to be tied to a tree and ritually killed after a year, his blood trickling into the soil as a sacrifice to feed the land. A new king would always be waiting in the wings to take his place, enjoying a life of ease and privilege until his turn came.

According to the traditional view, British history really gets going with William the Conqueror and the Norman invasion of 1066 – in other words, with an act of political violence. William's barons were of Viking stock, long settled in northern France, and they still had the Viking love of conquest. As the Normans drove their

The history of the monarchy

1625–49
A firm believer in the divine right of kings, the second Stuart monarch, Charles I, falls out with Parliament and pitches the country into a long Civil War ending in his own execution.

1689–1702
William III is invited, with Mary II, James II's daughter, to take the throne at the close of the Stuart era. He introduces a Declaration of Rights and defeats the Catholics in Ireland.

1760–1820
George III is a kindly soul, known as 'Mad George' because of attacks of severe mental illness, which worsen as he grows older. Britain loses its American Colonies in his reign.

sweating chargers up the slopes of Senlac Hill shouting their battle cries to engage the army of King Harold at the top, it would have been easy for a time-traveller to dismiss the scene as primitive, for all its heraldic gleam of clashing steel and flying arrows.

Yet the Battle of Hastings followed decades of complex dynastic shuttling. It had started with the Danish ancestors of both sides, who from the fifth to the eleventh century continually invaded England and settled there. In 911 a band of them crossed the English Channel to take root in the Seine Valley on land donated by Charles III of France (879–929), where their old designation as 'Northmen' was changed by French tongues to 'Normands'. These 'Norman' settlers prospered, intermarried with the French, and acquired land and property along with a new set of social customs.

A century later, the English king, Ethelred II (968–1016), was driven out by another Danish invasion, this time led by Sweyn Forkbeard, and took refuge in Normandy. Some years before, Ethelred had married Emma, sister of a Norman duke, in the vain hope of strengthening his hand against Danish aggression. By the time Ethelred died in 1016, the thrones of England and Denmark were occupied by Cnut, or Canute (995–1035), son of Forkbeard. Cnut proceeded to marry Ethelred's widow in order to cement the union of Danish and Anglo-Saxon lines. But the English crown passed to Emma's son by her first husband, Edward the Confessor (1003–66), who took the throne in 1042.

Edward reasserted the power of the Anglo-Saxon dynasty. Having grown up in Normandy, he also tried to impose the French language and customs on the English court, in the process cultivating his French favourites at the expense of Anglo-Saxon

King Cnut, or Canute, was credited with a legendary royal realism when he showed that the waves would not obey him – a disclaimer of regal divinity.

A thirteenth-century manuscript illumination depicting the burial of Edward the Confessor in his tomb at Westminster in 1066.

claimants – to the disgust of many, including his English father-in-law, Earl Godwin. When Edward died without issue, Duke William of Normandy (1027–87) proclaimed that he had been named Edward's heir some years earlier. But Harold Godwinson (1022–66), Earl Godwin's son, also staked a claim, insisting that Edward's dying words had vouchsafed the throne to him. Their quarrel was put to the Witan, a council of nobles and prelates required to choose a successor if a king died childless. The Witan chose Harold.

And so, long before their regal contest broke out into open war near Hastings, and Harold was felled by an arrow in one eye, the English throne had been the coveted prize in an intricate dance of dynastic rivalry originating at least 150 years before. The spot where Harold fell is still marked by a brass plaque. In many ways

Indeed, until the eighteenth century one of the most striking characteristics of the British monarchy was its instability. While the institution itself endured, the cast of characters vying for its power and privilege was ever-changing, and as often as not the ruling incumbents were under constant threat from forces at home and abroad.

A glance through the chronicle tends to bear this out. Duke William, offspring of a Norman duke nicknamed 'Devil', revealed an early instinct for royal PR by arranging his coronation on Christmas Day. He established the feudal system, earned loyalty through large gifts of land and commissioned the Domesday Book. In time, though, he was challenged by his eldest son, Robert Curthose, so called because of his short legs, who wounded his father in the hand when they fought after William had refused to let Robert rule in Normandy. William died in France, five weeks after rupturing his intestines on the pommel of his saddle. A fire broke out at his funeral, and when the pallbearers tried to force the king's swollen corpse into an undersized sarcophagus, the body burst open, emitting an abominable stench that emptied the church.

The throne passed to William's preferred younger son, William Rufus (1056–1100), who spent much time hacking about in Normandy until his death from a hunting accident in the New Forest. William II was succeeded by Henry I (1068–1135), younger son of William I and Matilda, who consolidated his position by marrying another Matilda, daughter of Malcolm, King of Scotland, but had to defend his kingdom against the still-rancorous ambition of his elder brother Robert. Henry's son William was drowned, while Henry himself died at Angers, Normandy, reputedly from eating a bad moray eel. The last of the Normans was Stephen (1097–1154), son of the Count of Blois and William I's daughter Adela. He won early popularity by handing out privileges, but had a talent for making enemies, notably David of Scotland, who invaded the North on behalf of his niece Matilda, daughter of Henry I. When his son Eustace died, Stephen accepted Matilda's eldest son, Henry Plantagenet (1133–89), as heir.

So began another dynasty. In 1154 Henry II embarked on his reign firmly, scrapping the self-serving favours granted by his predecessor, booting mercenaries out of the kingdom and

this early theme of power-struggle – the ceaseless manoeuvring, marital and martial, across international borders, tangled by plots and competing claims to legitimacy – is the key to much of the bloodshed that colours the history of Britain's monarchy.

The cultivated image of the monarchy as a pillar of stability, cautiously adjusting by small increments to changes in the society around it, is not at all true to its older historical antecedents.

founding the jury system, though he came to blows with the barons and his own sons. Richard I (1157–99) was a high-minded but feckless absentee, who spent a king's ransom on the Third Crusade and, indeed, literally required one when waylaid on the way home by Leopold I of Austria. His foreign travails left an opening for his cunning younger brother, John (1167–1216), who did a deal with Richard's arch-enemy, Philip of France, imposed heavy taxes on the English people and was excommunicated by the Pope after disputing the appointment of the Archbishop of Canterbury. He signed the Magna Carta at Runnymede under duress in 1215 and then did his best to renege on its terms.

Enter Henry III (1207–72). Having come to the throne aged nine, in the midst of a French rebellion, he did not take power until 16 years later. His reign was beset by troubles with clergy and barons, papal dues and the 'Mad Parliament' of 1258, which objected to the king's reliance on foreigners. Despite his acceptance of a part-elected baronial council in government, war followed. Henry was captured by Simon de Montfort, later killed in battle by Henry's son, the Black Prince. Though devout and temperate, Henry III was marked down by history as weak-willed.

Not so his successor, Edward I, dubbed the 'Hammer of the Scots' (1239–1307). After devoting the early part of his reign to some shrewd legal and administrative reforms, the forceful 'Longshanks' lost no time in stamping out rebellion in Wales, placing the country under English jurisdiction and inaugurating the title of Prince of Wales for his son, which has endured to this day. When the Scots invited him in to resolve a haggle over their throne by 13 claimants, Edward then proclaimed himself ruler and became embroiled in a lengthy struggle with a young nobleman, Sir William Wallace, whom Edward had hanged, disembowelled, beheaded and quartered in 1305.

Richard I, known as Richard the Lionheart for his bravery, leads Crusaders into battle against the Muslims at Arsuf.

Edward's ruthlessness left a lasting legacy of Scottish bitterness; he himself died on campaign in 1307.

Next up was Edward II (1284–1327), who suffered a shocking death by red-hot poker in the Tower of London in 1327 after alienating just about everyone, not least because of his infamous favourite, the petulant Piers Gaveston. Edward III (1312–77) spent much of his reign away fighting in Scotland or in France where, despite resounding victories at Crécy and Poitiers, he lost almost all of England's Norman lands. The last of the line was Richard II (1367–1400), who forfeited the throne when he unwisely seized the estates of John of Gaunt, Duke of Lancaster, and was deposed by the Duke's heir, Henry Bolingbroke (1356–1413), in 1399.

Hence the next dynastic chapter, the House of Lancaster. Bolingbroke was crowned Henry IV in 1399 on Richard's abdication. He defeated the Welsh rebellion of Owen Glendower and saw Parliament inch forward, gaining the right to disburse funds, and was succeeded by the dashing Henry V (1387–1422), who won glory at Agincourt, became French regent and set about anglicizing Normandy in the face of stiff French opposition. Henry was succeeded in turn by his infant son, Henry VI (1421–71). Power then passed to the Privy Council under parliamentary supervision until the king came of age, during which time England once more let slip virtually all its Norman holdings.

In 1453, when the king went mad, Richard, Duke of York, later Richard III (1452–85), became his Protector. But when Henry recovered York was shut out, setting the scene for the Battle of St Albans – the first engagement of the Wars of the Roses. Henry had an eventful time of it: imprisoned after a battle at Northampton and released following another at St Albans, by which time the Duke of York's son had been proclaimed king as Edward IV (1442–83), Henry then fled to Scotland, was locked up in the Tower of London, restored to the throne and, finally, returned to the Tower, where he was murdered in 1471. It was there, too, that Edward V (1470–83), the young Yorkist successor to Edward IV, met his end along with his brother – on the orders of Richard III, though his guilt was never proved.

The story of the Princes in the Tower and 'Crookback Dick' made Richard the classic stage-villain of British history. When he was trounced at the Battle of Bosworth Field in 1485 by Henry Tudor, it was the end both of the Wars of the Roses and of his

short-lived dynastic ambitions. Henry VII (1457–1509), though he was a descendant of John of Gaunt and the Lancastrians, founded a new dynasty. An astute, balanced and politically effective ruler, he dealt firmly with the divisive clamour of Yorkist pretenders, married Edward IV's daughter Elizabeth in a bid to reconcile the warring houses and gave Parliament its measure of power while keeping the nobles at bay through judicial proceedings in the Star Chamber.

His heir was an entirely different matter. Henry VIII (1491–1547) remains among the most notorious of English monarchs. His relentless desire for a male heir led him not only to marry six wives, divorcing two and beheading two more, but to break with Rome and trigger the English Protestant Reformation. Henry appointed himself head of the English Church by the Act of Supremacy in 1534; the Dissolution of the Monasteries followed two years later. Meanwhile, the international situation grew steadily more complex as England wove in and out of alliances, first opposing France along with Spain, Venice, the Pope and the Holy Roman Empire, then sealing an unpopular alliance with it, and, later, switching back to conflict. Two wars were fought with Scotland. Henry died in 1547, elephantine from sickness and consumed by paranoia.

The reign of Elizabeth I (1558–1603), though proudly invoked as a high point of English history, was also riven with anti-Papist paranoia. Plots and counterplots proliferated, with Spain taking a leading role in the anti-English intrigues, culminating in the defeat of the Armada in 1588. A steady procession of Catholics went to the scaffold through the long reign of the queen who came to be known as Gloriana. Plotters, real or imagined, suffered agonizing deaths, enduring torture by rack and red-hot iron as well as hanging, disembowelment

and public castration. Elizabeth's most prominent victim was Mary, Queen of Scots, entrapped by another plot. Yet Elizabeth was a skilful ruler, who had learnt to withstand danger in her youth and kept a cool head to the very end.

The Stuarts came to power with clear ideas about the monarchy. In a speech to Parliament, James I (1566–1625) set forth his ideas in terms that left no doubt as to his view of the future role and powers of the assembly: 'The state of monarchy is the supremest thing upon earth,' the king declared, '... God has power to create, or destroy, make, or unmake at his pleasure, to give life, or send death, to judge all, and to be judged nor accountable to none: to raise low things, and to

rights of a few powerful families against regal rapacity, but it became an important weapon in the intellectual armoury of those opposed to Stuart high-handedness.

Charles I (1600–49) was of one mind with his father in his view of the rightful powers of the king, and his relationship with Parliament was fractious and quarrelsome from the first. Between 1625, when he became king, and January 1629, Charles dissolved Parliament no less than four times. The rival factions argued over war and taxes, over Charles's predilection for aristocratic advice over parliamentary counsel, over his refusal to acknowledge the legitimate powers of the House. Then, for 11 years, Charles ruled without a Parliament, recalling it in 1640 only because he was broke.

On their return members insisted that Parliament must meet every three years, irrespective of the king. In the November of the following year, their grievances reached fever-pitch, leading to the 'Grand Remonstrance'. This rumbling catalogue of complaint was passed by the slenderest majority, occasioning such outrage that, in November 1641, swords were drawn in the House for the first time. And with that the country was well on the road to civil war. Running in two phases from 1642 to 1651, the English Civil War was a cruel, destructive conflict that claimed the lives of more than 200,000 people, from a total population of around 4.5 million. By the end of it, the king was dead.

From this crucible of violent disorder and social strife emerged a country polarized as never before. The Commonwealth and Oliver Cromwell's Protectorate, lasting just over ten years, did not heal the scars. When it collapsed in 1660, a Stuart monarch again became king. Charles II (1630–85) had his revenge against those who had condemned his father, while his indulgence towards Catholics sparked off a war with Holland but garnered financial support from France. James II (1633–1701) followed with a Catholic Declaration of Indulgence; then the birth of his son, raising the prospect of a Catholic heir, tipped the balance. William of Orange (1650–1702), who had married James's daughter Mary (1662–94), was invited to take the throne and landed with an army. James fled to France and William defeated his army in Ireland in 1690.

After this 'Glorious Revolution,' Parliament enacted laws to ensure linear succession and since then the English throne has been, in many respects, a much quieter place. Not that the

make high things low at his pleasure, and to God are both soul and body due. And the like power have Kings ... judges over all their subjects, and in all causes, and yet accountable to none but God only.'

In England in the first decade of the seventeenth century, this ringing resumption of the mantle of God's Anointed struck many as an unconscionable, even outrageous attempt to reassert absolute power on behalf of the Crown. And it was dumped straight into parliamentary laps almost four centuries after King John had been forced to concede a share of his earthly dominion to the barons by signing the Magna Carta at Runnymede. True, that ancient charter had done little more in 1215 than protect the

After being welcomed by cheers, the Duke and Duchess of Windsor, surrounded by soldiers and sailors, seat themselves at the 'Angel's Table' at the Stage Door Canteen in New York in 1943.

ensuing years were uneventful – from the Battle of the Boyne to the French Revolution, the Napoleonic Wars and the loss of the American Colonies, there was plenty to exercise the minds of reigning monarchs. The Hanoverians placed a growing reliance on their diplomats and politicians, while the ensuing Victorian era – an age of industry and empire – brought a long period of settled continuity.

Just how far the monarchy's star had fallen from its once-elevated course by the twentieth century can be seen in the story of Edward VIII's abdication. Edward (1894–1972) is the only monarch in English history to have abdicated voluntarily, and the issue was treated with the highest seriousness at the time.

It was, in a very real sense, a constitutional crisis. Yet the details of how and why he came to give up the throne have a kind of domestic banality alien to the high passions of the Stuart era. Charles literally lost his head, but Edward elected, in a symbolic sense, to fall on his own sword.

The cause of the abdication crisis was the king's desire to marry the American-born Wallis Warfield Simpson (1896–1986), whom he had met at a house party in January 1931 and who, by 1936, was in the throes of divorcing her second husband. The relationship flourished over the next five years. Mrs Simpson joined the future king for a holiday in Biarritz in the summer of 1934; later that year she attended a reception at

Buckingham Palace. Edward introduced his future bride to his mother, but his father, George V (1865–1936), refused to permit her to be presented – an early sign of trouble to come.

Baldwin, who served as Tory prime minister three times, was an upright Methodist. He had no inkling of the significance of Mrs Simpson's presence at their first meeting in May 1936. By August, when photographs of the king and Mrs Simpson on holiday together in the Aegean were splashed all over American and European newspapers, the truth was becoming clearer. Wallis moved into a house at Regent's Park rented for her by the king and on 27 October she was granted a *decree nisi*. Three weeks later Edward summoned Baldwin to inform him of his desire to marry her.

Baldwin immediately pointed out that if the king were to take this unprecedented marital step, Mrs Simpson would have to become Queen, and he was convinced that the British public could not accept this. Edward responded by raising the possibility of abdication. Nine days later the king came back to Baldwin with a compromise, proposing instead a 'morganatic' marriage that would make Mrs Simpson his consort rather than his Queen. But the idea was rejected out of hand by the Cabinet two days later. Then, on 2 December, Baldwin bluntly informed the king that he had three choices: break with Mrs Simpson; go ahead and marry her, in which case his government would resign; or abdicate.

Hushed up until then, the story hit the press the next day like a tidal wave. After a further week of agonizing, Edward made his choice. The Prime Minister came solemnly to the Bar of the House of Commons to read the king's statement, which began: 'After long and anxious consideration, I have determined to renounce the throne to which I succeeded on the death of my father ...' The text asked for understanding from his people, adding, with a touch of self-pity: '... the burden that sits on the shoulders of a sovereign is so heavy that it can only be borne in circumstances other than those in which I now find myself.' On 11 December Edward relayed his decision in person via the BBC, his reedy voice quavering out its message of resignation. Many sat rigid with shock, frozen like statues at their wireless sets.

The former king went on to marry Mrs Simpson in France on 3 June 1937, and during the rest of his life returned to England only twice. After the abdication the couple had to endure what

INSTRUMENT OF ABDICATION

I, Edward the Eighth, of Great Britain, Ireland, and the British Dominions beyond the Seas, King, Emperor of India, do hereby declare My irrevocable determination to renounce the Throne for Myself and for My descendants, and My desire that effect should be given to this Instrument of Abdication immediately.

In token whereof I have hereunto set My hand this tenth day of December, nineteen hundred and thirty six, in the presence of the witnesses whose signatures are subscribed.

SIGNED AT
FORT BELVEDERE
IN THE PRESENCE
OF

Edward RI

Albert

Henry.

George.

might in today's more informal climate seem the relatively minor smart of forfeiting the title of 'Royal Highness'. To Edward, though, this was a grievous affront to his wife that rankled until the day he died. They lived a footloose life of voluntary exile in Europe and the USA, enjoying the leisured pursuits of high society – yachts, golf, cocktail parties. Their exclusion from official circles and the petty snubs of the English might have stung, but they were hardly fatal.

There was a kind of inescapable futility in their gilded existence. Edward's much-quoted observation on America gives a hint of this. 'I like going there for golf,' he declared. 'America's one vast golf course these days'. More damaging to both of them in the 1930s and 1940s were the rumours that Mrs Simpson was a German sympathizer who might have passed over state secrets. Having taken the titles of Duke and Duchess of Windsor, the couple did not help matters, amid the rising international tension of the thirties, by paying a friendly visit to Hitler in 1937.

Yet the great irony of Edward VIII's life was that he had started out, as Prince of Wales, on a wave of popularity and public esteem. Though his childhood was marked by a lack of overt affection from both parents, he emerged from it a confident and popular young man. Unlike his diffident younger brother, the future George VI (1895–1952), who was afflicted with a stammer, Edward seemed to have charm and *savoir faire*. He also showed at least some awareness of the economic realities of Britain in the 1930s, remarking on a visit to South Wales in late 1936, 'These steelworks brought these men here. Something must be done to see that they stay here – working.'

By today's touchy-feely scheme of values, Edward's decision to put personal happiness before royal duty might seem understandable, even laudable. Yet he was on the throne only for 325 days, and lived on afterwards to the ripe old age of 79. Whatever sadness came to Edward was the sadness of a life lived out in a minor key; a life shaped to the burdens of state, which somehow finished up as a kind of extended holiday.

It might even be argued that the painful but inescapably comic spectacle of monarchy as soap opera – an unavoidable feature of the later years of the twentieth century – can be tracked back to Edward's abdication and its aftermath. For the Windsor drama of the 1980s and 1990s with Diana, Princess of Wales (1961–1997), at centre stage was not just the creation of

an intrusive popular press. It became a multimedia production, with which parts of the Royal Family were in active collusion. Did they toil? In their fashion, yes. But there was no doubt about the spinning. They were all at it, including the Queen.

True, Elizabeth II (b. 1926) has been disciplined, dedicated and dutiful in her efforts to promote the continuing value of the institution, making it more accessible and less costly to the public purse and bringing foreign exchange into the country through the proven tourist draw of royal pageantry. Constitutionalists argue that she has 'saved' Britain from a presidency. Yet some of her descendants still trail a whiff of Edward's faint but unmistakable air of futility. And the question they will have to face, now and later, is this: in the twenty-first century, what is a monarchy actually *for*?

Above: The Duke and Duchess of Windsor visit Hitler in Germany in 1937.

Left: Edward VIII's abdication document, signed in 1936.

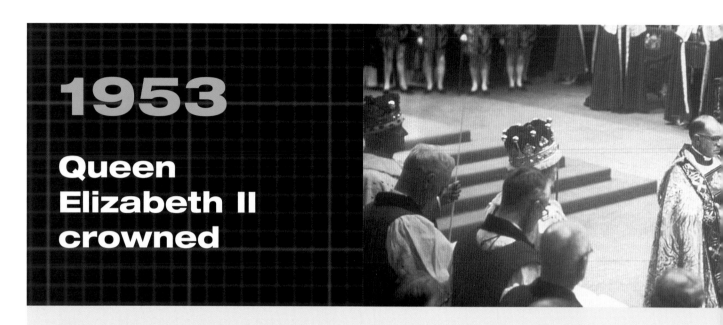

1953

Queen Elizabeth II crowned

2 June 1953. More than a year after her accession to the throne on the death of George VI, Elizabeth II prepares to take on the historic duties of the British monarch. At 27 she has two small children, Charles and Anne; when she herself was only ten, she lived through the crisis of Edward VIII's abdication. This day is not just about reaffirming an ancient institution; it is about lending renewed stability and continuity to the royal dynasty.

10:30 The Queen sets forth from Buckingham Palace alongside the Duke of Edinburgh in the golden State Coach, pulled by eight Windsor greys. They are last in an impressive procession of horse-drawn vehicles, creating a glorious spectacle for the crowds lining the route, many of whom have been waiting all night. It is estimated that three million people have turned out to witness the coronation.

Despite sunny forecasts, the weather is wet, but the mood of the crowd cannot be dampened, especially after the fortuitous announcement this very morning that Edmund Hillary, the New Zealand-born mountaineer, reached the 8,800 m (29,000 foot) summit of Everest with Tenzing Norgay in a British expedition just four days earlier. The State Coach pulls up outside Westminster Abbey to cheers, and the Queen alights. Upon her head, a diadem; under her ermine-trimmed robe of crimson velvet bordered with gold, a white satin gown threaded with gold and silver. The robe is strung with diamonds, crystal, opals and amethyst and embellished with floral motifs portraying the four national emblems: the Tudor rose, the Scottish thistle, the Welsh leek and the Irish shamrock. There is even a four-leafed clover, which the Queen can touch for luck with her left hand as she offers her right to loyal subjects or foreign dignitaries.

11:00 The Queen enters the Abbey and receives the greeting from the four corners of the building. It was here that William the Conqueror became the first monarch to be crowned within its walls some nine centuries earlier, on Christmas Day 1066. The Abbey is packed with more than 8,000 guests – royalty, prime ministers, presidents, Commonwealth leaders – all intent on the Queen's small,

solemn figure as she proceeds up the aisle. The Archbishop of Canterbury, Dr Geoffrey Fisher, asks if she will take the Oath; the Queen replies in a faint, youthful voice, 'I am willing.'

Divested of her robes, she stands in a simple linen shift. The archbishop anoints her with oil mixed to a formula devised under Charles I; then the golden robes of the Supertunica are wrapped about her and she takes her place on the seat of Edward I above the Stone of Scone. She receives the four symbols of authority – the Orb, Sceptre, Rod of Mercy and the Royal Ring of sapphire and rubies – and at last the Archbishop settles the heavy crown upon her head. A shout of 'God Save the Queen!' goes up as gun salutes boom out across the city, bells peal and crowds rejoice.

12:30 Once church leaders have paid homage, Prince Philip is next in line, then the peers of the realm. The Queen takes holy communion. Now it is time to leave the Abbey. On the route back the Queen carries Orb and Sceptre. Another queen, Queen Salote of Tonga, here as a guest, also wins the crowd's approval as she rides by smiling in an open landau through a very British downpour. In the afternoon there is a flypast and the Queen appears six times on the balcony to acknowledge her loyal people.

21:00 In a wireless broadcast the Queen tells the nation, 'Throughout all my life and with all my heart I shall strive to be worthy of your trust.' This is a day when television itself has been enthroned: in a British population of 36.5 million, it is estimated that more than 20 million have watched the ceremony live on television – almost double the radio audience – while many millions more have seen it abroad. In time it will be a power in countless lives. And it will not always be such a friend to monarchs as it was today.

Above left: Symbols of power: Queen Elizabeth II holds the Sceptre and Rod of Mercy as she sits on the Coronation Chair.

Above right: Historic pageantry: the Queen's golden State Coach dazzles the coronation crowds in June 1953.

1997

Diana dies in Paris smash

31 August 1997. Princess Diana is a media star, campaigner for good causes and mother of the future heir to the British throne. At 36 this beautiful woman has rebuilt her life after an acrimonious divorce from Prince Charles, which has seen both parties trying to sway public sympathy in the confessional of television. After a string of fleeting romances, she has fallen for Dodi Fayed, the son of the billionaire owner of Harrods.

21:45 **30 August.** Diana Spencer and Dodi Fayed arrive together at the luxurious Ritz-Carlton Hotel in Paris at the end of a ten-day trip to Europe. They have flown in from Sardinia to Le Bourget Airport in a Harrods Gulfstream private jet; their itinerary also included San Tropez and Monte Carlo. Anything that Diana does sets off fresh waves of media speculation: one theory is that during this trip Dodi went ashore in Monte Carlo to pick out an engagement ring for her. Self-appointed royal 'experts' insist the couple are deeply in love. Yet their bodyguard, Trevor Rees-Jones, who has accompanied them throughout the trip trying to keep photographers at bay, thinks they look subdued on arrival; he hears that Diana may have been crying as she entered the hotel. A good picture will sell for tens of thousands of pounds, and the Paris paparazzi are formidable.

As Diana and Dodi head off for dinner upstairs in the Imperial Suite, Rees-Jones and

another bodyguard, Alexander 'Kez' Wingfield, catch the opportunity to have a bath, a sandwich and a tonic water in the hotel. While they are relaxing they are joined by Henri Paul, acting head of security at the Ritz. According to Rees-Jones, Henri has something to drink – a 'yellow liquid' – but there is nothing to indicate that the drink is alcoholic or that Paul is in any way the worse for wear. Later reports allege significant amounts of alcohol in his bloodstream – equivalent to ten glasses of wine, according to one claim.

00:05 **31 August.** Dodi and Diana emerge behind the hotel, in a more cheerful mood than when they went in. They are going back to Dodi's apartment on the Champs-Elysées; Dodi has announced that they will leave in a single car, a black Mercedes 600, from the back with no back-up vehicle. The security men are not happy: they would prefer to leave by the front,

where the crowd is penned back and there are two cars. But Dodi is the boss, so with Paul at the wheel the Mercedes starts out from the back. Dodi does not bother with a seatbelt; neither do Diana nor Rees-Jones.

As soon as they are out on the road, paparazzi on motorbikes close in like pursuing wasps. Paul speeds up in an effort to shake them off, but they are persistent. The car increases speed again. As they enter an underpass beside the Pont de l'Alma, the heavy armoured Mercedes goes out of control, hits the concrete pillars on one side and overturns, flattening the roof. The speedometer is later reported found stuck at 193 km/h (120 miles per hour). Dodi is dead and so is Paul, but Diana is still alive. A photographer dismounts and hears Diana speak. He reaches in and takes her hand; an ambulance is called.

02:00 It takes two hours to cut the injured Princess free from the wreck. Doctors at Salpetrière Hospital fight for another two hours to save her from terrible chest wounds. But by 4 a.m. she is dead. The deaths stir up a viper's nest of conspiracy theories, including claims from Mohamed al Fayed, Dodi's father, that they were murdered by British intelligence. Questions are raised about a missing white Fiat Uno, thought to have collided with the Mercedes; about the crashing car's actual speed; about the true level of alcohol in Paul's bloodstream. But none of this alters a single, grievous fact: Diana's sons, William and Harry, have been left motherless at the ages of 15 and 12 respectively. Britain is swept by a tide of unrestrained grief and mourning.

Above left: Family grief: Princes William and Harry mourn their mother's death, flanked by Prince Charles and Diana's brother, Earl Spencer.

Above right: Like medieval pilgrims, countless mourners left flowers, cards, toys and pictures at Kensington Palace for Diana's funeral.

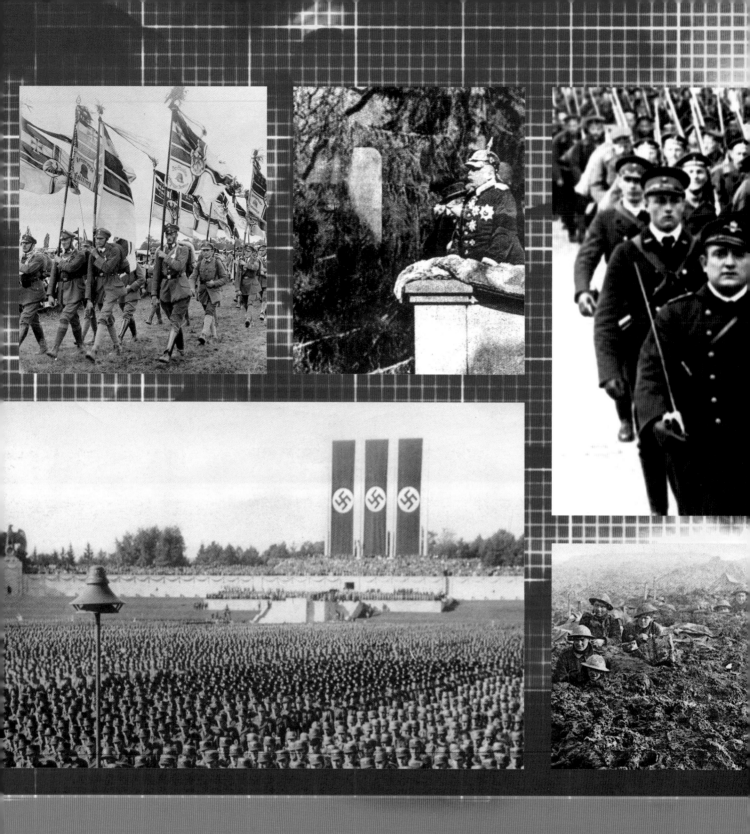

Tyrants and dictators invariably bring violence in the wake of their drive for power. World War I started in 1914 with the assassination of Archduke Ferdinand in Sarajevo; four decades later, at the end of World War II, after millions of lives lost on both sides, Adolf Hitler took his own life in a Berlin bunker.

[1914] : [1945]

TYRANTS AND DICTATORS

The shot that lit the fuse for World War I was fired in Sarajevo, capital of Bosnia Herzegovina, on the morning of 28 June 1914. The target was Archduke Franz Ferdinand (1863–1914), the Habsburg heir to the throne of the Austro-Hungarian Empire; the gunman was a Bosnian Serb named Gavrilo Princip, who belonged to a group called Mlada Bosna, or Young Bosnia.

Gavrilo Princip had been recruited to carry out the assassination, along with six other activists, by a Serb terrorist organization known as the Black Hand. This violent nationalist cell was secretly sponsored by Serbian military intelligence and controlled by its head, Colonel Dragutin Dimitrijevic (1877–1917).

Franz Ferdinand was riding through the provincial capital with his wife by open-topped car in the scorching heat of the Balkan summer when the attack came. The couple were on a tour of a more recent addition to the far-flung spread of Habsburg possessions – two provinces, situated just to the south of Austria, which until 1878 had been under the control of the Ottoman Empire. At that point Austria had wrested control of the region from the Turks under the Treaty of Berlin after Turkey's disastrous war with Russia, dashing hopes among the Bosnian Serbs for restored nationhood. Three decades later, in 1908, the region was annexed outright.

Behind this act of imperial consolidation, Austria's aims had been to undermine any Turkish hopes of reclaiming their former territory, to strengthen the boundaries of the imperial heartlands of Austria, and to reassert the pride and vigour of an empire that had long been mocked in other European capitals as 'the sick man of Europe'. In return Austria would

The history of tyrants and dictators

1871
Thanks to the efforts of Otto von Bismarck, Germany is united and the Prussian king, Wilhelm I, becomes German Emperor, appointing Bismarck Reich Chancellor.

1873
Bismarck stitches together the Three Emperors League, a three-way alliance between Germany, Austria and Russia – opening an intricate diplomatic chess game that lasts for 15 years.

1889
Bismarck is bitterly opposed to socialism and trade unions. When 150,000 Ruhr miners go on strike, he proposes harsh measures that lead to his political downfall.

Stark and simple, the stone crosses in the Douaumont cemetery in the Meuse region of France are lined up with the precision of a military parade. The cemetery holds the remains of 130,000 unidentified French and German soldiers from World War I.

such terrible consequences? The answer lies in the complex manoeuvrings on the chessboard of European diplomatic alliances during the last third of the nineteenth century. This period saw the transformation of Germany from a loose assemblage of free cities and independent states into a nation, thrusting with economic confidence and imperial ambition; and the emergence of revolutionary forces in Russia, which by the end of the war would have bulldozed the supreme power of tsarist monarchism aside and put in place a regime ultimately no less oppressive.

The rise of Germany as an imperial power had begun with the campaign of Prime Minister Otto von Bismarck (1815–90) in 1866 for a German Parliament to embrace all the country's regions in a federal system. This move was opposed by Austria, which had alliances with several German states and cities, and saw Bismarck's ambitions as a threat to the cohesion of its heterogeneous empire. A brief military

worse and more widespread military contagion: within a generation a second war would sweep the world anew, killing millions more and leaving great cities in ruins.

How, then, could a single political murder, in a strategically significant but minor outpost of a declining empire, generate

1939
After annexing Austria in the Anschluss and seizing Czechoslovakia by force, Hitler launches an all-out Blitzkrieg on Poland. Britain ends its policy of appeasement and declares war.

1941
German armies have conquered much of Europe as the Battle of Britain rages; atlantic U-boats exact a grievous toll. Hitler revokes his pact with Stalin and marches on Russia.

1945
Hemmed in by Allied forces and the Red Army, its cities reduced to rubble, the German Reich collapses. After Hitler's suicide the full horrors of the Holocaust horrors become clear.

struggle ended in a German victory: Hesse, Hanover, Frankfurt and Nassau were ceded to Germany as provinces. Four years later, in the Franco-Prussian war against Emperor Napoleon III, the German commander, Helmuth Von Moltke (1848–1916), used the speed and mobility of the railways to encircle the French and force them into a quick armistice. Thus was the stage set for German unification in 1871 and, with it, the creation of a new empire.

These developments occurred with the memory of Europe's political revolutions – of 1789, 1830 and 1848 – still fresh in the minds of its statesmen. The impact of the industrial revolution, too, was shaking the old social hierarchies and values. In Germany, though, there was a mood of confident optimism, forging ahead as wages rose from the 1850s onwards. The nation had prospered on the back of free trade; with a single currency and central bank under a unified set of laws, the boom looked set to last.

When it suddenly turned to bust in 1873, triggered by the collapse of the Vienna stock exchange and then, in quick succession, those of Berlin and Frankfurt, the national mood began to turn ugly. A full six decades before the rise of Hitler, anti-Semitic voices were raised in Germany, blaming Jewish manipulation for the financial *débâcle*; at the same time huge imports of wheat from Russia, the Ukraine and the United States, which brought German landowners to the brink of ruin, steered international economic policy away from free trade towards protectionism and tariff barriers.

In 1889, after a lengthy 28 years in power, the authoritarian Bismarck was dismissed over his hardline approach to a strike by 150,000 miners that took place in upper Silesia and the Ruhr. Once he was out of the way, the industrial transformation of Germany picked up apace, with a renewed emphasis on open markets and the value of technical education. By 1910

the country was unrecognizable. Interlaced with railways and telegraph poles, its cities lit by electricity and its homes filled with labour-saving gadgets, it was a new Germany built on coal and steel. The ban on socialist parties was dropped and trade unions were invited to play their part in the industrial life of the nation.

In the wider sphere of European diplomacy, Bismarck had fostered alliances with both Austria and Russia, culminating in the Three Emperors Alliance of 1873. Yet Russia's position grew tricky as the Tsar came under mounting pressure from pan-Slavic sentiment at home to support Serbia in its struggle to throw off the Turkish yoke, whereas Austria recoiled in horror at the prospect of outside intervention in the Balkans as a threat to its fragile imperial integrity. By 1876 the Tsar felt impelled to step in, with victory going to the Russians and Serbs the following year.

Above left: By his eightieth birthday in 1895, Bismarck had been a spent force in German politics for five years – but he still commanded pomp.

Above right: Germany's long naval build-up was underlined as its sailors marched into Brussels in 1914, although it failed to achieve dominance of the seas.

1914

Franz Ferdinand shot dead in Sarajevo

28 June 1914. Archduke Franz Ferdinand, nephew of the Habsburg emperor and heir apparent to the imperial throne, is on a visit to Sarajevo with his beloved wife Sophie. Serbian nationalist feeling is running high – this day marks an ancient defeat at the hands of the Turks, 525 years ago – and assassins with bombs and guns are waiting for him in the crowd.

09:45 As Inspector General of the Armed Forces, Franz Ferdinand has resolved to round off his review of imperial troops, at the invitation of Bosnia's military governor, General Oskar Potoirek, with a visit to Sarajevo. The manoeuvres are a gratifying show of Habsburg prowess, and the Archduke is in a good mood as he climbs into the open-topped limousine that will convey him to the city.

In Vienna the Serbian minister Jovan Jovanovic has warned the Austrian finance minister, Leon Bilinski, of plots afoot. It was a delicate mission, entrusted to Jovanovic by Serbia's Prime Minister; but Jovanovic's diplomatic indirection meant it was given little weight.

Besides, the rather charmless Franz Ferdinand, once described as 'the loneliest man in Europe', is a stubborn character. He showed it in his love match with the Countess Sophie Chotek von Chotkovota, marrying her against his family's wishes. It is almost exactly 14 years since they married, and Sophie will ride at his side, a freedom always denied her at home by the rigid dynastic protocol.

09:55 It is a beautiful morning as the motorcade sets off and Sarajevo presents a festive appearance with flowers and flags. There are six cars: in the lead are the mayor and the police chief; Franz Ferdinand and Sophie ride with Potoirek next; other dignitaries bring up the rear.

Mingling with the crowds along Appel Quay, beside the River Miljacka, are seven would-be assassins fired with a nationalist longing to see Bosnia Herzegovina reunited with Greater Serbia. All are afflicted with tuberculosis and have little to lose, recruited for the attacks by the Black Hand, a shadowy organization controlled by Serbian military intelligence.

10:20 Before reaching Cumburja Bridge the motorcade passes by the group's sole Muslim without mishap. A few yards on, Nedjelko

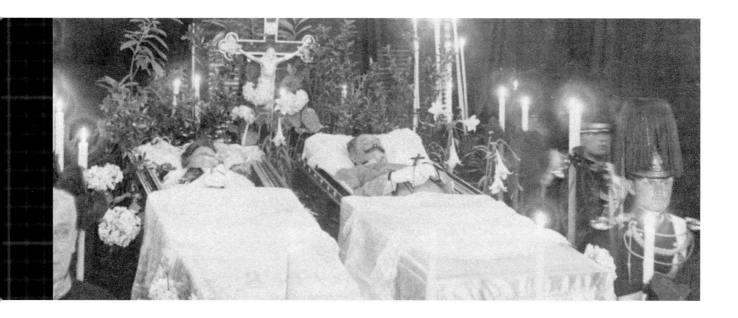

Cabrinovic hurls his bomb straight at the Archduke's car. The driver puts his foot down and the missile is deflected; it blows up in the street, injuring a dozen spectators, along with Potoirek's officer, Eric von Merizzi, and Count Boos-Waldeck in the car behind. Cabrinovic takes cyanide and jumps in the river, but the poison only makes him sick. He is arrested.

10:30 At the Town Hall, Franz Ferdinand protests to the mayor, 'Mr Mayor, one comes here for a visit and is received by bombs!' Then he recovers. The mayor, taken aback, sticks to his script: 'Our hearts are filled with happiness …' With the ceremonies over, Franz Ferdinand does not wish to cancel a planned visit to the museum, nor his lunch at the governor's residence, but first he wants to visit Merizzi in hospital, which means a change of route.

11:10 The motorcade sets off again. Heading back down Appel Quay, the mayoral car and the imperial car turn into Franz Joseph Street; Potoirek expostulates that they are supposed to continue along the quay and the chauffeur begins to reverse. Gavrilo Princip, another young Bosnian assassin, sees his chance.

He draws his revolver and fires twice from 1.5 m (5 feet) away, hitting the Archduke in the neck and Sophie in the stomach. A thin jet of blood from the mouth of the Archduke hits the chauffeur's cheek. Sophie exclaims, 'For heaven's sake! What has happened to you?' and dabs at his mouth with her handkerchief before sinking down between his knees. Franz Ferdinand pleads, 'Sophie dear! Don't die, for the sake of our children.' Soon after, he, too, is dead. Princip swallows poison, which only makes him sick; he tries to shoot himself but is overwhelmed by the crowd.

Above left: Imperial greeting: Franz Ferdinand and Sophie receive warm salutations from officials just one hour before their deaths at the hands of a Serbian assassin.

Above right: Side by side in death as in life, the imperial couple lie in state at the Habsburg Palace in Vienna.

Ce numéro contient en supplément : 1º Une gravure hors texte en couleurs : DEUX HÉROS, par Georges Scott ;
2º LE TABLEAU D'HONNEUR DE LA GUERRE (planches 145 à 148).

L'ILLUSTRATION

Prix du Numéro : Un Franc.   SAMEDI 29 JANVIER 1916   *74ᵉ Année. — Nº 3804.*

UN PETIT ÉCOLIER DE REIMS

Comment, dans une ville ouverte, il faut protéger les enfants contre les projectiles asphyxiants
que les Allemands font alterner avec les obus incendiaires.

Cliché de la Section photographique de l'Armée. — Voir l'article, page 118.

Further twists followed, as Bismarck tried to defuse hostility between Britain and Russia in the eastern Mediterranean, and occasioned ill-feeling in Russia by taking up the cause of Austria. This initiative culminated in 1879 in an alliance with the Austro-Hungarians to deter further Russian incursions in the Balkans. By the end of the next decade, however, Germany had a secret 'reinsurance' pact with Russia, promising mutual neutrality in the event of war with France or Austria. A year later, in 1891, the sands shifted again. France struck a military alliance with Russia and, later, took on the former role of Germany, supplying the Tsar's huge armies with weapons and injecting large amounts of cash into Russia's capital markets, by way of loans charged at above-par rates, to finance large-scale industrialization.

Competition among leading European states in the last two decades of the nineteenth century had been sharpened by a virulent imperialism, with Britain, France, Belgium and Germany all swept along in the feeding frenzy as they vied for the colonial spoils of Africa and Asia. Two further developments helped lock the European powers on course for war. In 1904 France and Britain struck an Entente Cordiale, which became a device for curbing the ambitions of an increasingly self-assertive Germany; then, in 1905, the Schlieffen Plan, which envisaged fighting wars against France and Russia almost simultaneously, was adopted by Germany. The idea was to win a quick victory against France in the west before then pulling troops back east by train to take on the Russians – a strategic doctrine for which the country was later to pay dearly.

By 1907 Britain and Russia had settled their long-standing dispute in the Far East and the 'Great Game' of the British Empire drew to a close. France's alliance with Russia was thriving.

Germany, intoxicated by greedy visions of imperial glory under Kaiser Wilhelm II (1859–1918), no longer saw the need to seek out new alliances and was instead going all out to build a navy to rival that of Britain. The Austrians, in spite of their continuing alliance with Germany, felt ever more insecure. And so, when Archduke Franz Ferdinand met his violent end in 1914, they felt that the very survival of the Habsburg Empire was at stake. A strong gesture was needed; the pretext was an ultimatum to the Serbian government, demanding an end to all anti-monarchist propaganda, swift trial and sentence for the assassins, and a purge of the military.

Despite a placatory response from the Serbs, the Austrians declared war on 28 July 1914. This left the Tsar no option but to bow to 'the wish of the people' and act on his treaty obligations by ordering the mobilization of the Russian army in Serbia's defence. Germany took this as an act of war against its Austro-Hungarian ally, declaring war on Russia on 1 August. Two days later France, in turn, felt obliged to enter the fray under the terms of its Russian alliance. And when the Germans then mobilized their armies on 4 August in a massive advance on the Western Front, they marched roughshod over Belgian neutrality to reach Paris by the quickest possible route. So the chain of mechanistic cause and effect clanked inexorably on to reach Britain, which dispatched its expeditionary force to France on 22 August.

The colossal horror and futility of World War I has been graphically documented in countless books, novels, photographs and documentaries. The Germans lost the initiative almost at once, when unexpectedly strong resistance by the Belgians at the Siege of Liège and the ensuing 'Miracle of the Marne' put them on the defensive, while modern artillery and machine guns forced troops on both sides to take refuge in trenches. The first engagement between German and British forces was fought at Mons on 23 August; thereafter a grim litany unfolds: the gruelling first Battle of Ypres in 1914; Ypres again in 1915, where chlorine gas was first used by the Germans; then Loos a few months later, where the British replied in kind but the gas blew back on to the British lines.

Elsewhere other battles stand out in the record. These include Tannenberg on the Eastern Front, where the Russian general Aleksandr Samsonov (1859–1914) shot himself in a wood in 1914 after the Germans took 95,000 Russian prisoners and killed or wounded some 30,000 more; Gallipoli in 1915, where Turks and Germans held out for ten months against repeated Allied attempts to seize the Dardanelles Straits, throwing British, French, Australian and New Zealand troops against the rocky heights again and again; the desert battles with the Turks in Palestine, Iraq and Arabia; and the Battle of Jutland in 1916, which was the biggest naval engagement of the war.

By the end of 1917, the Bolsheviks had withdrawn Russia from the war, thereby enabling Germany to redeploy more than a million fighting men from the Eastern Front. But the entry of the USA tipped the balance in favour of the Allies. In 1918 Allied tanks appeared in force on the Western Front – some 800 to a paltry 20 or so on the German side – along with fresh US troops. As a new, centre-left government was hastily convened in Berlin, the abdicating Kaiser decamped by train for Dutch exile. But already Lenin's hopes of a revolution in industrially advanced Germany, long foreseen as the catalyst of worldwide revolution, seemed primed to bear fruit.

Even before the Armistice was signed on 11 November 1918, sailors in the German fleet had mutinied, setting up workers' councils, and red flags were flying over German cities within days. The head of the provisional government established a Council of People's Deputies, but strikes and marches erupted across the country in a ferment that lasted from 1919 to 1923. When an armed insurrection by 50,000 workers in the Ruhr in 1920 threatened civil war, the provisional government turned to the army to head off the danger. The Ruhr uprising was bloodily put down, and concessions were offered to the workers, including better wages and shorter hours.

Apart from Germany's troubles at home, there was also the impact of the Treaty of Versailles. By the end of the Great War, the German, Austro-Hungarian, Russian and Ottoman empires were in the dust. The conflict had left 8.5 million men dead and 16 million more wounded, with more than 37 million casualties in all. Even more relevant to the real agenda at Versailles, however, was the fact that its ruinous economic cost had left all the European combatants flat broke. Huge war bonds had to be repaid.

The losers were not among the 27 states invited to the Paris Peace Conference, which was to agree a general peace, redraw the map of Europe and establish a League of Nations. The Versailles talks were to have been conducted on the basis of the 14 Points of US President Woodrow Wilson (1856–1924) – an idealistic blueprint for postwar capitalist democracy, that was drawn up as a challenge to the appeal of communism – but they subsided into bickering over territorial carve-ups and the payment of reparations. Germany was saddled with the individual responsibility for the war and with a correspondingly stupendous bill; so large, in fact, that long-term economic recovery looked doubtful. Perhaps the British economist John Maynard Keynes (1883–1946) was not alone in worrying that this peace contained within it the seeds of a future war.

Back in Germany there was one veteran of the Western Front who took in the state of his country in the aftermath of war and felt a burning resentment: Adolf Hitler (1889–1945). Having seen frequent action as a regimental runner and won the Iron Cross, Hitler had ended the war a lowly corporal. In November 1918 he found himself, homeless and jobless, in an exhausted nation where communists and Jews were seeking power. In Munich a Bavarian republic was proclaimed after an uprising by workers and soldiers led by a left-wing Jew, Kurt Eisner (1867–1919), whose murder precipitated a coup and the declaration of a Soviet republic, again led by Jews. Hitler witnessed the demolition of this revolutionary beachhead when the army, aided by irregular Freikorps troops, massacred hundreds of leftists. Within months he was proposing 'planned legal opposition to and elimination of the privileges of the Jews'.

No man's land: soldiers of an Allied machine gun company take shelter in fox-holes amid the devastated landscape around Passchendaele Ridge, captured by Allied forces during the third Battle of Ypres, November 1917.

The story of Hitler's rise to power in the 14 years from the end of World War I to the parliamentary elections of July 1932 remains an extraordinary one. From the start his concept of leadership meant 'being able to move the masses'. Long before he developed any real ideology or political strategy of his own, this animal-loving, vegetarian teetotaller was immersed in that lurid stream of prewar European ideas that nourished the pretensions of fascism. His was a potent cocktail of racial superiority, Social Darwinism and anti-Semitism, given an extra twist by a Teutonic cult of the irrational and a belief in war as the elemental bringer of 'renewal by destruction'.

Hitler joined the German Workers Party in late 1919, taking charge of recruitment and propaganda. At a meeting in Munich's Hofbräuhaus the following February, he dominated an unruly crowd of almost 2,000, announcing a 25-point programme and appending the words 'National Socialist' to the party name, later abbreviated to the simpler 'Nazi'. Discharged from the army in April 1920, he set about building a vehicle to drive the party's new agenda forward, coupling his proven power of oratory with a set of symbols that had been chosen for maximum visual impact – the blood-red banners, the swastika and the raised-arm salute – and were to reach their ritualistic zenith in the overpowering spectacle of the Nuremburg rallies of the 1930s.

By July 1921 Hitler was sure enough of his position to elaborate his *Führerprinzip*, a credo of unconditional personal loyalty to himself as leader that left him free to take unilateral decisions untrammelled by rules or procedures. It was a

Far left: Corporal Hitler, the future *Führer* (right) ended World War I still low in the German ranks, though he won the Iron Cross.

Left: On the rise: Hitler flanked by supporters in Munich, 1930, three years before achieving real power in a right-wing coalition.

an attempted putsch in Bavaria – a miscalculation. Arrested and tried for treason, Hitler turned the tables on his accusers, defending himself in court with a rhetorical panache that brought him widespread publicity. The ensuing months in jail gave him leisure to start writing *Mein Kampf*, or *My Struggle*.

From 1924 it took another six years to build the Nazi party into a national political force, eventually achieved through a centrally controlled network of diligent local activists. From 1929 support was boosted by the Depression, which brought higher unemployment and sharpened the postwar privations. By September 1930 the Nazi share in national elections had rocketed from 800,000 in 1928 to 6.4 million – a 19 per cent share – and in 1932 it more than doubled to 13.75 million. The Nazis were now the second-largest party in the German Parliament, the Reichstag, though these trappings of legality were merely a cloak for more grandiose ambitions.

It was not until 1933 that Hitler's cunning paid off in full. By then he was the dominant partner in a right-wing coalition government. Early in the year SA violence increased sharply in Prussia, where Hitler's deputy, Hermann Goering (1893–1946), was in charge of the civil service; then came the Reichstag fire, blamed on a Dutch ex-communist. Hitler seized the opportunity: German communist leaders were arrested en masse and imprisoned without trial. Hitler was now chancellor; Josef Goebbels (1897–1945), the new minister of information and propaganda, announced a 'Day of National Uprising' as Hitler invoked emergency-enabling laws to place constitutional, legislative and foreign policy-making powers at the exclusive disposal of his Nazi cabinet.

somewhat arbitrary mode of organization that was to endure to the end, when Hitler would burst into furious rants in his Berlin bunker against the rank disloyalty of the generals, the army and, finally, even close associates. It also meant that the party's high command would develop as a patchwork of competing fiefdoms, ruled by patronage and prone to disintegrate once the purposeful forward thrust of military conquest turned to defeat.

At this point, though, no such doubts clouded his mind. His next step was to create the SA, or Brown Shirts, a paramilitary force of uniformed thugs who would act as a political spearhead in the 'coming struggle for freedom'. They became central to the Nazis' calculated use of violence. But in November 1923, still short of money and members, the party overreached itself with

Show of strength: Hitler
used the Nuremburg rallies
to reinforce Nazi myths
of invincibility, marshalling
huge banners and
regimented ranks.

At last the Nazis were in the position they had coveted so
long. And for the next five years, they pursued a narrow set of
objectives with fanatical determination. Their key priorities
were rearmament, foreign policy, full employment, military
indoctrination of the young and 'the Jewish question';
economic ownership and big business were largely left alone.
The Nazis were quick to tighten their political grip, banning the
Communist and Social Democrat parties, replacing trade
unions with a 'Labour Front' to represent all workers, and
instituting their own system instead of wage-bargaining. The
conventional machinery of government was often bypassed
as the Third Reich set up its own dedicated agencies to pursue
key projects, cutting across ministerial boundaries. Not long
after Hitler took power, too, the first concentration camps
were opened by the SA in regional locations such as
Oranienburg, Esterwegen, Dachau and Lichtenburg, seemingly
on an ad hoc basis rather than as official party policy.

In 1934 Hitler merged the roles of chancellor, president and
Führer, proclaiming himself 'Supreme Judge of the German
People'. By September Adolf Wagner (1890–1944), the
gauleiter of Bavaria, ringingly declared at Nuremburg that
the Reich would last a thousand years. By then the leadership of
the SA, the political street bullies left over from the party's rise
to power, had been ruthlessly liquidated by the SS. Hitler had
concluded that its leader, Ernst Röhm (1887–1934), was
undermining the party's relationship with the army. Under
Heinrich Himmler (1900–45), the SS grew into a still-more
arrogant killer elite – sporting black uniforms, death's head
emblems and lightning flashes – that would in time take the
leading role in the dirty work of the Jewish 'Final Solution'.

On the international front Germany had pulled out of the
1933 Disarmament Conference and the League of Nations,
while Hitler secretly charged Goering to build a powerful
airforce, the Luftwaffe, in defiance of Versailles. In 1934 he set
up a non-aggression pact with Poland, an expedient that
enabled him later to court other countries, one by one, and so
sabotage efforts at collective European security. Though Russia
was one of the very first to recognize the Nazi government,
along with the Vatican, Germany's rabid anti-Bolshevik rhetoric
quickly soured relations. Meanwhile, an abortive Nazi coup in
Austria obliged Hitler to disown the entire operation.

By the mid-1930s, with words of peace on his lips, Hitler had succeeded in thoroughly confusing his opponents, chiefly Britain and France, which became caught up in the diplomatic dance of appeasement in the mistaken belief that Nazi ambitions could be held in check. Just how wrong they were began to be apparent by 1935, when the scale of German rearmament gave rise to serious international concern, as did Hitler's ambitions in Czechoslovakia and Poland. In that year, too, Germany tightened the screw on the Jews, banning racial intermarriage, banning Jews from public places as *untermenschen* (subhumans) and excluding them from citizenship.

Elsewhere in Europe the fascist regimes of Italy and Spain began to show their teeth: the armies of Benito Mussolini (1883–1945) marched into Abyssinia in the autumn and General Franco's defiance of the republican government in Spain tipped over into civil war the following summer. But Hitler himself was not ready. In 1936 the Berlin Olympics, planned as a triumphant display of Aryan superiority, backfired thanks to the four gold

Left: Prime Minister Neville Chamberlain arrives in London in 1938 holding the Munich Agreement signed by Germany, France, Britain and Italy. It was a fatal illusion.

Right: Red Army troops raise the Red Flag on the Reichstag above the ruins of Berlin, May 1945.

medals taken by a superb black American athlete, Jesse Owens. Then, in 1937, German planes intervened in the Spanish Civil War to bomb Guernica. Later that year Hitler spoke at Nuremburg of the German need for *lebensraum*, or living space. He shared a platform with Mussolini, who was still talking of European peace.

By 1938 pressure in Europe was rising fast. First came Germany's annexation of Austria – the Anschluss – an action backed by almost 100 per cent of its people in a referendum that was held after the fact. Next, Hitler's demands over Czechoslovakia provoked a crisis, prompting Britain and France to warn that any invasion would inevitably lead to war. In late September, however, the British prime minister, Neville Chamberlain, flew back from his infamous meeting in Munich, clutching a piece of paper, to claim 'peace for our time'. The price was to be paid by the unhappy Czechs, who

were required by the agreement to cede a large chunk of German-speaking territory in the Sudetenland.

This Nazi success served only to make their territorial appetite keener. By March of 1939 the Germans had completed their takeover of Czechoslovakia; their next target was Poland and the recovery of the remaining lands lost in the postwar settlement. That summer Hitler sealed his non-aggression pact with Stalin, which gave him a free hand to invade Poland without fear of Soviet retaliation. In September he did so, launching a *Blitzkrieg* in defiance of pledges by Britain and France to defend the country. A fortnight later the Russians invaded, too, and Poland was chopped in half.

At last, after much prevarication and disagreement among British politicians, Britain and the Commonwealth entered the war alongside France. From then on the pace moved fast and furiously. German U-boats inflicted immediate casualties on Allied

shipping and British troops landed in France, but 1940 brought a volley of German victories: Denmark and Norway were invaded in April, Holland and Belgium in May, and the Fall of France meant victorious German troops marching down the Champs-Elysées by June, only ten days after the Allied evacuation from Dunkirk.

Winston Churchill (1874–1965), taking over from Chamberlain in 1940, told the British he had 'nothing to offer but blood, toil, tears and sweat', a stark warning soon borne out by the Battle of Britain. Heavily outnumbered British fighters engaged the Luftwaffe in a desperate but determined defence; then came the Blitz, when thousands of tons of German high explosive rained down on London, ending only when the bombers switched to other cities. In the Atlantic, U-boats inflicted grievous casualties on convoys criss crossing the ocean to keep the war effort supplied. In spite of a few British victories, notably in North Africa, the Germans kept coming; Greece and Yugoslavia fell in April 1941.

And yet 1941 was the year when the tide turned. Now Hitler was to make his greatest mistake – convinced that he was invincible, especially to an 'inferior race' of Slavs, he broke his 1939 pact with Stalin and committed to an invasion of Russia. The Germans came within 48 km (30 miles) of Moscow, but their army was finally broken at the Battle of Stalingrad, costing some three-million Russian lives and about half that number of Germans.

From then on, slowly but surely, the Germans were driven back. Later that year, after Pearl Harbour, the USA entered the war, joining the fight for Europe as well as the Pacific. It was a long, gruelling struggle. Yet by the time the Red Army closed in on Berlin, its buildings in ruins and its people defeated, the once-mighty *Führer* had been reduced to moving buttons about on a table in his underground bunker, as if he still had armies to command. But they were gone – and so, soon enough, was he, with the aid of a bullet fired through his temple by his own hand.

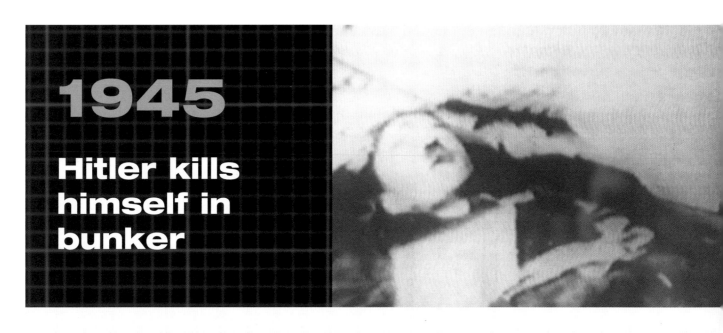

1945

Hitler kills himself in bunker

30 April 1945. As the Red Army closes in on the ruins of Berlin, instructed by Stalin to raise the Red Flag above the Reichstag by May Day, Adolf Hitler is still holed up in the bunker at the Chancellery. He has veered for a week from hysterical rage at the treachery of his generals to the grandiose rhetoric of his will, both personal and political, settling the imaginary Nazi succession. Just 15 people remain behind in the *Führerbunker*.

03:30 **29 April.** The rage and hysterics of recent weeks are spent. Hitler has married Eva Braun – her reward for loyalty after so many other desertions – just hours after the summary execution of her brother-in-law for desertion. After a glass or two of champagne, Hitler puts the final touches to his last testament. He claims Germany never wanted war in 1939; it was provoked by international politicians 'who either came of Jewish stock or worked for Jewish interests'; he will stay in Berlin with the people, worn down by Stalin's 'army of blind automata', and keep faith with them by choosing death voluntarily.

Next, his will expels Goering and Himmler from the party. Through secret negotiations with the enemy, attempts to seize power and their treachery to him, they have brought 'irreparable shame on the country and the whole people'. In a gesture of incongruous sentimentality, he bequeaths his paintings to the founding of an art gallery in Linz, and commends Eva Braun as the woman 'who, after many years of true friendship, came to this town, already almost besieged, of her own free will, to share my fate'.

04:00 The documents are signed and Hitler retires to bed. Josef Goebbels, the Nazis' chief propagandist, stays awake. He retires to his apartment to compose an appendix to Hitler's testament, stating that for the first time, 'I must categorically refuse to obey an order of the *Führer*', claiming that his wife and children concur. Invoking 'feelings of humanity and loyalty', he declares that if they were to obey Hitler's order to leave, he would 'appear for the rest of [his] life a dishonourable traitor and common scoundrel'.

12:00 A conference in the bunker, attended by Hitler, Bormann, Goebbels and seven others.

The Russians are advancing fast; it is agreed that three officers will try to get through to the army of General Wenck, on which Hitler had placed such hopes, travelling by boat down the River Havel to the Wannsee Peninsula. Later, news comes in that the Italian fascist leader, Mussolini, is dead. Hitler has his pet Alsatian, Blondi, put down with cyanide and gives poison capsules to his secretaries for use *in extremis*.

02:30 **30 April.** Hitler bids farewell to the women in the outer bunker. His eyes look hollow and glazed; one secretary thinks he might be suffering from Parkinson's disease. He walks stiffly down the passage, shakes hands with each in silence and departs. The mood lifts suddenly and a party begins, with dancing until the early hours. Bormann, plotting to the last, sends a telegram to Dönitz, commanding him to 'proceed at once, and mercilessly, against all traitors'. It adds, 'The *Führer* lives and is conducting the defence of Berlin.'

15:00 Hitler has taken lunch – a bland affair of spaghetti and salad. By now a chauffeur has been ordered to bring 200 litres (44 gallons) of petrol to the garden. After lunch, and a

further round of farewells, Hitler retires with Eva Braun to his suite. A single shot is heard: Hitler is found slumped on a blood-soaked sofa, having shot himself in the right temple. Eva Braun has taken poison, though she, too, has a pistol. The bodies are taken up four flights and, in the midst of a Russian bombardment, placed outdoors, doused with petrol and set on fire with a burning rag. Next day, as others plan escape, all six Goebbels children are poisoned by injection, which they are told is to stop them getting sick; their parents march upstairs in silence and are shot in the garden by an SS man. They, too, are burned.

Above left: Final forgery? This picture of the dead Hitler, which the Russians claimed was taken from authentic military footage from the Moscow archive, may have involved the use of a double.

Above right: Allied experts examining Hitler's bunker.

From the emancipation of the serfs in 1861 by Tsar Alexander II and the rise of the Bolsheviks, to the fall of the Berlin Wall in 1989 in the wake of the radical new initiatives of *glasnost* and *perestroika*, Russia was the epicentre of the most far-reaching attempt in world history to engineer a new society.

[1917] : [1989]

THE RISE AND FALL OF COMMUNISM

In 1861 Tsar Alexander II of Russia (1818–81) abolished serfdom, thereby in theory ending two centuries of slavery for the illiterate Russian peasantry. The previous 200 years had been a period in which landowners could buy and sell whole peasant families, and the supreme symbol of status among the landed gentry had been the number of serfs they could afford to own.

The peasants lived at the whim of their masters, who more often than not had little idea of how to run their vast estates. Instead they chose to spend lavishly on their mansions, filling them with costly French furniture and pictures and embellishing their gardens with fine statuary. They gave parties and balls, quaffed brandy and champagne, and, not surprisingly, often ran up massive debts.

Rural Russia had long been administered by provincial governors, remote from the centres of power, who collected taxes and maintained law and order through ill-disciplined local police forces. As embodiments of the inscrutable powers of an autocratic Tsar – instruments of his God-given will – they were entitled to reward themselves handsomely from imperial tithes culled from their regions. Often, too, these privileges

The history of communism

1881
Tsar Alexander II, having abolished serfdom 20 years earlier, is assassinated by a member of The People's Will on the very day he signs a liberalizing decree.

1894
Nicholas II becomes Tsar but shows no disposition to continue the reforming policies of his forebear, instead reaffirming the traditions of autocratic rule.

1903
The Bolsheviks, with Lenin as their leader, emerge at the Second Congress of the Russian Social Democratic Labour Party, held outside Russia to avoid the tsarist police.

РОСТОМ КОЛХОЗОВ и СОВХОЗОВ УКРЕПИМ СМЫЧКУ ПРОЛЕТАРИАТА с КРЕСТЬЯНСТВОМ

were exacted with a heavy hand, marked by injustice, brutality and unconcealed acquisitiveness. In effect, they were a law unto themselves.

All that the peasants had to insulate them from the caprices of the ruling elite was their faith in Orthodox Christianity, floating like a votive candle on a darker undercurrent of paganism and superstition. They also had a strong tradition of communal

Above left: Nicholas II at the Duma, a body over which he kept effective control.

Above right: Russian peasant women demonstrate in the 1930s in support of the removal of class distinctions between workers and peasants.

1905
The Russian Empire is shaken by armed rebellions, strikes and mutinies after soldiers shoot unarmed marchers on 'Bloody Sunday' in St Petersburg, leaving many dead.

1906
Nicholas II accedes to pressure for reform and the first Duma parliament is elected, but real power stays in the hands of the Tsar and his ministers.

1917
In February a mutiny in St Petersburg grows into full revolution; then, in October, Kerensky's Provisional Government flees, leaving the Bolsheviks to fight a civil war.

organization – a vital survival strategy against natural hazards such as crop failure, sickness or starvation. For village life in Russia was far from a bucolic idyll. It was harsh and uncertain, riven with drunken feuds and violence, directed by conservative patriarchs who dominated group decisions and often placed private interests above those of the community. By honoured custom, though, the peasants could send petitions directly to the Tsar, convinced that he knew and cared about each detail of their lives, and that his benign authority would set right any complaints about injustice or hardship.

At its worst, the words of the seventeenth-century English political philosopher Thomas Hobbes seem perfectly to describe the life of a Russian peasant in the first half of the nineteenth century: it was indeed, very often, 'poor, nasty, brutish and short'. Yet Russia was also a challenge to Hobbes's preferred solution. His cynical belief was that natural human wickedness could be checked only by a king's authority, exercised with a stern, unbending will. But Russia was already on a very different trajectory. And it was one that would, within little more than half a century, bring 300 years of Romanov rule crashing down in ruins.

At the centres of imperial power, in Moscow and St Petersburg, the lead of Alexander II in emancipating the peasantry lurched to a halt when he was assassinated in 1881. His reforms had, crucially, failed to address the insatiable hunger for land among the former serfs, and after several attempts on his life he was killed by a bomb thrown by a member of the People's Will, an offshoot of the Populist movement. He died on the very day he signed a decree

The backward-looking Alexander III, Tsar of Russia from 1881, with his wife, *née* Princess Marie Dagmar, and their family.

The history of communism

1924
Lenin dies. He had had second thoughts about handing the succession to Joseph Stalin, but Stalin has built an impregnable power base as party general secretary.

1936
After a deadly famine and the slaughter of kulaks, along with collectivization and the first Five-Year Plan, Stalin makes growing use of state terror, including show-trials.

1953
When Stalin dies the new leader, Nikita Khrushchev, raises hopes for a new era. These are dashed in years to come as protests in Soviet satellite countries are brutally crushed.

granting limited new powers to local authorities. His efforts were swiftly repudiated by his successor, Alexander III (1845–94). A man of formidable appearance – over six feet tall, black-bearded, with broad shoulders and powerful hands – the new Tsar lacked neither intelligence nor willpower. Yet he embarked on a disastrously backward-looking course, reaffirming the ancient prerogatives of the despot and centralizing power in his own hands, just at a time when Russian society was modernizing swiftly. Industrialization was transforming the cities; education was spreading rapidly to the new social classes. There were anguished calls from the landowners, who were hard hit by a severe agricultural depression, for constitutional government, the rule of law, a parliament and civil liberties.

Alexander III met such demands with lofty insouciance, insisting on the divine right of the Tsar to behave as a feudal lord, born to rule all Russia as his personal property – a private fiefdom vouchsafed to him by God. Bombastic, forceful and high-spirited, he was always a heavy drinker, and drink was to prove his undoing. When he contracted kidney disease and was instructed by the Tsarina to give up alcohol, he kept a flask hidden in a special hollowed-out boot and would whip it out for a roguish toast as soon as her back was turned. He died in 1894, aged just 49.

His heir, Nicholas II (1868–1918), was a very different character. Shy, punctilious and impeccably well mannered, Nicholas had a rather infantile streak and had been dismissed as a dunce by his father, which he was not. However, Nicholas led the imperial parade even further into the archaic shadow of his forebears, eventually trapping himself and his dynasty in a fatal tapestry of medieval illusion woven from the reimagined glories of the Romanov past. He had, moreover, grown up in an imperial court that was largely ignorant of peasant Russia. If the nobles had a view on it at all, they were inclined to regard the vast Russian hinterland with faint contempt, as a region of backwardness and dirt. They looked to France as the icon of civilized elegance, and decamped whenever they could for its glittering boulevards to while away their leisure time. Arms deals and development loans from French banks and industry reinforced the links.

More significantly, Nicholas failed dismally to reform the time-hardened imperial administration in Russia, which was obsessed with the petty insignia of rank. It offered a rigid, predictable order of promotion to well-born beneficiaries that inevitably stifled any real talent. Nicholas dutifully applied himself to minor issues when strategic boldness, a clear head and firm political decisions were urgently required. Instead of rationalizing the rigid bureaucracy of the civil service, or addressing the chaos of overlapping responsibilities between rival ministries, he played them off against each other to ensure that none might impinge upon his role as Tsar and father to the nation.

Such was Nicholas's well-bred disposition to agree in conversation that he developed a chronic inability to take issue with anyone. This tendency inspired a joke in Russia: 'The most powerful man in Russia is the last man to have spoken to the Tsar.' Yet chief among those with a more enduring influence over him was a woman: his wife Tsarina Alexandra

1961
Trying to stem a rising tide of East German emigration, especially by its younger citizens, Khrushchev orders the Berlin Wall to be built, which cuts the city in half.

1982
Mikhail Gorbachev sets about reforming the Soviet system through glasnost and perestroika, ending decades of suspicion and secret wars between communist and capitalist worlds.

1989
As East Germans decamp in their thousands for Hungary, its newly opened border with Austria giving access to the West, Berliners from both sides destroy the Wall.

Above: The Tsar and Tsarina visit Queen Victoria at Balmoral. (From left to right) Tsarina Alexandra Feodorovna, the infant Grand Duchess Tatiana Nicholovna Romanov, Nicholas II, Queen Victoria of England and Albert Edward, Prince of Wales.

Above right: Rasputin practises his heavy, hypnotic gaze among a crowd of his adoring ollowers.

(1872–1918), the German granddaughter of Queen Victoria of England. She firmly endorsed Nicholas's views on the proper conduct of a Tsar, urging him, almost comically, to 'be more autocratic than Peter the Great, sterner than Ivan the Terrible'. In the domestic sphere, meanwhile, she took after her grandmother, presiding over a regime that was stuffy and somewhat joyless. Alexandra was unpopular in Russia, for she, too, lacked ease or grace in public. As she began to keep out of society, she gained a reputation for being aloof, even cold, compounding the offence with a lofty dismissal of the relevance of Russian high-society opinion to her actions.

Having given birth to four daughters, the Tsarina had prayed fervently for a son and heir to the imperial throne, and her prayers seemed to have been answered when she was delivered of a baby boy, Alexei. Sadly, the boy was afflicted with haemophilia, an inherited condition then prevalent among the royal houses of Europe. Thereafter his mother lived with the constant anxiety that a minor bump or fall could bring on internal bleeding that would kill him. And so, having already shown herself susceptible to self-styled mystics peddling dubious treatments, she fell under the influence of Grigori Rasputin (1871–1916), a peasant 'holy man' of decidedly murky antecedents.

After a misspent youth devoted to drink, lechery and horse-thieving, Rasputin claimed to have heard the call of God. Despite his long, greasy hair, filthy beard and goatish stench, he totally enthralled the upper-class women of Moscow with his deep, penetrating gaze, and they submitted eagerly to his ministrations. Whether or not his fearsome sexual reputation had any basis in fact – after death his genitals were found to have shrunk almost to nothing – he did have an unexplained power to arrest the Prince's bleeding. His position at court thus became impregnable, and Rasputin exploited it with gusto, accepting bribes and sexual favours, his drunken rampages incurring

Left: An early twentieth-century family of Russian peasants sit outside their cabin, one woman weaving on a loom and another checking the head of a child for lice.

Right: Voice of command: A poster from the Russian Revolution instructs the viewer: 'You – Still Not a Member of the Cooperative, Sign Up Immediately!'

public outrage. Yet such was Rasputin's hold on the Tsarina that Nicholas not only refused to do anything about him; he let him acquire a huge political influence over him, feeding Nicholas's autocratic fantasies with mumbo-jumbo about fate and destiny.

Outside the imperial court larger social forces had picked up momentum. Nicholas's refusal to countenance the reforms that liberals had been pressing for left the way open to more radical influences. Nationalist stirrings in many parts of the outlying empire, emerging at first over issues of language and culture, mutated into more overt political strains as the imperial authorities responded with a harsh and often cack-handed policy of 'Russification'. The Jews in particular suffered

severely: a great many of them were killed or forced to flee the country in the wake of savage state-inspired pogroms.

In 1901 the Socialist Revolutionary Party was founded in succession to the Narodniks, the forerunners of the Populist movement, who had agitated in the countryside during the 1870s in a vain attempt to adapt socialism to the conditions of rural Russia. In 1903, a time of mounting labour unrest, the Bolshevik Party was formed by Vladimir Ilyich Ulyanov (1870–1924), otherwise known as Lenin, at the Second Congress of the Russian Social Democratic Labour Party. The First Congress, held at Minsk in 1898 while Lenin was still in Siberian exile, had ended with the arrest of all but one of its delegates.

Coming the year after Lenin's famous pamphlet, *What is to be Done?*, the Second Congress was convened in Brussels, beyond the reach of the tsarist police, but switched to London after a ban by the Belgian authorities.

The Bolsheviks, meaning 'majority', opposed the Narodniks, arguing that peasants and proletariat must unite to establish socialism in Russia; at the same time a disagreement at the Congress over party membership widened into a major split with a more moderate faction dubbed the Mensheviks, or 'minority'. This group believed in making the base of party support as broad as possible, whereas Lenin argued for keeping 'professional' revolutionaries separate from legal trade unions, lest both be trampled down indiscriminately in a general repression. Later, the Mensheviks cooperated with the Provisional Government, formed after the Tsar was toppled by the February Revolution of 1917; later still, Lenin had them all shot.

In 1903, however, the declared aim of the Bolsheviks was Marxist: to advance in stages from feudalism, via capitalism and 'bourgeois democracy', to full-blooded socialism. But this pseudo-scientific vision of an orderly historical progression was brought up short when, early in 1905, a wave of armed rebellions, strikes, mutinies and rural attacks convulsed the empire. The flashpoint was 'Bloody Sunday', an infamous incident in which soldiers fired on a peaceful march through St Petersburg led by an Orthodox priest, killing hundreds. This was on top of strong opposition to the ill-advised Russo-Japanese war of 1904, which inflicted a humiliating defeat on the Russian side, along with heavy casualties, stirring up activists into a hornet's nest.

Among the political parties seeking reform was the Constitutional Democratic Party, made up of liberals, landowners and professionals from the Union of Liberation. They had joined with Finns, Poles, Georgians, Armenians and Russians in the Socialist Revolutionary Party to campaign against the autocracy, and were known collectively as Kadets. Under pressure from his chief minister, Count Witte, Nicholas issued the October Manifesto, raising hopes for a constitution and some civil liberties. This despite the fact that ministerial government would still be answerable to Nicholas rather than to the proposed national assembly, the Duma, whose policies would remain subject to the approval of both the Tsar and the old State Council, now serving as an Upper House.

Despite continuing outbreaks of terror instigated by both left and right, the government somehow managed to regain its equilibrium. Some 60,000 political detainees were executed and Nicholas sacked Count Witte. The first Duma, elected in 1906, was dominated by Kadets, who struck a crusading tone on land reform; the Duma was duly dissolved by the Tsar. New elections filled out the political spectrum, this time admitting the left in force after the main parties dropped an earlier boycott. Amid rhetorical fireworks, the assembly was once again dissolved. The third Duma, in 1907, was doctored to ensure conservative dominance; then in 1911, after four more years of infighting, the Prime Minister and would-be reformer, Pyotr Arkadevich Stolypin, was shot dead.

hedonism. Vintage champagne was swilled by the case, caviare gobbled by the bucketload. Rasputin was poisoned, shot, stabbed and drowned in December. As the economic crisis deepened, a wave of arrests decimated the Bolsheviks, and Lenin called for an armed proletarian revolution to end Russia's involvement in the war.

In late February 1917, after weeks of bread shortages in St Petersburg, the moment came. And again it took revolutionary leaders by surprise. First, some 100,000 people massed in the streets for International Women's Day on 23 February, their numbers swelling to 150,000 by the next day. An almost festive mood prevailed. The third day, a Saturday, brought even larger crowds, 200,000 and more, this time waving red flags and shouting defiant slogans. A general strike was declared and the city came to a standstill. A young girl offered a symbolic bunch of red roses to a Cossack officer on Nevsky Prospekt; he accepted with a smile to cheers from the crowd. But then the Tsar took the fatal step of ordering his commanders to suppress the demonstrations by force. His troops opened fire on the crowds the following day, killing dozens.

Then there came an insurrection by a group of about 100 soldiers who, putting their sympathy for the people before their oath of loyalty, shot back at the police. When they were arrested, the misgivings of other young conscripts spilled over into mutiny. The arsenal was ransacked by rebel soldiers and workers, yielding thousands of rifles; thousands more were seized at weapons factories. In the ensuing street battles, imperial snipers picked off the rebels from church towers as commandeered vehicles careered crazily through the streets, bristling with armed revolutionaries.

As government buildings were seized and prisons smashed open, an impressive discipline shown by soldiers and workers on

When Germany declared war on Russia three years later, the nation seemed to rally in defence of the motherland. Strikes came to an end, political agitation subsided. But a series of military setbacks – due in no small part to the army's failure to modernize or to provide its men with adequate training and munitions – soon snuffed out this brief glow. A huge number of Russian soldiers surrendered rather than go on fighting in June 1915. And when Warsaw fell soon after, Nicholas, urged on by his wife, assumed personal command of the armed forces, despite an almost total ignorance of military matters.

By 1916, in a toxic atmosphere of anti-German paranoia, conspiracy theories and mounting hysteria, even the rich sensed revolution in the air, plunging into an orgy of last-chance the streets was offset by outbreaks of rape, robbery, drunkenness, looting and arson. There was a bloody showdown in the luxurious Astoria Hotel after roof-top snipers fired on the crowds below; the revolutionaries came back with machine guns, mowing down tsarist officers and their families through ground-floor windows before storming in with bayonets for a desperate hand-to-hand struggle amid the smashed glass and fallen chandeliers.

To the writer Maxim Gorky, this was chaos, not revolution; others saw the excesses as an inevitable byproduct of the people's liberation. Yet the irony of the February Revolution was that its most important leaders and thinkers were elsewhere when it happened. Lenin was in Zurich, Trotsky (1879–1940) in New York. It was left to Alexander Kerensky (1881–1970), scrambling to keep up with events, to declare the 'Provisional Executive Committee of the Soviet of Workers Deputies' at St Petersburg, though this body incorporated not one factory worker. Some 4,000 tsarist officials were locked up in the old Romanov stronghold, the Peter and Paul Fortress, but political stalemate set in as the Soviet leaders tried to pursue the prescribed revolutionary course by forcing parliamentary government on the Duma instead of taking power directly.

What of the Tsar? Confronted by the failure of his commanders to put down the revolution, his will seemed sapped. By 2 March 1917 it was not hard for his generals, who were satisfied that a new government would be based on the Duma rather than the Soviet, to persuade him to abdicate. Until his son Alexei came of age, the throne would pass to the Tsar's younger brother, the Grand Duke Mikhail (1878–1918). In his opulent imperial railway carriage, Nicholas greeted the recommendation of his commanders in silence, then rose and said that he had been 'born for misfortune'. As more telegrams arrived, confirming the generals' view, he sat and smoked. At last, he agreed. Yet Mikhail declined the crown after a day or so of reflection, and this refusal meant more than the end of Nicholas's reign: it was the end of the Romanovs.

Lenin returned to Russia one month later. The Germans, still bogged down on two fronts, offered him safe passage from Switzerland. He arrived by night at the Finland Station, then within the boundaries of Russia's empire. After 17 long years of exile, he marched into Petrograd and turned the Marxist credo upside down with an electrifying set of new propositions. He asserted that there was no longer a need for a 'bourgeois' phase of revolution: power should now pass directly to the proletariat through the Soviets, under the simple but inspiring slogan of 'Peace, Bread and Land'.

By September the Bolsheviks had gained a majority in the Petrograd Soviet. Then came the October Revolution. Knowing that the German forces were rapidly advancing, Kerensky ordered half the garrison to move out of the city into defensive

positions and closed down Bolshevik presses as a prelude to suppressing the party's embryonic Military Revolutionary Committee. Armed revolutionaries seized control of key strategic points in the city, including bridges and stations; workers and sailors joined forces to storm the Winter Palace, and Kerensky fled, unable to muster his own troops in time.

What followed in Russia alone would require a vast canvas in itself, but for the Tsar this Bolshevik takeover foretold something

Demonstrators on the crossroads of Nevsky Prospekt and Sadovay Street in Petrograd on 4 July 1917 flee from government troops firing into the crowd.

far worse than the earlier loss of imperial privilege and power. Kept in comfortable detention at a palace east of the Urals since the abdication, the former Royal Family found themselves by early 1918 being treated with less kindness by their guards. Their butter and coffee disappeared; new rules were imposed. Hardline Bolsheviks at Ekaterinburg were unhappy with the easy life that was still enjoyed by the Romanovs: some wanted the ex-Tsar jailed or executed. But the party's Central Committee had other plans – a show-trial in Moscow, starring Trotsky as chief prosecutor. So the local commissar was instructed to bring them back to the capital, travelling via Ekaterinberg to avoid arousing local suspicions.

Nicholas and Alexandra arrived there at the end of April, the rest of the family about three weeks later. Inside their new quarters, a white house encircled by a specially erected fence, their captors were now openly insolent. The family were kept in their rooms constantly except at mealtimes and escorted to the lavatory; obscenities were scribbled on the walls, property was filched from the garden shed. By July, in any case, the party leadership's plans had changed. As Trotsky later disclosed, Lenin had decided that the former Tsar could be 'a banner' for the royalist Whites, a risk that should now be eliminated.

Accordingly, not long after midnight on 17 July, all 11 members of the unsuspecting household, comprising Nicholas and Alexandra, their five children, the royal physician and three servants, were taken down to the basement and shot. The bodies, thrown on a lorry that night and dumped in mineshafts, were removed next day because the shafts were not considered deep enough. The communists' great fear was that the bodies might, if recovered, become sacred relics of a cult of royal martyrdom. Acid was thrown on the faces to prevent identification and the corpses were buried in a shallow grave. The site remained unknown and unmarked for many years. When it was dug up, decades later, two of the skeletons were missing.

So ended a dynasty that had lasted more than 300 years – a sad and ignominious end, in part the outcome of Nicholas's blind devotion to the rule of autocracy, and in some ways a mirror image of the fate of many nameless Russians who had sought to overthrow that rule, democratically or not. Yet it is noteworthy that while the tsarist secret police executed some 14,000 people in the last 50 years of their rule, their Bolshevik

In Leningrad, *c*.1940, Vladimir Lenin, Bolshevik leader and founder of the Soviet State, addresses a May Day crowd.

successors, the Cheka, are estimated to have disposed of at least 200,000 by the time of Lenin's death in 1924.

Lenin was much admired by fellow communists for his hard, unswerving faith that revolutionaries must kill, without doubt or remorse, to defend the revolution from its enemies. The six years that elapsed between Nicholas's murder and Lenin's death in 1924 were years of civil war and state control over industry, of famine and peasant revolt against the party's requisitioning of grain. Lenin showed himself willing to act ruthlessly again and again, allowing no deviation from policy imperatives.

Lenin had initially cultivated Joseph Stalin (1879–1953), admiring his efficiency, but he had growing doubts about him in his last days after suffering a stroke. By then, though, it was too late. Stalin had already used his position as party general secretary to build a formidable power base, manoeuvring his supporters into key positions and skilfully isolating or eliminating opponents. When he took power in 1924, he immediately set about neutralizing other top Bolsheviks, concentrating above all on Trotsky, his main rival for the succession, who years later was assassinated at his desk in Mexico on Stalin's orders by a local agent who drove an ice-pick through the back of his skull.

In 1928 Stalin launched a policy of forced collectivization, imposing five-year plans for industry and agriculture. Peasants had to pool their equipment and livestock on the new state-run farms; their produce was taken by the government, leaving workers to subsist on low wages or eke out such meagre supplies as were left to them. The result was a devastating famine. Many *kulaks*, propertied peasants of rural Russia, destroyed crops and animals rather than hand them over: five million were slaughtered or starved to death in a savage retribution, and a similar number of peasants died of famine between 1932 and 1934.

1918

Massacre of the Romanovs

17 July 1918. Nicholas Romanov, the former Tsar, has been held for 78 days with his family at Ipatiev House, Ekaterinburg, under an increasingly harsh regime. The Bolsheviks thought of bringing him to Moscow for trial; now, with White Russian forces closing in on the Urals, Lenin sees the family's existence as a dangerous rallying point for royalists in the civil war.

Evening

16 July. The Romanovs gather for supper. This simple family ritual is the last social life left to them, their roster of elaborate ceremonial duties vanished since the abdication of Nicholas II 15 months earlier. Mealtimes are now the only hours they can spend together, in a place designated by their captors as a 'House of Special Purpose'. Apart from their brief daily exercise periods, they are confined to their rooms on the top floor. Even on visits to the lavatory, they are escorted by the Bolshevik guards – a source of no small discomfort and embarrassment to the women and girls.

Around the table are Nicholas himself, his face lined with the strain of uncertainty; his wife Alexandra, also looking older; and their children: Olga, 22, Tatiana, 21, Maria, 17, Anastasia, 16, and Alexei. A month short of 14, Alexei is heir to the lost throne of the Romanovs, and his haemophilia has always been a worry to his parents: his mother was terrified during his boyhood that a bump or scratch might set off fatal bleeding. After supper Nicholas says prayers and the family disperse to their rooms.

00:05

17 July. They are woken by the guards, led by Jakob Yurovski, who orders everyone to assemble in a cellar in readiness for a move to new quarters. The girls cram jewels in their underwear – many things have been stolen since they came to Ekaterinburg. Joined by the family physician, Eugene Botkin, the lady-in-waiting, Maria Demidova, as well as a footman and a cook, they troop down to the cellar on the far side of the house. The children scoop up their pet dog and carry it with them.

Once gathered in the cellar with its striped walls, they wait, subdued but anxious. Suddenly the door is thrown open and a squad of assassins appears. They are armed with rifles, bayonets fixed, and pistols.

There is one killer for each member of the royal party. As Yurovski reads out the execution order, Nicholas steps forward in disbelief, stuttering 'What? What?' ... He dies first, shot in the face.

The rest of the squad start firing. At first the bullets seem to bounce off the girls' bodies, deflected by the jewellery hidden in their clothes, but blood eventually sprays the walls as the guns keep blazing, ricocheting in the confined space until the cellar is filled with smoke. The killers check the heap of bloodstained bodies to see that all are dead. When Anastasia and Maria Demidova stir, groaning, they are bayoneted repeatedly, while Yurovski finishes off Alexei with two shots through the ear. The bodies are carried upstairs and thrown on the back of a truck.

02:30 The truck is driven to the disused Four Brothers iron mine in the forest near Koptiaki Road. In a glade the bodies are stripped, relieved of jewels from the girls' corsets, and thrown down a flooded mineshaft. Because the water is shallow, they are still partly visible from above, so the killers throw larch branches on top, burn the clothes and drive away in the dark.

Morning **18 July.** Bolshevik officials from Ekaterinburg tell Yurovski the bodies must be moved – if found they could become icons in a cult of royal martyrdom. Much later, the dead are dragged out and loaded back on the truck. An attempt is made to burn the Tsar, Tsarina and Alexei, but they are wet from immersion. The truck gets stuck in mud, so the soldiers decide to bury the corpses under the road at a remote crossing. Sulphuric acid is thrown on the faces to prevent recognition; interred in a shallow grave beneath some planks, they remain undiscovered for 73 years. When they are dug up in 1991, two skeletons are missing, promoting claims that Anastasia survived.

Above left: Nicholas II pictured with his family: Duchess Olga, Duchess Maria, his wife the Tsarina, the Grand Duchess Anastasia, the Tsarevitch Alexei and the Grand Duchess Tatiana.

Above right: Late obsequies: after decades of lying hidden in the earth at a remote forest crossing, the nine bodies found lie in state at last – but two are still missing.

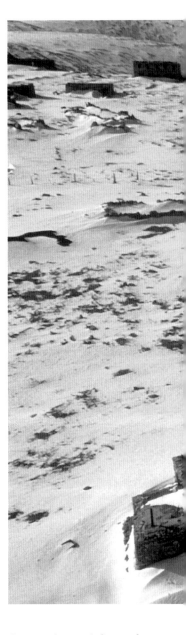

Left: Joseph Stalin attends a meeting in 1935 commemorating the completion of the Moscow Underground.

Right: Like iced-over tombs in a frozen graveyard, the buildings of a former Soviet gulag still stand in Pevek, Russia.

By the 1930s, Stalin's terror had reached its zenith, deploying the full totalitarian apparatus of party purges, spies, secret police investigations, informers, nocturnal disappearances, show-trials, torture, execution and exile to the gulags – bleak prison camps, often in Siberia, where inmates died in their millions from slave labour, hunger, cold and disease. Yet Stalin assumed the old tsarist mantle of 'father of the nation', twinkling for the cameras as he received peasant delegations in Moscow and tousled the hair of small children. For many Russians, especially those from the countryside, it was a strangely convincing imposture.

In June 1941 Hitler broke his non-aggression pact with Stalin and invaded the Soviet Union in a desperate gamble to seize the Baku oilfields on the Caspian. The Red Army's heroic defence of Stalingrad, costing some three million lives, turned the tide of the war – but it also gave Stalin the chance to push westwards, all the way to Berlin, vastly enlarging the Soviet Empire's domain. In Winston Churchill's later phrase, an 'iron curtain' had fallen across Europe. And from 1945 countries within the new communist bloc soon learnt the cost of defying the will of their Soviet masters.

Although Stalin's death in 1953 ushered in the era of Nikita Khrushchev (1894–1971), who in February 1956 made public acknowledgement of Stalin's murderous excesses, it was still the height of the Cold War. Yet Khrushchev's liberalizing drive seemed genuine as Stalin's man in Hungary, Prime Minister Rakosi

(1892–1971), was removed and thousands of Russian troops were withdrawn. But the thaw did not last. On 23 October 1956, following a lead from the Poles, crowds of students and workers demonstrated in the capital, Budapest. They toppled statues of Stalin, yelled slogans and issued a set of 16 Points that included demands for food and personal freedom, the scrapping of the secret police and an end to Russian control. When the new prime minister, Imre Nagy (1895–1958), announced a week later that Hungary would quit the Warsaw Pact, his foreign minister, Janos Kadar, resigned in disgust and proclaimed an alternative government, loyal to Moscow, in the east of the country. Russian tanks rolled into Budapest in November, crushing the rebels with

frightening brutality, even dragging dead bodies through the streets as a deterrent to any further dissidence. Up to 30,000 Hungarians lost their lives; 200,000 more fled the country.

Five years later, in the early hours of 13 August 1961, East Germany sealed its border with the West. A white line painted across the road at the Brandenberg Gate was the first signal, but it was replaced by strands of barbed wire. Within days a solid barrier went up, built from the same concrete slabs used in the East's monolithic grey apartment blocks. Tanks swivelled their turrets at key junctions, truckloads of armed police and soldiers were stationed at the roadsides. This was the start of the Berlin Wall, ordered by Khrushchev to stem a mounting flow of refugees.

Berliners woke to the deafening racket of pneumatic drills and jackhammers as 25,000 'factory fighters' from the East, backed by armed police and three Red Army divisions, were mobilized to cut the city in two. They cauterized 193 roads at the city's heart and cut the number of crossing-points from 81 to a dozen. Underground and train links to West Berlin were halted, telephone lines disconnected. East Berliners could no longer travel to the West, including 53,000 workers with jobs on the other side and 12,000 school children.

It was not the first time Berliners had seen Russian tanks on the streets. They were there when the Red Army first stormed into the ruined city in 1945, and in June 1953 they had opened fire on demonstrators in the Potsdamer Platz. Yet as the disparity between life in the Soviet sector and the affluence of the West became glaring, by 1953 the numbers leaving had reached 6,000 a week. In all almost 200,000 people had gone by the time the Wall went up. This human haemorrhage was an economic liability – more than half of those leaving were under 25 – and an embarrassing propaganda failing for a system still trumpeting its superiority over capitalism.

As soon as the Wall was in place, people started trying to tunnel underneath or escape over the top. One such exit route was located in a cemetery, where 'mourners' would appear with flowers and then, without warning, vanish into the earth. A woman with a baby stumbled on the entrance by chance and got away, leaving her pram behind; it was spotted by police and the tunnel was sealed. Still people contrived to escape, bribing guards with cigarettes or money. At one point the sale of rope and twine was prohibited when a few intrepid souls clambered over the top. In all, during the 28 years of the Wall's existence, around 5,000 people tried to get away. More than 150 perished in the attempt, mostly gunned down by border guards; at least 3,000 of these attempts ended in failure.

Within a year the partition extended to almost 150 km (93 miles), with 12 km (7 miles) of solid wall across the city centre, reaching an average height of 4 m (13 feet); the rest, running through surrounding fields and meadows, was made of twin rolls of wire up to 70 m (76 yards) apart. The Wall was surmounted by a bulging coping or barbed wire, with a trench behind to stop the passage of vehicles. Then came a patrol road, a guard-dog run, arc lights, watchtowers and machine-gun bunkers. After that a second wall. The area between was

the 'death strip', a barren concrete trench in which several would-be escapers bled to death; the main crossing-point to the US sector in West Berlin was Checkpoint Charlie, 200 m (220 yards) west of the Brandenberg Gate.

Communism maintained its grip in Eastern Europe through new crises: the Cuban missile crisis of 1962 saw the world on the brink of nuclear war; the crushing of Alexander Dubček's Prague Spring in 1968 left another gloomy monument on the *via dolorosa* of Soviet repression. After Khrushchev, Brezhnev (1906–82) came and went, ushering in the era of *détente*; then, in 1982, he was succeeded by Mikhail Gorbachev (b.1931), a bold reformer who saw that Russia's economic plight required radical new initiatives. His policies of *glasnost* and *perestroika* transformed relations with the West.

Even more importantly, they transformed expectations on the other side of the Iron Curtain. So much so that by the summer of 1989, the Soviet empire was unravelling fast. Thousands of East Germans were slipping away via Hungary; elsewhere the system was crumbling. At last, on 9 November, the dam burst. A tidal wave of East Germans, wielding sledgehammers, chisels, penknives, nailfiles, anything – even tearing at the concrete with their bare hands – swarmed over the Wall in an ecstasy of hope and celebration. The pent-up energy of a downtrodden people burst forth in a spectacular demonstration of just how far communism had strayed from its original ideals. For the East Berliners of 1989 were, in a sense, indistinguishable from the people of St Petersburg, who threw off the yoke a lifetime ago in those far-off, heady days of February 1917.

East Berlin police build the wall that divides the city. East German leader Walter Ulbricht famously declared, 'Nobody intends to build a wall', before it was first erected in August 1961, separating East and West Berlin for more than 28 years.

1989

Tearing down the Berlin Wall

9 November 1989. For 28 years the Berlin Wall has stood as the symbol of a divided world. For Germans, Berliners especially, that division was painful. While capitalist West Berlin lay inside Soviet-controlled East Germany, the Wall was a reminder not only of the gulf between systems, but also of a nation cut in half. But by late 1989 the Soviet Empire is falling apart.

18:55 **9 November.** In East Berlin, Party spokesman Günther Schabowski slips a surprise announcement into a routine press conference: citizens of the DDR, he says, are now free to enter and leave the country at will. One journalist, unable to believe his ears, asks when this decree takes effect. Schabowski replies, 'Comrades, I was told a statement has been made. According to my information, from today – immediately.'

This news, incredible given East Germany's postwar history of repression, is less so in the light of recent events. Since September, when Hungary opened its borders with Austria, East Germans have been slipping away to the West in their thousands, and Czechoslovakia has recently followed suit; three weeks ago, after 18 years as president, the old-style hardline president, Erich Honecker, was ousted by the Politburo in favour of the more liberal Egon Krenz. All over the communist world, previously unimaginable changes are taking place.

20:30 It hasn't taken long for the news to spread. On the Western side of the Wall, decorated with colourful graffiti, satirical artwork and pointed political comments, the reaction is one of celebration. In the East, where it is screened off by barbed wire, arc lights, guntowers and bleak concrete killing-zones, it takes longer to conquer old fears. No-one has informed the border guards – and since the Wall went up in 1961, those guards have shot down hundreds trying to escape. From the West a bold few clamber on to the bulbous coping and peer over. Cautious at first, they start to gain confidence and call out to the anxious crowds on the Eastern side, still facing guards who are equally unsure what to do.

23:30 For the East Berliners it appears that their officials meant to say only that travel permits will henceforth be issued on demand. But now this is nowhere near enough. The

East German guards are wavering, as nervous as the crowd. At last one commander takes the lead and orders some gates to be opened; the action is repeated at other crossing-points. East Germans begin to stream through, a flood of dazed, happy people. They are greeted by ecstatic Westerners on the other side, who hug and kiss them, cracking open bottles of beer, wine and champagne.

02:30 **10 November.** The mood is now indistinguishable on both sides of the Wall – like two pent-up waves, rushing together in a tumult of pure celebration. More and more people climb on the Wall. They dance and drink and chant and shout, waving frantically to those still on the far side, imploring them to come up. Crowds attack the Wall with anything to hand – hammers, picks, penknives, even nailfiles. They gouge, chisel, scrape, pry and smash off lumps of concrete for souvenirs, punching holes through the poor-quality cement blocks, intended a lifetime ago for new apartment blocks.

Security is a shambles – a Dane shows his cat's vaccination certificate in response to an East German border guard's request for documents and it's enough to get him through in his car. Guard towers stand empty, barbed wire shoved aside in heaps. A stream of headlights along the *autobahn* turns night into day as the destruction of the Wall gathers pace, thousands of people now joining in.

05:00 Heavy machines have now been brought into play. A giant industrial drill punches holes in the Wall, raising loud cheers every time a new one appears. East German guards peer through. Fireworks go off, lighting up the sky in brilliant colours, along with flares and rescue rockets. The Wall is now like a Swiss cheese – full of holes. Germany is reunited, and the celebrations continue for many days and weeks to come.

Above left: Seeing the other side – through a crack in the old concrete barrier.

Above right: 'Something there is that doesn't love a wall,' wrote Robert Frost, the US poet, and Berliners show how right he was.

The dream of flight is one of mankind's most enduring, and there are many notable days in the history of aviation. Two that stand out, separated by just 20 years, are Chuck Yeager's 1947 flight to break the sound barrier and Donald Campbell's 1967 attempt to set a new landspeed record in Bluebird.

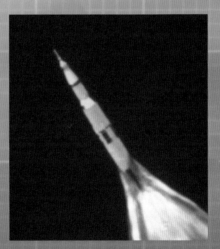

[875] : [2003]

THE HISTORY
OF FLIGHT

The dream that men might fly like the birds that swoop upon the aerial currents of the sky is an ancient and compelling one – some would say it is an obsession as old as humankind. Ancient pictographs clearly portray the magical ability, long credited to tribal shamans and shape-shifters, to transform themselves at will from human into animal form.

These mystical figures could change into bears and wolves and fish and, sometimes, into birds. Indeed, there are cave paintings dating from as far back as the Upper Palaeolithic era well over 10,000 years ago that show winged men and women with long, birdlike beaks protruding from their faces.

Whether these transformations were seen as literal, with actual claws, beaks and feathers sprouting from the body, or spiritual, involving the departure of the soul from its physical vehicle to take wing under its own power, flight has also been an enduring mythical theme. The early Christians gave their angels wings. In ancient Greece the story of Daedalus and Icarus, who escaped from captivity in Crete on wings fashioned from wax and feathers, is coupled with a warning against hubris – the overweening ambition of mortals to match

The history of flight

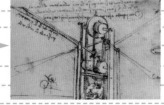

875
Abbas Ibn Firnas, a Moor living in Spain, takes off from a mountain near Cordoba on a glider and glides some distance through the air before crashing to earth.

1490
Leonardo da Vinci starts producing sketches for all manner of possible flying machines. He concludes that the secret must lie in the ability to glide, observed in bats and birds.

1680
Giovanni Borelli's study of animal motion contends mistakenly that birds owe their ability to fly to the movements of individual feathers, which human beings can never hope to replicate.

their powers against those of the gods. Icarus, intoxicated by the experience, soared too close to the sun, whereupon his wings melted and he plummeted to his death in the foaming waters of the Aegean far below.

Leonardo da Vinci (1452–1519) is the most celebrated among the early visionaries who began to develop the ancient dream into a more practical set of ideas in the last part of

Angels ascending: detail of a fresco depicting '*Noli Me Tangere*' from the life of St Mary Magdalene, attributed to Palmerino di Guido, *c.*1309.

1783
The Montgolfier Brothers send aloft a hot-air balloon made of silk, carrying a sheep, a cockerel and a duck the first time and then two men in the basket below.

1903
The Wright brothers make the first powered flight in a heavier-than-air machine at Kitty Hawk, North Carolina, achieving a distance of 260 m (852 feet).

1909
French aviator Louis Blériot wins a £1,000 prize after becoming the first man to fly the Channel, travelling in a modified Type XI monoplane.

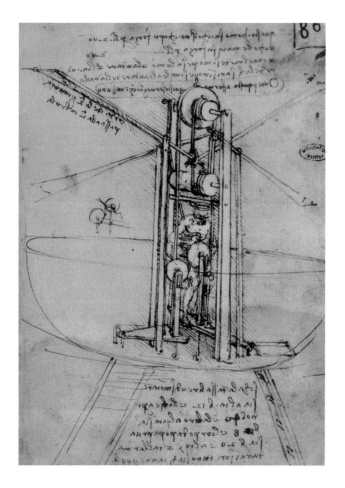

Not so much a flying saucer as an airborne breakfast bowl, this machine was one of Leonardo da Vinci's more fanciful designs.

the fifteenth century. In 1490 he drew a number of sketches in order to illustrate his theories, quickly latching on to the idea that the best way to get a man airborne was to use wings that would exploit the ability to glide, observed in birds and bats, rather than attempt to harness the power of human anatomy directly.

Leonardo had been obsessed with birds from his youth. In the *Codex Atlanticus* he recalled: 'This writing distinctly about the kite seems to be my destiny, because among the first recollections of my infancy, it seemed to me that, as I was in my cradle, a kite came to me and opened my mouth with its tail, and struck me several times with its tail inside my lips.' There has been considerable speculation since about whether he also constructed prototypes to test out his designs in person, though it is generally accepted that his celebrated 'ornithopter' never got off the drawing board.

Whatever the truth of this last line of inquiry, Leonardo was certainly not the first on to the launch-pad in Europe. Almost two-thirds of a millennium before him, two adventurous Moors living in Spain had become equally fascinated with flying. And so it was that in 852 a certain Armen Firman stitched a cloak into the shape of a wing and leaped from a tower in Cordoba. Though the cloak was not enough to keep him aloft, it was just sufficient to break his fall, and Firman escaped with minor injuries.

More successful was Abbas Ibn Firnas, also resident in Cordoba at around the same time. Having studied chemistry, physics, astronomy and glassmaking, as well as building a device to demonstrate the movements of the planets and

The history of flight

1919
John William Alcock and Arthur Whitten-Brown make the first non-stop transatlantic crossing in a Vickers-Vimy, flying from Newfoundland to Ireland.

1927
Charles Lindbergh becomes the first man to achieve a non-stop solo transatlantic flight, crossing from New York to Paris in The Spirit of St Louis.

1932
Amelia Earhart becomes the first woman to fly alone across the Atlantic Ocean – on the fifth anniversary of Lindbergh's epoch-making flight and just days after his son's abduction.

inventing a new chronometer, in 875 he constructed a glider that was capable of carrying a human being. The people of the city gathered on a mountaintop to watch as Ibn Firnas took off and drifted quite a way before crash landing. He attributed his sudden, uncontrolled descent to a failure on his own part to take account of how birds use their tail feathers in the air. But, having damaged his back quite badly on his first outing, unsurprisingly he did not feel up to applying this avian insight to a second attempt.

The example set by birds may have been inspiring, but it was not, in these early days, especially helpful. Besides, by 1680, Giovanni Alfonso Borelli (1608–79) was thought to have arrived at the definitive view on the matter. In his posthumously published *De Motu Animalium*, he surmised – wrongly, as it turned out – that a bird's ability to fly comes from the motion of each individual feather, twisting and turning in flight, combined with an intricate choreography of wing flaps, and he claimed to offer clear proof that the human musculature was far too feeble to emulate this approach.

In fact, the principles of bird flight were not entirely understood until the twentieth century, but this did not deter the more intrepid pioneers. Historian Clive Hart documented more than 50 attempts to fly before 1800 in his book *The Prehistory of Flight*, despite the fact that only about a dozen are reckoned to have got even briefly airborne. One example of these attempts is the case of Besnier, a locksmith from Sable, France, who attached a pair of wings made from wood and taffeta to his back and then flapped them energetically by means of ropes that were attached to his hands and feet.

Besnier proudly trumpeted his success, and while many doubted whether he had got off the ground at all, his boasts helped to keep others trying.

In any case, there were other angles to explore. It did not require a huge stretch of the imagination to observe that kites, flown for recreation and at religious ceremonies in the East since ancient times, might be scaled up to carry passengers. Then, in 1783, the brothers Joseph Michel Montgolfier (1740–1810) and Jacques Etienne Montgolfier (1745–99) had a breakthrough with the first hot-air balloon by blowing heated air into a large silk bag that was attached to a specially designed basket below.

Since hot air rises, the balloon rose, too, carrying with it a sheep, a cockerel and a duck – farmyard precursors of the dogs and monkeys to be launched into space on the test flights of the future – for about 1.6 km (1 mile), floating up to a claimed height of 1,825 m (6,000 feet). The first manned flight followed quickly on 21 November 1783, with Jean-François Pilâtre de Rozier (1756–85) and François Laurent (1742–1809) taking the glory. The military, meanwhile, was not slow to see a battlefield role for the balloon, and it was successfully deployed against the Austrians by the French at the Battle of Fleurus in 1794.

Despite these early efforts, the man hailed as the 'father of aerodynamics' was an Englishman, Sir George Cayley (1773–1857). For more than half a century, from 1799 until his death, Cayley experimented with wing design. He distinguished between the forces of lift and drag, advancing new concepts for rudders as well as tail surfaces, rear elevators and air screws. His practical work was done with gliders, and he sent a boy up on the first true manned glider flight. Cayley sought continually to improve his

1947
Chuck Yeager, a World War II fighter pilot, breaks the sound barrier – going beyond Mach 1 – in the Bell X-1 test plane, a kind of winged rocket.

1961
Yuri Gagarin becomes the first man in space, orbiting the earth three times in Vostok 1. This Soviet achievement triggers the space race.

1969
US astronauts Neil Armstrong and 'Buzz' Aldrin walk on the surface of the moon – 'one small step for a man, one giant leap for mankind', in Armstrong's words.

designs, trying out different wing profiles to improve air flow or adding a tail for greater stability. He even tried out a biplane variant for structural strength.

While Cayley was impressively advanced in his recognition that engine power would be required for sustained flights, his three-part paper *On Aeriel Navigation* displayed further exceptional foresight by suggesting that fixed-wing aircraft, driven by powered propulsion and with a tail to improve handling, would be the airborne method of the future.

Lighter-than-air flight was one thing, however; heavier-than-air flight quite another. It was not until the last two decades of the nineteenth century that those driven to fly turned in earnest to the central problem of manned flight, defined in Mike Spick's *Milestones of Manned Flight* as 'controlled flight in a powered, heavier-than-air machine'. We might say, without being too fanciful, that they were seeking the equivalent, in the much thinner medium of air, of Archimedes' bathtime discovery of the principle of water displacement, which eventually made possible the building of iron ships. But people do not float in air as they can in water. They simply fall out of the sky.

Thus the next stage brought forth a fresh crop of eager would-be pioneers, touting ideas that ran the gamut from the eccentric and the wrong-headed to the ingenious or even inspired. Inevitably this phase also brought its fair share of accidents. The luckier ones got away with cuts, bruises and broken bones; the less lucky lost their lives amid the splintered wreckage of their frail and rickety machines.

Foremost among them was Otto Lilienthal (1848–96), who became known as 'the bird man of Europe'. An engineer and a methodical thinker, Lilienthal was convinced that the problem of heavier-than-air flight could not be solved by a single breakthrough alone. He argued that it has to be broken down into its component parts, each of which must be investigated fully to have any chance of success. Yet he also had a clear kinship with the earliest dreamers, for he was much taken up with the study of birds.

Lilienthal undertook almost 2,000 glider test flights from 1881. Beginning with a tailless model that was really just a simple pair of wings, which he tested by jumping from a board, he graduated to more ambitious designs with cambered wings and a fixed tailplane. All were in essence hang-gliders – the pilot's head and

shoulders stuck out above the wing while his body dangled below, exerting limited control over the plane's movements by swinging the legs and hips. Lilienthal came up with no less than 15 monoplane and three biplane designs, building a cone-shaped artificial hill at Lichterfelde, near Berlin, to ensure optimum launch conditions irrespective of wind direction. Then, in 1889, he published *Birdflight as the Basis for Aviation*, highlighting the curvature of a bird's wings as the master secret of lift.

For all his scientific diligence, Lilienthal was at heart a born airman, remarking once, 'To invent an airplane is nothing. To build one is something. But to fly is everything.' Yet he was only too well aware of the dangers. In his essay *Practical Experiments for the Development of Human Flight*, he observed: 'The manner in which we have to meet the irregularities of the wind when soaring in the air can only be learnt by being in the air itself. At the same time, it must be considered that one single blast of wind can destroy the apparatus and even the life of the person flying.'

And so it proved. By 1896 Lilienthal decided that the time had come to attempt powered flight. So he fitted out a glider with a small, handmade motor, powered by carbonic gas, to make the glider's wingtips flap. But on 9 August he crashed, fracturing his

spine, and he died the following day in a Berlin hospital. As he had said some time before, with a certain prophetic irony, 'Sacrifices must be made.'

Yet he did not die altogether in vain. For Lilienthal's efforts had attracted worldwide attention, thus helping to make the means of heavier-than-air flight a respectable subject for scientific study rather than the absurd or semi-suicidal domain of crackpots, dreamers, daredevils and showmen. And among the would-be flyers whom he inspired were two American brothers from Dayton, Ohio. These two were destined to succeed where Lilienthal had failed, initiating the first powered flight in a heavier-than-air machine. They thus earned themselves a place not just in the annals of aviation, but in world history, ushering in a century that would see countless millions travel the world, as casually as they had once hopped on the tram across town.

Wilbur Wright (1867–1912) and Orville Wright (1871–1948) were the two youngest of four sons born to Milton and Susan Catharine Wright. Their father was a bishop in the United Brethren Church, a devout Christian who had served as a preacher, school teacher and missionary before becoming a professor of theology and editor of the sect's newspaper, *The Religious Telescope*. The upbringing of the Wright children was strict but loving, with lots of intellectual stimulus. Their home had two libraries – one for divinity, another for general knowledge – and their father would bring back mechanical toys from his travels, including a top that could spin like a helicopter. It was this, reputedly, that first fired the boys' interest in flying.

Wilbur was an outstanding student, whom his parents planned to send to Yale. But their hopes were dashed first by the poor health Wilbur suffered after a skating accident, then by the illness and death of the boys' mother. Orville was merely

average at school, known more for pranks than intellectual prowess. He did not complete his senior college year; instead he left at 18 to set up a printing business with his 22-year-old brother, using the Wright Brothers name professionally for the first time. Three years on, in 1893, they switched to bicycle repairs; in another three years they were producing their own brand of bicycles in two different models.

In 1896 Orville fell ill with typhus. While nursing his brother, Wilbur read of Lilienthal's death and began to take an interest in flying. In May 1899 he wrote to the Smithsonian Institution asking for information on aeronautical research. He quickly identified the key criteria: wings for lift, a power source for propulsion and an adequate control system. But Wilbur had an insight of his own, missed by other early aviators: the control must extend to all three axes of motion – pitch, roll and yaw. Hence his concept of 'wing-warping', or twisting the wing surfaces in response to the wind, which should, he surmised, produce set changes in the flight path.

Using a bicycle-tube box as an improvised prototype, Wilbur tested his idea successfully on a small kite. Wing-warping was combined later with adjustable rudders for improved lateral control. In August 1900 the brothers tested their first manned glider at Kitty Hawk, a remote stretch of flat sands in North Carolina with an average wind speed of 21 km/h (13 mph). Their first attempt produced indifferent results, but they were not deterred. They came back a year later with a fresh design – it had a 6.5 m (22 feet) wingspan but it, too, performed badly – and then again in 1902. After some careful testing in a wind tunnel, this effort fared much better, flying up to 188 m (620 feet).

By 1903 the brothers had developed a propeller, along with a lightweight, four-cylinder petrol engine generating about 12 hp. These were fitted to a biplane, with wings of cotton on willow spanning around 12 m (40 feet). On 14 December the brothers tossed to decide who would go first. Wilbur won, but the plane crashed at take-off. Repairs took two days, plus a day

Almost there: the Wright brothers' No. 3 glider is launched at Kill Devil Hill, North Carolina, USA, with Orville lying on the wing.

of rest to respect the Sabbath. At last, at 10.35 a.m. on 17 December, in a 44 km/h (27 mph) wind, assisted by four lifeboatmen and a boy, it was Orville's turn. And this time – success. The plane travelled 36 m (120 feet), staying airborne for 12 seconds. Then Wilbur, making his second attempt, reached 53 m (175 feet); on the third trial Orville made 61 m (200 feet). And on the fourth and final flight, Wilbur covered no less than 260 m (852 feet) in 59 seconds. It was somehow fitting: the younger brother went first, while the older went farthest.

Orville recalled of his maiden 36 m (120 feet) voyage 'I found the machine pointing upwards and downwards in jerky undulations. This erratic course was due in part to my utter lack of experience in controlling flying machines and in part to a new system of controls we had adopted, whereby a slight touch accomplished what a hard jerk or tug made necessary in the past. Naturally, I overdid everything.' But the Wrights had done what no-one else had done before: instead of employing a ramp, as earlier pioneers had done, they took off from level ground in a powered, heavier-than-air machine and flew with an acceptable degree of control for a short distance to land at the same level from which they had first taken off. Six years later they sold a Wright flying machine to the US government for $25,000, plus a $5,000 bonus for exceeding the specified speed of 65 km/h (40 mph).

From here the history of flight climbs to ever-greater heights and velocities, though the achievement of long distance took a little longer. Airspeed records may have been modest in the early days, and for that reason they did not last long. Glenn Curtiss (1878–1930) set a record at 70 km/h (43.35 mph) on 23 August 1909, but lost his title the next day to a Frenchman, Louis Blériot (1872–1936), who hurtled to 74 km/h (46 mph) in Rheims. Blériot's new record came just one month after he had landed a £1,000 prize, offered by an English newspaper, the *Daily Mail*, for the first cross-Channel flight: on 25 July 1909 he took off in a modified Type XI monoplane from Les Baraques, near Calais, and landed 36 minutes later in Northfall Meadow near Dover – a distance not far short of 39 km (24 miles).

French pilots and designers then remained the undisputed champions of airspeed until 1922. At that point Billy Mitchell (1879–1936) snatched the record away from them by opening up the throttle to reach 359 km/h (223 mph) in a Curtiss HS D-12 near Detroit, USA, only to see another Frenchman, Sadi Lecointe, regain the record four months later in a Nieuport-Delage 29. Nor was the French love of flying confined to winged aircraft. Paul Cornu (1881–1944), like the Wright brothers another bicycle maker, became first to get off the ground in a helicopter in November 1917, at Lisieux, France.

World War I saw the emergence of the air aces – crack pilots who fought out their balletic dogfights in bi- or triplanes with open cockpits, notching up 'kills' on their machines. At first they hurled darts or bombs by hand or fired single revolver shots; later came machine guns mounted on the upper wing or fixed to the nose, with firing-speeds timed to the propellor revolutions. One of the pioneers was Sir Thomas Sopwith (1888–1989), who crashed on his own maiden flight in 1910 but went on to design that mainstay of the British airforce in World War I, the Sopwith Camel. On the German side the best-known makers were Fokker and Albatros.

In an early example of the lack of forward strategy for which the military leaders of World War I would later become notorious, General Ferdinand Foch (1851–1929), professor of strategy at the Ecole Supérieure de Guerre, pronounced in 1911: 'Aviation is fine as sport, but as an instrument of war it is worthless.' The emergence of a new breed of daredevil hero during the conflict was to prove how wrong he was – aces such as Ball, Boelcke, Fonck, Immelmann, Lufbery, McCudden, Mannock, Nungesser, Rickenbacker, Richthofoen and Voss. Von Richthofen (1882–1918), famed as the 'Red Baron', achieved an extraordinary reputation for his skill and ruthlessness, but Rickenbacker (1890–1973) was perhaps the more far-seeing when he observed, 'Fighting in the air is not sport; it is scientific murder.' By the end of the war, engine power had gone from a modest 80 hp to the much more muscular 400 hp churned out by the 12-cylinder American Liberty engine, while bomber aircraft attained wingspans of 30 m (100 feet) and more.

Within a year of the end of the Great War, John William Alcock (1892–1919) and Arthur Whitten-Brown (1886–1948) made the first non-stop transatlantic crossing, taking 16 hours 28 minutes to fly a Vickers-Vimy from Newfoundland to Clifden, Ireland, where they flopped down in a bog. They, too, won a *Daily Mail* prize, ten times the value of Blériot's. Then Charles Lindbergh (1902–74) did it solo, flying from New York to Paris eight years later. He made his epic journey in a Ryan NYP monoplane named *Spirit of St Louis*, and became one of the first truly global celebrities – though he paid a tragic price five years later when his baby son was kidnapped from his home in New Jersey. The kidnappers left a note demanding $50,000; ten weeks later the infant's dead body was found in a wood. Less than a fortnight after this grim discovery, on the fifth anniversary of Lindbergh's flight, Amelia Earhart (1898–1937) became the first woman to fly solo across the Atlantic, at the controls of a Lockheed Vega, completing the journey in 13 hours 30 minutes. Later, she flew the Pacific, from Hawaii to California.

A Messerschmitt Bf 109E-3 fighter doing a banked turn over Germany in 1939. This model of the Bf 109 ruled the skies over Europe until the early 1940s, when it first encountered the Spitfire.

As air races, displays and flying circuses became popular forms of entertainment, a boom began in US airport construction, and the 1930s are known as aviation's golden age. Seaplanes competed at ever-increasing speeds for Europe's Schneider Trophy, which was won three times running by the British; the Italian Macchi MC72, powered by a massive 2,800 hp engine, set a new record of 709 km/h (440 mph) in 1934, which stood until the end of World War II. Inevitably the quest for speed inflicted casualties. In the USA the top competitions were the Bendix Trophy for coast-to-coast flight and the Thompson Trophy. Especially risky were the USA Gee Bee racers, which claimed the lives of several top aviators. Among those who made their names in this high-stakes era were Benny Howard (1904–36), Roscoe Turner (1895–1970) and Jimmy Wedell (1900–34), who established an air service between Houston and New Orleans but later died in a crash. Howard Hughes (1905–76) made his name first as a flyer, setting a land-speed record and flying coast to coast before turning tycoon, a figure of immense glamour until he became the wild-haired, claw-nailed, hypochondriac recluse of later years.

World War II hatched a lethal swarm of legendary fighter aircraft – the Spitfire, the Messerschmitt Bf 109, the P-51 Mustang – as well as the world's first jet plane, Germany's Heinkel He-178. The Spitfire, powered by a Rolls-Royce Merlin engine, was the creation of Reginald Mitchell (1895–1937), son of a Yorkshire printer, who died of cancer before seeing the vital role played by his fighter aircraft in combat with the Messerschmitt during the Battle of Britain. The Merlin engine was astonishingly successful: it also powered the Hurricane, Mosquito, Mustang and Lancaster bomber. Germany's Heinkel He-178, designed by Hans von Ohain (1911–98), made its maiden flight just days before war was declared, whereas the British jet-engine designer Frank Whittle (1907–96), who had filed a patent in 1930, had to wait until 1941 to see his design in action on a Gloster E.28/39 thanks to the dim-wittedness and delay of British bureaucrats. In 1944 Messerschmitt brought the first jet fighters – the Me-163 Komet and the Me-262 – into action, albeit to limited operational effect.

Yet it was only two years after the war ended that Chuck Yeager (b.1923), hero of Tom Wolfe's *The Right Stuff*, became the first man to break the sound barrier. He was a certified wartime ace with a dozen 'kills' to his name, including an Me-262, and had escaped across the Pyrenees disguised as a peasant after being shot down over France. Newly trained as a postwar test pilot at Wright Field in Dayton, Ohio, he was assigned to the XS-1 project in California. On 14 October 1947, in spite of a cracked rib, Yeager was launched from the bomb bay of a B-29 in the Bell X-1 jet-propelled plane to fly at Mach 1 – a feat many had thought impossible, as the prototype plane would start shuddering uncontrollably well before it hit the speed of sound. The first passenger jet airliner, the De Havilland Comet 1, rolled out in 1949.

Britain's Gloster Meteor had set a new record of 975 km/h (606 mph) in late 1945, capped by 990 km/h (615 mph) the following year by a de Havilland Vampire, but in 1947 the lead was taken by the USA in a Lockheed P-80 Shooting Star at 975 km/h (623 mph). From the 1950s onwards the Cold War set off an explosion of ever-faster and more manoeuvrable jet fighters able to take off under their own power: the USA's F-86 Sabre and F-100 Super Sabre; then Britain's Fairey Delta 2, which lifted the threshold from 1,322 km/h (822 mph) in 1955 to 1,822 km/h (1,132 mph) in 1956. By 1958 the F-104A Starfighter was powering along at 2,259 km/h (1,404 mph) – faster than Concorde's 2,172 km/h (1,350 mph) cruising speed more than a decade later. Then came the Russians, at 2,386 km/h (1,483 mph) in October 1959 in the Sukhoi E-66 and a couple of months later the US Convair F-106A Delta Dart at 2,454 km/h (1,525 mph).

Yet the Cold War had another consequence, too. By the late 1950s, the old impulse to fly, now satisfied, had become eclipsed by a still more ambitious urge – to send rockets into space, and to place men inside them. So, rather than merely rising above the clouds, the objective now fell nothing short of the stars.

1947

Chuck Yeager breaks the sound barrier

14 October 1947. Chuck Yeager grew up in a small town on Mud River, the son of a gas driller in the West Virginia coalfields. Wiry and tough, he was a World War II pilot at 20 and shot down more than a dozen German planes, including a new jet fighter, from his prop-driven P-51 Mustang. Today he is trying to break the sound barrier in an army test in the Mojave Desert.

Morning **13 October.** Chuck Yeager wakes after a fitful sleep. His right side is hurting badly, and no wonder. At around eleven o'clock the night before, he had taken his wife Glennis to Pancho's Fly Inn, a rundown bar close to the windswept X-I testing base at Muroc, with a decrepit piano and signed photographs of pilots behind the bar. They had some drinks and decided to go for a gallop in the desert on horses owned by the proprietor, Pancho Barnes; on the way back Yeager rode smack into the corral gate and went flying.

But he's damned if he'll see an army doctor at the base – if he does his flight will be cancelled for certain. So he takes his beaten-up motorbike into the nearby town of Rosamond, wincing each time he hits a rut, and the doctor there tells him he has two broken ribs. He needs to keep his right arm immobile for a fortnight and avoid any unnecessary exertion – then he should be OK.

Dawn **14 October.** Yeager is already dressed, having risen before daybreak; his side is still hurting like hell. During training they used to call him 'a natural stick-and-rudder man': on his very first flight in the X-I, he performed an unauthorized roll with a full tank of *lox* – a mixture of alcohol and liquid oxygen – and then went into a vertical climb in the bullet-shaped, bright orange aircraft, with its stubby, straight, almost undistinguishable wings, reaching Mach .85 before levelling out. The test pilots all found that things start to get very bumpy around Mach .8 and it was no different for Yeager; however, it doesn't bother him much. Today he's due to go past Mach 1 – the 'sound barrier' – though Yeager himself doesn't really believe in any such thing.

Glennis drives him to Muroc. The ground crew are filling the X-I's tanks with *lox*; it screams aloud as the liquid oxygen, stored at -297°C (-502°F), starts boiling off when it

hits the air. Yeager goes to the hangar and realizes that he won't be able to reach over and shut himself inside the X-I's tiny cockpit with his broken ribs, so he discreetly tells flight engineer Jack Ridley, an ex-pilot from Oklahoma, who gets the janitor to saw off a length of broom handle for him. Yeager hides it in the X-I.

Yeager hauls himself aboard the converted B-29 'mother-ship', where the X-I is now suspended in the bay like a bomb; the B-29 takes off. At 2,133 m (7,000 feet) he clambers down into the cockpit of the X-I and, with the aid of his broom handle, slams the hatch shut. He pulls on his outsized football helmet – a cushioned thing as big as a pumpkin to stop his head knocking around the cockpit. At 7,925 m (26,000 feet) the B-29 dives and releases the X-I as if dropping a bomb; Yeager is dazzled by bright sunlight but fires up the four rocket chambers immediately. He has about two and a half minutes worth of fuel.

The X-1 shoots straight up like a bat out of hell and disappears, bucking furiously at Mach .87 but settling again at Mach .96. As Yeager surges on, travelling faster than any man before him, the sky darkens – he's seeing straight out into space. Down on the ground a tremendous boom rolls across the desert. Chuck's done it: Mach 1.05. He does victory rolls on the seven-minute glide back down to earth.

Above left: The Right Stuff – Chuck Yeager strapped in at the controls of the X-1, ready for the challenge of Mach 1.

Above right: All four cylinders fire up as the Bell X-1 roars away at the first powered take-off of the supersonic plane in 1949.

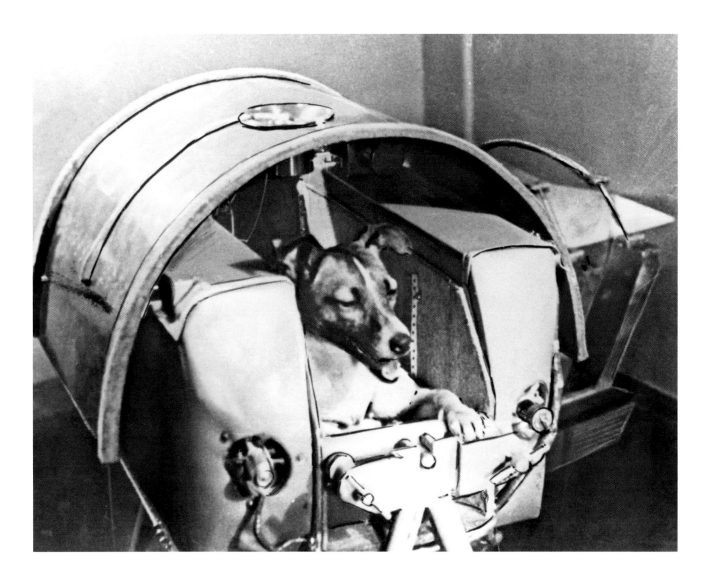

Space became a dark mirror for what was happening on the earth: science-fiction writers explored themes of galactic colonization by rival powers, film-makers scared the pants off punters with tales of invasion by alien life-forms. Back in the real world, an incendiary mix of white-hot technophilia, ideological rivalry and political paranoia powered the emergence of the space programme.

Rockets had in fact originated as a branch of ballistics, quite separate from the dream of flight. Simple, solid-fuel rockets were being used by the Chinese at the start of the thirteenth century. They soon turned up in Europe, too, where they evolved along parallel tracks – as a branch of military ordnance and as a recreational aid to royal revels. Yet the key twentieth-century event that opened the way for the US–Soviet space race was probably Germany's development and deployment of the unmanned V-2

rocket late in World War II, and the subsequent defection to the USA of Hitler's top rocket scientist, Wernher von Braun (1912–77), who was welcomed for his grasp of modern weaponry.

What really galvanized the US drive into space, however, was the Soviet Union's launch on 4 October 1957 of the first manmade satellite, Sputnik, followed less than a month later by Sputnik 2, with the celebrated space dog called Laika on board – a canine pin-up for the space age. Coming as they did at the height of the Cold War, these two triumphs sent a jolt of competitive fury through the US administration, coupled with the gnawing fear that the Russians might also be secretly planning to shape their astonishing technological breakthrough to military ends. Besides, Soviet successes flew in the face of the USA's complacent faith that capitalism simply worked better.

Far left: Laika, the space dog, yawns unsuspectingly inside the Soviet satellite Sputnik II in 1957 before becoming the first living creature to orbit the earth.

Left: At the age of 27, on April 12, 1961, Russian Air Force Major Yuri Gagarin became the first man in space. Gagarin orbited around the earth and returned safely.

The US Congress rushed to fill the gap, and in July 1958 President Dwight D Eisenhower signed the National Aeronautics and Space Act, formally establishing NASA, the National Aeronautics and Space Administration, on 1 October of that year. Its official mission was, 'To provide for research into problems of flight within and outside the Earth's atmosphere, and for other purposes', while shifting the prime responsibility for aerospace research from military to civilian hands and subsuming the older National Advisory Committee for Aeronautics (NACA).

From that point the race was on in earnest. For a time the Russians maintained their early lead. They landed a Luna probe on the dark side of the moon in 1959 and brought back pictures; two years on, in April 1961, they launched Yuri Gagarin (1934–68), the world's first cosmonaut, on a successful flight into space. He orbited the earth three times in Vostok 1, ejected from the capsule on his way down, and floated safely back to terra firma by parachute to land in a field near the village of Smelovaka. In his bright orange suit, smiling with down-to-earth peasant warmth and the gracious modesty of a truly great man, here was a Soviet hero for all humankind.

The gloom at NASA, which had felt so sure of getting its man Alan Shepard into orbit ahead of the Russians, was like a choking cloud of dust. John Glenn, who won fame as an astronaut the following year by orbiting the earth three times in a one-man Mercury capsule, summed up their dismay: 'They beat the pants off us, that's all. There's no kidding ourselves about that.' But John F Kennedy, the popular, young new president, urgently needed something big to rally the dented confidence of the US people after the Bay of Pigs fiasco – a failed invasion of Cuba that left the self-styled champions of Western freedoms looking corrupt, cynical and hopelessly incompetent, which had happened in the same month as Gagarin's mission.

The boundless frontiers of space were the ideal distraction from terrestrial political *débâcles* – a bold, aspiring cause – and Kennedy jumped at the chance to restore his lustre by declaring his full support for the space programme. There was also a fear that the Soviet Union would adapt spacecraft to military purposes and attack the USA. From then on the USA started to make up lost ground. NASA did get Alan Shepard into orbit, one month after Gagarin's epoch-making flight, in a craft pointedly named Freedom 7. NASA pressed on quickly from Project Mercury, a research programme to gauge the prospects for human survival in space, to Project Gemini, which developed spacecraft able to accommodate two astronauts. Next up was Project Apollo. With this NASA had set itself by far its most audacious target yet: one to put the Soviets firmly in their place. For their new goal was nothing less than landing on the moon.

This vaulting ambition exacted a heavy price en route to success: four astronauts died in a flashfire that broke out in January 1967 inside the command module of an Apollo-Saturn rocket during a launch-pad test for the craft's first manned flight. But the momentum was too strong even for such a tragic setback as this to stop or even significantly delay the programme. Thus in 1969, almost six years after President Kennedy's assassination in Dallas, the Apollo 11 mission to the moon was ready to go. By that time the Cold War point-scoring of the early space programme had given way to an intense, highly focused effort involving thousands of people to master the various daunting technical and human challenges of such an unprecedented venture. Those enlisted in the project had simply become caught up in the sheer enormity of the adventure.

And so, at 9.32 a.m. on 16 July 1969, Apollo 11 was launched on a Saturn V rocket, with three astronauts tucked inside their womblike capsule: commander Neil Armstrong; Michael Collins, operating the command module, Columbia; Edwin 'Buzz' Aldrin, pilot of the lunar module, Eagle. Four days later, having made one and a half orbits of earth without mishap, the mission went out of radio contact as it swung round the dark side of the moon. Tension rose palpably in Houston.

At last, at 4.18 p.m. on 20 July, Armstrong's famous message, 'The Eagle has landed', came out loud and clear over the speakers at Houston. At 10.39 p.m., more than five hours ahead of schedule, Armstrong opened the hatch and started to climb down the ladder. As he placed his boot on the soft dust of the moon's surface, he radioed back to earth with the celebrated words, 'That's one small step for a man, one giant leap for mankind.' Buzz Aldrin followed him out just 15 minutes afterwards.

On their return to earth, they were welcomed by President, Nixon who declared in a fit of ecstatic hyperbole: 'This is the greatest week in the history of the world since the Creation … as a result of what you have done, the world's never been closer together … we can reach for the stars just as you have reached so far for the stars.'

In many ways this was the emotional zenith of the space programme, one that has never been matched since. True, there have been subsequent achievements – Skylab in 1973; the two Viking Mars probes launched in 1976, and the landing there, 21 years later, of the robotic exploration module Sojourner; the exit of Pioneer 10 from the solar system for deep space in 1997. Yet there have also been harrowing disasters, such as the Columbia Space Shuttle disasters of 1986 and 2003. For in the terrible images from the first of those traumatic events – a spacecraft spinning to instant extinction in a wild corkscrew of white smoke, killing seven astronauts – some may see an echo of the fate of Icarus. And it is also fair to ask whether, if ever other intelligent life-forms are discovered on other worlds, there is any guarantee they will want to know us.

Flames steam from the booster rocket as the Apollo 11 craft streaks across the sky during the Saturn V moon launch on 16 July 1969.

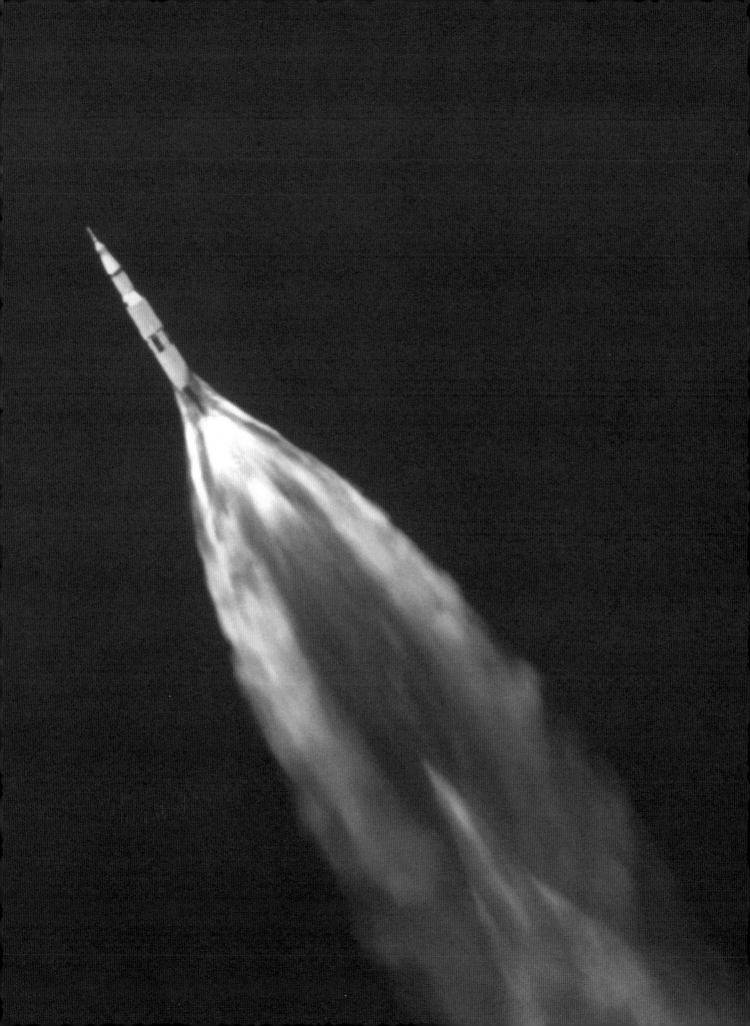

1967

Campbell aims to top 300 mph in Bluebird

4 January 1967. Donald Campbell has an insatiable hunger for speed – like his father Malcolm, he wants to 'fly' in elements other than air. Malcolm Campbell set landspeed records from 1924 and waterspeed records from 1937; Donald made it a family double – first in 1964, holding both at once after a successful trip to Australia. On this day he hopes to top 300 mph (483 km/h) on Coniston Water in the Lake District.

Evening **3 January.** Trying to relax after several wintry weeks at the Sun Hotel in Coniston, waiting for the right conditions, Donald Campbell draws a bad hand at cards. He and his wife Tonia are superstitious. In 1964 in Australia they stumbled on a legend that Lake Eyre had been cursed by a 'witch doctor', a story that appeared to gain substance when the normally dry lake they were using for the landspeed attempt began to flood.

So Tonia took the Aboriginals for a picnic and sang to them to dispel bad luck. Half-jokingly, they told each other afterwards that it must have worked, for Donald set a new water record of 276.33 mph (444 km/h) at Lake Dumbleyung. Though Campbell, who is 46, feels at home in Coniston, having set water records there on four previous occasions between September 1956 and May 1959, he takes his poor cards as an inauspicious omen.

08:30 **4 January.** The morning is cold but calm; *Bluebird K7* stands ready at the quayside. Powered by turbojet, it is the boat Donald built to replace his father's vessel, the K4, in the wake of a disastrous outing at Coniston in 1951. When he inherited K4 it ran on jet power; he had it modified to solve an engine-cooling problem, then to prevent the stern lifting by using a propeller, and finally to stop the craft 'corkscrewing'. Just when the boat seemed to be running well at last, it hit an underwater obstacle and sank. The new boat cost him £18,000 – a sum he could raise only by remortgaging his house.

Campbell checks the boat over. The engine, a Metropolitan Vickers Beryl, provides 3,750 lb of thrust. Since he took possession of the boat, a lot more tinkering has gone on: weights were added after buoyancy tanks failed to work; the engine was moved nearer the stern; deflector panels were fitted to induce 'planing'.

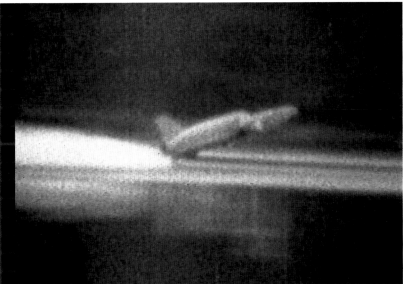

Further adjustments were made after tests on a model in a wind tunnel at Imperial College, London. Since then he has made seven record-breaking outings in K7, five of them in the Lakes, and overcome serious injuries after a bad smash during a landspeed attempt in Utah.

08:55 Campbell straps on his helmet and settles into the cockpit. The engine powers up; he opens the throttle and takes off across the long, straight lake just like a waterborne rocket, tracing an arc of silver spray behind him. On the first leg he hits 297 mph (478 km/h), makes a tight turn without waiting for his wake to settle, and roars off once again. This time he exceeds 300 mph (483 km/h) – initial estimates suggest 320 mph (515 km/h) – but suddenly the nose of the boat lifts too high. K7 flips 50 feet (15 m) into the air, somersaults and crashes down again, disintegrating on impact. It sinks into more than 120 feet (36 m) of water; later, the mangled remains of the boat are found, but there is no trace of Campbell.

Above left: Donald Campbell shows off his speedboat to members of the 14th Field Regiment, Royal Artillery. He hopes to break his own speed record of 239.07 mph (384.75 km/h).

Above right: *Bluebird*'s nose lifts from the surface of Coniston Water just before the craft flips 50 feet (15 m) in the air and crashes to the bottom of the lake.

In a long history of prejudice and oppression, Jews were treated with suspicion even in ancient times, accused of occult practices in the medieval age, exploited or expelled by monarchs and subjected to the horror of the Nazi years. Even Israel, their homeland, remains a land riven with conflict.

[300 BC] : [1948]

JEWISH SUFFERING, JEWISH FREEDOM

In many parts of eighteenth-century Western Europe, the Enlightenment brought hopes for a new dispensation to the Jews after centuries of hatred, suspicion and persecution. The emphasis placed by this new era on the power of human reason, on scientific method as opposed to religious superstition and, above all, on the idea of universal human rights, appeared to Jews and non-Jews alike as a promise of deliverance from the darkness of the past.

For the Jews this was an especially significant period, as these influential European thinkers and writers began to espouse their cause. While such advocacy was often mingled with the expression of older, more intractable prejudices, it looked as though the seed of European humanism planted by the Protestant Reformation might at last bear fruit. This would then allow the Jews to enter unreservedly into societies that for hundreds of years had rejected them as pernicious and destructive outsiders, a view often coupled with the assumption that they were in league with Satan.

France was the epicentre of this new spirit. The social and political philosopher Montesquieu (1689–1755) argued in 1748 that the Jewish talent for commerce had been warped by Christian restrictions on their rights of ownership since the Middle Ages and

The history of the Jews

1275 BC
Moses leads the Exodus from Egypt – a story of divine deliverance to the Jews. A thousand years later an Egyptian insists they were expelled because of disease.

4th century
Church Fathers such as John Chrysostom begin a major assault on the reputation of the Jews, blaming them for Christ's death and blasting them as heretics.

1096
During the First Crusade Jews are massacred in Germany while taking refuge in a bishop's palace. They are rumoured to spread plague and practise witchcraft and ritual murder.

that Jews had in fact levied generous contributions to Christian royal purses. They should be treated, he concluded, in the same way as Christians would wish others to treat them. Even that terror of the French Revolutionary tribunals, Robespierre (1758–94), observed, 'the Jews' vices are the ones you have plunged them into; they will be good when they can find some advantage in so being.' Rousseau (1712–78) urged tolerance, while also

Above left: Weight of tradition: Zion Huvra, 13, works on a page of a scroll of the Books of Esther for the synagogue of Boys Town, Jerusalem.

Above: Beckholen Synagogue, containing a wall-painting of the seven-branched candelabrum or menorah.

1492
When Ferdinand and Isabella expel the Moors from Spain, Jews who have lived there for centuries are forced to leave without taking their personal wealth.

1656
Baruch Spinoza is excommunicated by rabbinical edict after rejecting ideas of a 'Chosen People', insisting that all religions should be judged by the Light of Reason.

1748
Enlightenment thinkers such as Montesquieu begin to defend the Jews against centuries of slander, though some of these tracts still show anti-Semitic thinking.

condemning the Jews as 'the vilest of peoples'; Voltaire (1694–1778) railed against them as 'ignorant and barbarous', though he did also express a similar contempt for the bigotries of the Catholic Church and added, on a more rational note, 'We should not burn them' – the Jews, that is.

France was not the only place where a new toleration was in vogue. Earlier, in England, the Irish-born free thinker John Toland (1670–1722) held that 'the true Christianity of the Jews was overborne and destroyed by the more numerous gentiles.' He also supported Jewish immigration, thus earning the ridicule of Alexander Pope (1688–1744) and the scorn of the satirist Jonathan Swift (1667–1745) as 'the great Oracle of the anti-Christians'. Even in Germany, in the later years of the century, theatre-goers were treated to the novel spectacle of plays featuring idealized Jewish characters in thinly veiled dramatic pleas for religious tolerance, while a Prussian historian, Christian von Döhm (1751–1820), argued strongly for the removal of restrictions on Jewish entry to professions other than commerce.

These changes were more than just the utopian musings of a few visionaries. For they pointed to far-reaching changes in politics, too. In 1782 the Holy Roman Emperor Joseph II (1741–90) issued an Edict of Tolerance recognizing the right of Jews to become naturalized citizens, seeking to blend together the diverse peoples of the Austro-Hungarian Empire and bring harmony to its scattered dominions. Less than a decade later, in 1791, the emancipation of the French Jews was declared. Thereafter Napoleon Bonaparte (1769–1821), though he had no regard for a people he considered 'chicken-hearted', went further. He introduced a formal rights bill, albeit with some stringent restrictions on Jewish business activities, and in 1807 summoned Jewish leaders from all over France to review their civil status, culminating in a grand Jewish council in Paris called the Great Sanhedrin. For a time France was hailed as the saviour of European Jewry.

In parts of Germany, too, new horizons were opening up for Jews after the entry of some of their richer brethren into Berlin's higher social echelons by the end of the eighteenth century. This was coupled with moves by the Jews themselves to adapt traditional patterns of worship to contemporary conditions, to translate sacred texts or even to accept Christian baptism, heralding a vigorous debate about 'assimilation' among Jew and gentile alike that still continues. During the nineteenth century the old link between religion and nationhood was increasingly set aside. Jews in France or Germany spoke of themselves as Frenchmen or Germans, Jewish by religion, rather than in the old way, as members of the dispersed Jewish nation residing for now in those countries.

A key figure in these upheavals was himself a Jew, Baruch Spinoza (1632–77), a radical seventeenth-century Dutch-born thinker who was excommunicated by rabbinical edict for his anti-religious polemics. Spinoza was an optical-lens polisher who gradually built up a formidable intellectual reputation; his writings rejected any notion of a 'Chosen People' and contended that all religions should be judged solely by the Light of Reason. So great was the eventual transformation wrought by the Enlightenment that the German-Jewish writer Moses Herschel exulted: 'Thanks to our philosophical century, the age of barbarism has passed away, when one must expect

The history of the Jews

1807
Napoleon calls a council in Paris of the leaders of French Jewry, a Grand Sanhedrin, and provokes rumours of a Jewish plot to seize world power.

1881
Amid violence and mass expulsions, the first wave of Russian pogroms breaks out following the assassination of Tsar Alexander II. Two more will follow.

1897
A notorious forgery, 'The Protocols of the Elders of Zion', is published in Russia to 'prove' a Jewish world conspiracy; the first Zionist conference is organised by Theodor Herzl.

Jewish philosopher Baruch Spinoza became an outcast among Orthodox Jews when he rejected the idea of a 'Chosen People'.

a contemptuous grimace at the mention of the word 'Jew.' And yet, three centuries before Hitler's rise to power, this grateful hymn of thanks for the illuminating force of reason and its benign social consequences was to turn out to have been fatally over-optimistic.

In the semi-feudal reaches of Eastern Europe, the situation at that time was very different. Despite a long tradition of peaceful Polish cohabitation dating back to the Middle Ages, there were savage Cossack massacres in Poland and the Ukraine in the late seventeenth and early eighteenth centuries. Here the Jews were seen by the peasants as agents of a greedy and oppressive aristocracy. The Polish Jews also resisted attempts to convert them by force. In Russia, meanwhile, Jews had been officially barred from entering the country for more than two centuries under the Tsars. Those who fell beneath the Russian writ after the annexation of the Polish territories in 1772, however, were later permitted to take up residence in the 'Pale of Settlement' between the Baltic and the Black Sea. They lived there under conditions of considerable local autonomy, only to find themselves forced out 50 years later when they were blamed for the abject poverty of the peasants and the decay of rural Russia's feudal system.

As the eighteenth century gave way to the nineteenth, the prospects for these two groups of Jews seemed widely divergent. In the East the Cossack massacres had galvanized the emergence of a new sect, the Hasidim, condemned by Orthodox rabbis for their Kabbalistic beliefs and strange rituals. And when the slaughter provoked Jewish hunger for a Messiah, a claimant emerged on cue, though he was later to confound his

1938
The Nazi campaign against Jews erupts in violence all over Germany. On Kristallnacht, 91 die and 26,000 more are sent to concentration camps.

1942
At the Wannsee Conference top Nazis finalize the details of the 'Final Solution'. Millions of Jews are transported to Poland to perish in death camps over three years.

1948
As the British pull out of Palestine, the Jewish state of Israel is declared by David Ben-Gurion, to implacable hostility from Arabs living in Palestine and beyond.

followers by converting to Islam. In the West, however, the current seemed to be flowing towards integration with a more secular European civilization. And yet, within 150 years both groups, in the east and the west, were engulfed by a common cataclysm – the Holocaust – that made a grotesque mockery of eighteenth-century hopes.

As Gabriel Riesser (1806–63), a Jew, grimly observed of German co-religionists who embraced Christianity to improve their social standing or enhance their careers: 'Believe me, hate like the angel of death can find its man, can recognize him by whatever name he calls himself.' Yet the broader question remains: how could two groups of people on such seemingly distinct social and historical trajectories come to share an identical fate within such a relatively short span of time? For many Jewish historians the answer lies embedded in the history of prejudice and oppression that had dogged the footsteps of God's 'Chosen People' since before the birth of Christ.

Though the term 'anti-Semitism' was not used until 1879, the phenomenon to which it refers is far older. Some historians invoke alternative words – 'Judaeophobia' or plain old 'Jew-hatred' – and trace its earliest manifestations right back to ancient Egypt. In the third century BC, a thousand years after the event, Manetho, an Egyptian high priest living in Alexandria, left a rather less ennobling account of the Jews' exit from ancient Egypt than the stirring Hebrew tale of divinely ordained deliverance in the Old Testament Book of Exodus. He claimed the Jews had actually been expelled because, just like many ragged migrants on the loose in Pharaoh's realm, they carried contagious diseases, including leprosy. In Manetho's view this, not the Jews' proud self-image as a people set apart by divine favour, was at the root of their tendency to stay aloof from others – they had once been banished from Egypt as pariahs.

While Jewish historians identify varying expressions of distaste for the Jews among writers in the classical world, it was the scorn of the early Church Fathers that laid the ground for the persecution of the Jews in Europe. Though Jesus and his disciples had been Jews, the Jewish authorities at the time of his death were seen as bearing the bitter burden of collective guilt for his suffering, torment and death. A corrupt priestly establishment had wilfully rejected the new covenant of Jesus and given him over to execution, thus exiling themselves from

God's grace. For this reason their descendants would be reviled for ever, by God and man alike, unless perhaps they might repent of their wickedness and accept Christ. The feuds and retribution that rumble through the Old Testament, a text shared by Judaism, Christianity and Islam, became not merely legends of the past but prophesies of the future.

Among the most venomous of the early accusers was the fourth-century bishop of Constantinople, John Chrysostom, who claimed that the Jews had renounced their beliefs since the time of Moses. He portrayed the synagogue as a whorehouse and branded the Jews as drunkards and gluttons: treacherous, lustful, rapacious and murderous, they were the polluters of all purity and gave up their own children as burnt offerings to the devil. By the fifth century the Church's identification of the Jews

with the forces of Satan was enshrined in Christian teachings throughout Europe, setting the scene for their moral vilification and their physical persecution as outcasts and blasphemers during the Middle Ages.

In medieval times the lurid litany of offences attributed to the Jews expanded to include the ritual murder of children for magical or medicinal purposes; profaning the Host, a heinous crime at a time when the belief that the communion bread and wine became Christ's body and blood was still taken literally; and spreading the Black Plague by poisoning wells. An early European pogrom, or massacre of Jews, broke out in 1096 at Speyer in the German Rhineland as Christians gathered for the First Crusade, when other Jews living at Worms got wind of the trouble and took refuge in the bishop's palace. Armed

attackers burst in and stripped the Jews naked before dragging them away; some are said to have killed their own children to avoid baptism. In all some 800 were massacred over two days, followed by another 700 in Mainz a few days later, with Jewish families again rumoured to have taken one another's lives to evade their tormentors.

While the overt aim of the Crusades was to liberate the Holy Land from the infidel, they invariably provoked assault on Jews living in Europe. In 1146 news of the Second Crusade brought attacks on Jewish communities across a number of towns and cities in both Germany and France. Later in the century the Third Crusade was attended by massacres in England in London, York, Norwich, Stamford and Lynn. A set pattern of anti-Jewish looting, desperate bids to escape by the terrified victims, and outbreaks of mass suicide endured right into the thirteenth and fourteenth centuries, recurring whenever the banners were raised for a new expedition to Jerusalem.

As hysterical accusations of Jewish ritual murder mounted towards the end of the twelfth century, the mass burning of Jews became a new outlet for popular hatred, in spite of papal attempts to defuse the violence by citing Jewish biblical taboos against killing or even touching dead bodies. The fear and hatred reached such a pitch that Jews were required to wear special clothing to make them instantly identifiable: red-and-yellow hats in Germany, green pointy ones in Poland. Much later, interestingly, some Jews insisted on hanging on to these signs of outward differentiation, when a new generation of rulers wanted to play down the distinctions.

At a time when European merchants were starting to make inroads into commercial trades formerly run by Jews – the

maritime traffic in spices, silks and exotic foodstuffs, for instance – the Jews responded to the precariousness of their lives by shifting their assets into gold, silver, jewels and other forms of portable wealth. These could facilitate a rapid getaway and a swift resumption of prosperity elsewhere, as against stark penury in a strange place where they might find themselves equally unwelcome. Thus they became known as usurers, lending money at interest and always exacting their 'pound of flesh', while they were squeezed in turn by greedy monarchs, desperate to bolster their funds after costly foreign adventures.

In England, King John demanded a gigantic contribution from the Jews in 1210 to meet bills for his foreign wars and subsidize his struggle with the barons. When they pleaded inability to pay, he locked them up. Some were tortured, including a certain Abraham of Bristol, who had his teeth pulled out one by one until he could stand it no more and killed himself. A special Exchequer to the Jews was set up to siphon off Jewish wealth for the Crown, fleecing them for more and more until, in 1290, England became the first country to expel them wholesale after Edward I (1239–1307) had stripped them of any remaining

Far left: Jews condemned to be burned at the stake under the Spanish Inquisition, which sought evidence of backstabbing among Jewish converts to Christianity.

Left: An illustration of the persecution of the Jews under Philip II of France, who arrested the entire Jewish population and would release them only on payment of a ransom.

property. Other continental monarchs played the same game. In France, Philip II (1165–1223) arrested the Jewish population and would release them only on payment of a large ransom; France, too, expelled them in 1392. With persecution rife across Western Europe, in Germany and later in Spain, many fled to Poland.

When the Black Death struck like a scourge across Europe in the mid-fourteenth century, the general populace often took the ravages inflicted by the rat-borne plague as a sign of divine displeasure, or, worse, a conspiracy of Satan in collusion with the Jews. Trials and executions ensued, spreading from Savoy to Switzerland; the German peasantry took matters into their own hands and massacred Jews in seven major cities. Europe began to resemble a madhouse as obsessional bands of nomads went from town to town inciting murder and Jew-burnings wherever they went as the Jews called in vain on their God for vengeance. It was in vain for papal authorities to protest that many Jews had died of the plague as well.

During the next century the diabolic image of Jewry became still more fantastical and frightening as Christians convinced themselves that Jews combined the attributes of both devil

and witch. Apart from their alleged smell, they were seen as powerful sorcerers, possessed of fearsome occult powers. Yet they were also regarded as physically weak or deformed, requiring liberal applications of healthy Christian blood to cure their afflictions. The men as well as the women were believed by some to menstruate, a condition that, again, could only be relieved by the use of Christian blood. These collective delusions led to frequent assaults. The Jews were not the only people to suffer from accusations of witchcraft or black magic, but they were an easy target – easy to identify, easy to envy if they were prosperous, and, with no-one to defend them, easy to kill. It was, moreover, a madness that endured for many centuries: Adolf Hitler wrote in *Mein Kampf* 500 years later that 'the personification of the devil as the symbol of all evil assumes the living shape of the Jew.'

Spain was a special case, at least initially. Under the Moors, who conquered the Iberian Peninsula early in the eighth century and retained a powerful presence there for nearly eight centuries, the Jews had prospered, attaining a high level of culture and scholarship in the Moorish capital of Cordoba. In the fourteenth century their position began to worsen as Spain was swept by successive fevers. First came the Crusades, then the Black Death. The Jews were subjected to the same accusations as elsewhere, with much the same results: village massacres become commonplace. A civil war in Castile, where the losing king, Pedro the Cruel (1334–69), was rumoured to have been a Jew, swapped at birth for the rightful heir, only made worse their woes. The winner, Pedro's illegitimate brother Henry, pushed the legislative body, the Cortes, into denouncing the Jews as 'evil and rash men, enemies of God and of all of Christianity', who 'cause numerous evils and sow corruption with impunity'.

Accordingly Jews were excluded from official posts and tax collection, banned from riding on horses or dressing in fine clothes, instructed to wear special insignia and, in a seemingly contradictory demand, required to 'christianize' their names. The reaction of many was to embrace Christianity. While this saved them from immediate persecution, it split Spanish Jewry into opposing camps and rebounded viciously on them with the advent of the Spanish Inquisition in 1478. Some of these *conversos* turned into keen persecutors of Jews who had stuck with the old faith, while others became atheists; others still turned away from all Christian allegiance, sometimes draping crucifixes over their backsides in a gesture of defiant obscenity. The Spaniards came in their turn to denigrate the *conversos* as *marranos*, or swine. It was a name that stuck.

As the Inquisition grew unstoppable in the late fifteenth century, even those who were sincere in their switch of traditions were suspected of continuing to practise secretly as Jews, as others did, or of urging fellow converts to do so. Many were tortured in the remorseless drive for confessions; many burned at the stake. In 1492 Spain's rulers, Ferdinand and Isabella, signed an edict of expulsion. The Jews were given four months to sell up and go, but were forbidden to take any money or precious metals. A new wave of conversions followed. Some Jews fled to destinations around the Mediterranean, including Turkey, Italy and North Africa; others married off all their children aged 12 and over, hoping to shield their daughters in the care of a husband. Then they bartered their possessions and set off on despairing journeys to nowhere, many dying of hunger and thirst along the way. Those who took refuge in Portugal were driven out again when the Inquisition set up operations there, too.

From the sixteenth century traditional forms of Jew-hatred began to intermingle with commercial rivalry. There was a clear conflict of interest in many European countries between the aristocracy, who increasingly saw Jewish expertise as a useful tool in managing the complexities of international finance and economic policy, and the emerging middle class, to whom they were simply commercial competition. Expelled from Vienna in 1670, a select group of wealthy Jewish families was invited to Germany by the Prussian Elector, but their arrival provoked the ire of Christian merchants, resulting in attacks on synagogues.

While the Jews were still seen as a profoundly negative influence on good Christian morals, the considerable incentives of financial gain felt by the ruling elite secured their readmission to European capitals.

England and France both revoked their medieval edicts against Jews. The French did so under Louis XIII (1601–43) early in the seventeenth century, though there were protests afterwards that resulted in new curtailments. By the middle of the century, England under Cromwell (1599–1658) allowed a colony of Marranos to settle unofficially in London in the face of bitter popular opposition, still strong enough a century later to effect a hasty repeal of new Jewish naturalization laws. By the mid-seventeenth century, too, the Inquisition had reached as far as Brazil, and Jews in flight from its merciless hounding found a welcome in New York. While American Puritans may have been anxious to convert them, the country was a haven of sympathetic tolerance in comparison to Europe.

If the Enlightenment had opened up a dream of civic freedom for the Jews in Europe, its aftermath slammed the gates shut with a resounding clang. The great irony of its liberalizing influence throughout the nineteenth century was that it fostered a definite resurgence of anti-Semitism. This time, though, it took new forms. Napoleon's summoning of the Great Sanhedrin in 1807 fuelled rumours of a Jewish conspiracy to seize world power. In Russia the Church claimed that the gathering was a signal of messianic ambitions on Napoleon's part. Fears of Jewish plots for world domination surfaced repeatedly during the nineteenth century, culminating almost 100 years later in an infamous forgery instigated by the tsarist police, *The Protocols of the Elders of Zion*. This was widely read in Europe and purported to show that the Jews were secretly manipulating European state policy to usher in a new world order founded on gentile slavery.

Western Russia was home to some four-fifths of all Europe's Jews by the start of the nineteenth century. The tsarist authorities were alarmed by their rapid multiplication, which they saw as a threat to the Slavic peasantry. They therefore took measures that were ostensibly in tune with the European trend to assimilation: secular education for Jewish children, European language studies, university entry and – for some 50,000 Jewish boys aged 12 and over – up to 25 years of compulsory military service in the Russian army. Traditional Jewish local government

was scrapped, but Jews were still required to collect taxes on behalf of the tsarist authorities; Jewish dress and hairstyles were banned. A wave of deportations convinced the Jews that the true agenda was to erase their presence. As Russia was forced to open up and revolutionary ideas began to gain a foothold, the first wave of pogroms broke here in 1881, when the Jews were blamed for Alexander II's murder. Two more followed, the second occurring under the Bolsheviks.

Elsewhere in Europe, in 1819, the climate of post-Napoleonic Jewish paranoia triggered off riots in Germany, France, Holland

and Denmark, where gangs of thugs whipped up the crowds and smashed up synagogues. It was the old story, all over again. Older strains of anti-Semitism erupted periodically later on in the century. And yet a defiantly positive view of the Jewish contribution to history and culture began to be promoted as well. Queen Victoria's Jewish prime minister, Benjamin Disraeli (1804–81), expressed this pride in his novel *Coningsby* by extolling the virtues of 'the living Hebrew intellect'.

As the century wore on, a new strain took hold in the intellectual fashion for racial anthropology, paving the way for a

Russian pogroms: a Jew is dragged off by a crowd in Kiev, *c.*1880. There had been savage Cossack massacres in the seventeenth and eighteenth centuries.

109

new hostility that was based on race rather than religion. Drawing on the ideas of the German philosopher Immanuel Kant (1724–1804) and, later, the scientific discoveries of Charles Darwin (1809–82) – neither of whom advanced any concept of racial hierarchy – elaborate theories were drawn up to 'prove' the innate superiority of white Europeans and of the Aryan racial type in particular. One theorist argued that the fair-haired, blue-eyed Germans were destined to conquer 'inferior' Slavs to the East. Another key influence was eugenics, pioneered by an Englishman, Francis Galton (1822–1911). His ideas were taken up by German scientists who went on to advocate selective breeding, sterilization and infanticide to protect the 'racial stock'. While this kind of thinking is now dismissed as gibberish, it was then a cornerstone of the Nazi racial programme, underpinning both Hitler's attempt to eliminate the Jews and his belief that Russia would inevitably fall to the superior might of the German people.

Long before then, however, other events were to convince some Jews that their position in Europe could never be secure, prompting the first steps on the Zionist road back to Israel. Two high-profile scandals played a part: the so-called Damascus

1919: Jews march in London in protest at a reported massacre of Jews in Poland. Before the start of World War II, Poland had a Jewish community of 3.5 million, the second largest in the world.

Moses Hess (1812–75), arrived at the view that anti-Jewish feeling in Europe was inescapable and Jews must therefore embrace their own national identity. In 1860 a group of young Jews began to promote settlement in Palestine. Almost 25 years later Leon Pinsker (1821–91), a Polish-born doctor and lawyer who had been shaken by the Russian pogroms of 1881, founded the Hibbat Zion movement, based on his conviction that Jews could never be truly assimilated. The first Zionist congress was held in 1897 under the leadership of Theodor Herzl (1860–1904). In 1914 Baron Edmond de Rothschild supported new agrarian settlements in what was to become Israel.

After the Russian Revolution – which, compounding already festering suspicions of Jewish international financiers, was widely blamed on the Jews – the preponderance of Jews in the Bolshevik leadership helped spawn a whole new set of conspiracy theories. Devious manipulations by international Jewish capitalists were believed to be central to the destruction of the tsarist regime. Prominent Western capitalists such as Henry Ford (1863–1947) in the USA spoke out strongly against worldwide Jewish economic power. In Germany anti-Semitic political trends, which had flourished since the late nineteenth century, were given a new lease of life when the Jews were held to account for the plight of the country during the Great Depression. Anti-Jewish parties were active in Habsburg Austria, where the Jews were portrayed as the capitalist enemies of a vanishing peasant idyll. In France both Zionism and the perceived collusion of a 'Judaeo-German syndicate' with European Bolsheviks and socialists came under strong attack. With the onset of the Edwardian era in the early part of the twentieth century, anti-Semitism began to stir again in England, too, albeit in a somewhat milder form than in other parts of the world.

Affair of 1840, when the disappearance of a Capuchin monk in the Syrian capital revived the old medieval suspicions of Jewish ritual murder; then, 50 years on in 1894, the Dreyfus Affair in France. A blameless Jewish army officer was convicted of treason on the basis of his handwriting alone and exiled to Devil's Island. In spite of clear evidence of his innocence, he was kept incarcerated through the use of forgeries; his eventual exoneration and release produced a huge reaction throughout Europe.

The earliest Zionist stirrings began in the mid-nineteenth century, when a Swiss-born journalist with socialist leanings,

1938

Kristallnacht

9–10 November 1938. To innocent or unknowing ears, the German word *Kristallnacht* might suggest something from an old Christmas carol. Yet even its English translation – the night of broken glass – is testimony to the Nazi gift for euphemism. For this is the night when the Nazis unleash a reign of terror against German Jews – looting, burning, destroying property and killing, while thousands are taken off to concentration camps.

21:00 **9 November.** At an annual dinner held in Munich to commemorate the Nazis' failed beer-hall putsch of 1923, when Hitler tried to topple the regional government of Bavaria with 600 stormtroopers, news arrives from Paris. A minor German embassy official, Ernst vom Rath, has been shot dead by a Jewish teenager, Herschel Grynszpan, enraged by the plight of his father, Zindel, who is now living in a refugee camp after the family's expulsion from Germany. Hitler confers urgently with his propaganda minister, Josef Goebbels, and hurries out, grim-faced, without delivering his customary speech.

Goebbels takes the podium. He conveys the news of vom Rath's murder and alludes to recent anti-Jewish violence in Germany. The propaganda minister explains that Hitler has no wish that such actions should be 'prepared or organized' by the party, but the *Führer* has indicated that if demonstrations 'erupt spontaneously', they should not in any way be hampered. His audience understands the coded message: the party is being directed to attack Jews, but the intention is to make this look like an outburst of unpremeditated anger by the German people in response to a Jewish crime.

The Nazis' well-organized communications network goes into overdrive. The message is rapidly distributed to regional and local headquarters as well as to police stations – their part will be to stand back while Jews are assaulted and Jewish property is plundered or destroyed. SS units tour beer halls and cinemas to whip up anti-Jewish feeling among the crowds. More beer and schnapps is downed, inhibitions thrown aside. Many who heed the call are supplied with hammers, chisels and petrol.

02:00 **10 November.** Goebbels receives news of the first Jewish death. There is a momentary frisson – should something be done to stop further bloodshed? The propaganda minister lets it be understood that there is nothing to be done. It is the will of the people.

02:30 The pogrom is now in full swing. Jewish businesses are attacked, their windows crashing in jagged splinters, their stock stolen in the orgy of destruction. Synagogues are surrounded by jeering crowds in towns and villages; sacred relics are tossed into heaps, doused with petrol and set on fire. Then the buildings themselves are burned. Cemeteries are desecrated, the gravestones daubed with Nazi insiginia.

In one synagogue the entire local Jewish population is herded inside and forced to sing the Nazis' 'Horst Wessel' song, over and over again, while petrol is sloshed round them by laughing Germans. Only right at the last minute, just before the building goes up in flames, are they shoved out again into the street. The doors of Jewish homes are kicked in, men are dragged out and attacked with anything to hand – such as lead pipes and bricks – or they are arrested. There are reports of German women holding up small children to watch Jews being beaten senseless. Other Germans are appalled but dare not speak out, for the mood of the crowd is ugly and even the police are doing nothing to stop it.

Once *Kristallnacht* is over 91 Jews have died and 26,000 are on their way to concentration camps at Buchenwald, Sachsenhausen and Dachau, the forerunners of millions more who will suffer the same fate. Some 7,000 businesses have been ransacked, 1,500 synagogues left destroyed or damaged. The Reich demands one billion marks from the Jews in 'reparation' and insurance payments to them are confiscated.

Above left: A man clears away broken glass from the Jewish Kaliski Bedding Emporium. More than 7,000 Jewish businesses were attacked.

Above right: The murders and violence and the destruction and burning of Jewish property during *Kristallnacht* took place in retaliation for the murder of Ernst vom Rath, a young Polish Jew.

The rise of Hitler is charted in Tyrants and Dictators (see pages 41–5), but for the Jews it was at first a stealthy, insidious process. Nazi intentions were plain – the party had declared as early as 1920 that no Jew could be a German national – yet many did not take Hitler seriously at first. Nazi objectives were achieved by a gradual wearing down that left many Jews unsure whether to leave or not until it was too late. It started with a boycott of Jewish shops in April 1933. Slogans were daubed on windows, customers berated and proprietors beaten up, storm troopers egging on such acts. 'Non-Aryans' were then barred from all government jobs, which also covered university academics; the inheritance laws were revised to end Jewish ownership. A wholesale redefinition of German citizenship followed under the Nuremburg Laws in 1936. Two years later, after the murder of an embassy official in Paris by the son of a Polish Jew, who was angered at his father's expulsion from Germany, the Nazis struck. Baying about conspiracy, they unleashed a nationwide wave of anti-Jewish violence. Some 90 Jews were killed; synagogues were defaced, buildings wrecked, books and relics burned, thousands arrested.

This was *Kristallnacht*, the 'night of broken glass'. Yet it was still a long way from here, via the mass deportations of Jews to the East and the forced labour camps, to the Wannsee Conference of January 1942 and the Final Solution, the Nazi plan to exterminate the Jewish people. The bare statistics of that ghastly industrial slaughter tell their own story. Along with many others – Poles, gypsies, homosexuals, communists – about half of the six-million Jews murdered by the Nazis during World War II were killed in extermination camps on Polish territory. More than a million died at Auschwitz; 974,000 at Treblinka; 600,000 in Belzec; 250,000 at Sobibor; 225,000 in Chelmno; 60,000 at Majdanek – most of them gassed, then incinerated. Though the horror and cruelty of these hellish places has been exhaustively documented in the ensuing years, and there have since been other holocausts elsewhere, it remains hard for the human imagination to encompass.

The present tensions between Arabs and Jews living in Israel, witnessed in the Palestinian intifada uprisings, the spate of suicide bombings, and the harsh retaliations of the Israeli military, can be dated back to the Balfour Declaration of November 1917. Around 90,000 Jews were settled in the Holy Land by the

outbreak of World War I, their numbers having grown ninefold over a period of some 60 years. At that point Jews and Arabs alike were still under the Turkish rule of the Ottoman Empire.

By the time the country was liberated by the British in 1918, the Jews had already obtained consent from the British government to create a Jewish national home in Palestine. Britain took on the Palestinian Mandate from the League of Nations in 1919, though it always insisted its plan had never implied the founding of a Jewish state. The Arab majority held that Palestine was for the Arabs, as the Jews had not lived there in almost 2,000 years. They objected to the fact that there were

Jewish ministers in the British cabinet, and Zionist colonial administrators on the ground to do the bidding of the British government, whereas they were merely a subject people lacking any such political clout. The Jews feared that any representative bodies would inevitably be Arab-dominated; political initiatives fell repeatedly flat.

After 1939, when the British restricted Jewish immigration to 75,000 over the next five years, and none thereafter without Arab consent, the Jews turned to terrorism in 1945. Two years later, when the UN voted to partition the country, thousands died in the ensuing urban warfare. And yet, with Arab forces

Death camp inmates: fifty years after the liberation of Auschwitz in 1945, camp survivor Elie Wiesel recalled it as 'a place of darkness and malediction' where 'earth and heaven are on fire'.

115

The arabic text on the podium reads: قمة البحر الأحمر

THE RED SEA SUMMIT

massing threateningly beyond Palestinian borders, Prime Minister David Ben-Gurion (1886–1973) proudly declared independence at Tel Aviv on 14 May 1948. For good or ill, modern Israel was born – an ill-omened birth that soon led to a troubled life. In some sections of the European left, recent actions by the Jews have been likened to those of the Nazis – a charge that provokes fury and disgust in Israel.

Today the country's problems can be usefully compared with those of Northern Ireland: both tell, in effect, a tale of two minorities. The Jews fear obliteration by the wider Arab world, while the Palestinians, crushed by superior military force and driven off their land by aggressive settlement policies, have turned to terrorism. A fence is now being erected to separate the two communities – another Northern Irish parallel, which is reminiscent of Belfast's infamous 'peace line'. During the Iraq conflict in 2003, the US president, George W Bush, pledged to address the minefield of Israeli politics. Both he and the British prime minister, Tony Blair, were also preoccupied with finding weapons of mass destruction in Iraq, still undiscovered at the time of writing, to justify the decision to go to war.

As for Israel's future, more than 50 years after it was first mooted in the UN, partition is once again on the agenda. To pessimists, or perhaps simply to weary realists, this fact may suggest a third Northern Irish analogy: the tragic, futile circularity of its politics. And yet the gains of the latest Irish peace process, snail-like but significant, might just offer a glimmer of hope. If so, we may still have to wait another 250 years for peace. In Northern Ireland the Troubles date back at least as far as 1690, and Bloody Sunday in 1972 signalled that they were back with a vengeance.

Above: Show of hands: George Bush with Israel's Ariel Sharon and Mahoud Abbas at the Red Sea Summit, Jordan, June 2003.

Right: One week later – the aftermath of a Palestinian bomb attack on a bus in Jerusalem, one in a spate of bombings and suicide attacks.

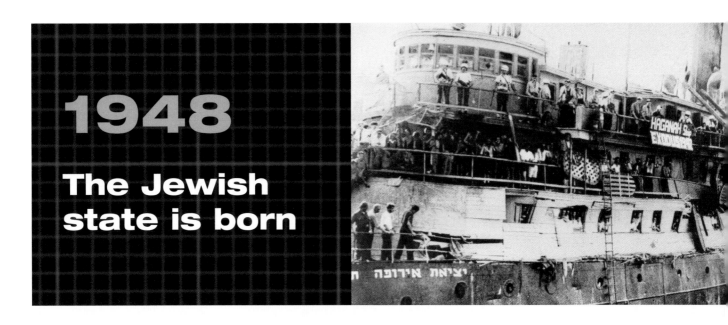

1948

The Jewish state is born

14 May 1948. Since the USA agreed in late 1947 to Britain's giving up the Palestine Mandate, a UN resolution to partition the country has led to renewed fighting between Jews and Arabs. The UN split endorses the formation of a Jewish state alongside Arabs in the rest of Palestine, with a separate regime for Jerusalem. Now the British have brought forward their leaving date.

00:00 As midnight strikes in Jerusalem, the British Mandate has just 24 hours to run. Seven hours behind, in Washington, it is late afternoon and the Americans are urgently seeking a transitional arrangement in order to forestall the risk of immediate bloodshed. They are convinced that the UN plan is, as it stands, a certain recipe for war between the Jews and Arabs in Palestine. What they have in mind is a ceasefire, to be brokered by the UN and followed by a UN Trusteeship, with an appointed mediator to take control pending further talks. The proposal will go before the Assembly first thing in the morning.

The UN partition plan took its lead from a British proposal originally mooted in 1937; it now envisages a territorial patchwork, based on demographics, that would still mean some 350,000 Arabs living in a Jewish state of about 600,000 people. The Arabs, including those in neighbouring Arab states, remain bitterly opposed to partition. The Zionists – though dissatisfied with the amount of land that has been allotted to them, with the seeming indefensibility of borders across three separate chunks of territory, and with the fate of Jerusalem – have still welcomed its recognition of their right to a Jewish state.

Golda Meir, of the Jewish provisional government, went disguised as an Arab to meet King Abdullah of Jordan but came away in no doubt that Jordanian forces will invade if an Israeli state is declared. King Abdullah has warned, 'All our efforts to find a peaceful solution to the Palestine problem have failed. The only way left for us is war. I will have the pleasure and honour to save Palestine.' In Washington, Moshe Shertok, Israeli foreign minister and ambassador in waiting, has been warned by Secretary of State George Marshall, who opposes a Jewish state, that if the Jews go it alone the USA will not come to their aid. The Jews see no other option but to do so.

02:00 News comes in of a massacre of Jewish *kibbutzim* at Kfar Etzion, near Hebron, where defenders have been besieged for weeks by the Arab Legion. Like many other places in Palestine, it is hotly disputed, having been settled by Jews first in 1927, in 1935, and then for a third time in 1943. Orchards were planted and light industry established; a synagogue was built. It is symbolically and strategically important to the Jews, guarding the road to Jerusalem. The defenders had been overwhelmed the day before, when 127 were slaughtered, bringing the death toll to 240, including 20 women, but the bodies are not found until later by a British patrol. Survivors surrender later in the day, around 10 a.m., under Red Cross auspices, and are taken prisoner.

16:00 In Tel Aviv, David Ben-Gurion, soon to be prime minister and defence minister of Israel, has redrafted the declaration. Debate shuttles back and forth all day inside Independence Hall – the issue of including references to God is troublesome until a compromise, 'the Rock of Israel', is agreed. The document excludes any territorial definitions. Ben-Gurion starts reading out his text; by 4.32 p.m. he is done. Members sign a blank paper, later stitched physically to a fair copy of the declaration. In Washington, as the UN debate gets going, a letter is drafted to the US government seeking formal recognition. So great is the haste to deliver it that the name 'Israel' has to be written in on the way. Eight hours later President Truman recognizes the new nation. It has been a difficult birth, and more bloodshed will inevitably follow on both sides.

Above left: Some 4,500 Jewish refugees set out for Palestine from France in the ship *Exodus 1947*, but were forced to return to Hamburg after the ship was rammed by a British destroyer.

Above right: Members of the Arab League go into a huddle at a meeting of the UN General Assembly in November 1947 before the long and bitter debate on the partition of Palestine into Arab and Jewish states.

Slavery has existed since ancient times and formed a major part of the world economy until the nineteenth century. Long after the success of abolitionists, charismatic campaigners such as Martin Luther King and Nelson Mandela dedicated their lives to fighting its legacy of injustice in the twentieth century.

[73 BC] : [1990]

CIVIL RIGHTS

Slavery has a long and lamentable history. It has existed throughout the world since ancient times; in parts of Africa and Asia, it still exists today under the guise of debt bondage or indentured labour. In its earliest form it was a system of brutal simplicity: slaves were routinely taken among the spoils of war, uprooted from their ransacked homes along with any valuables, property, goods or chattels that could be plundered by a conquering people.

Younger women from the losing side were taken for sexual gratification or as domestic servants; the men were set to back-breaking toil in the fields, to dangerous or menial tasks such as mining and sewage disposal, or to further the military ambitions of their conquerors to subdue a new set of victims.

The Romans, for instance, were not the only people to use their captives as galley slaves, straining under the lash to row armoured warships with heavy oars across the seas. Nor were children exempt: those who survived initial attack without being speared or having their brains dashed out would grow up to become slaves in their turn. Freed slaves were a rarity and uprisings were stamped down with the utmost savagery. Spartacus was a Thracian gladiator who in 73 BC led a slave revolt against the Romans and defeated them in battle several times before being

The history of civil rights

1441
The date of the first-recorded African slave transaction by the Portuguese – three decades later Spain recognizes Portugal's monopoly in the African trade, although this does not last.

1619
More than a century after Columbus took slavery to the islands of the West Indies, a first cargo of 20 slaves is swapped for food with a Dutch captain at Jamestown, Virginia.

1652
A supply station is established in Table Bay, South Africa, by the Dutch East India Company, opening the way for Boer settlement, in which local tribes lose their land.

captured and crucified alongside his fellow insurgents. His celebrated story is testimony both to the desperate courage of the runaways and to the iron brutality of their masters.

Earlier still, the democracy of ancient Athens, traditionally held up in Europe as one of the glories of classical civilization and an illustrious example to future ages, had been founded on slave ownership among the small farmers of the Athenian *polis*.

Above left: In ancient Egypt slaves helped build the pyramids. Here they haul a stone into position with a wooden lever and ropes.

Above right: African slaves march to the coast, yoked with branches or roped together; many died en route.

1790
A census discloses that there are 700,000 slaves in the USA – more than a sixth of the population. A year later, in Haiti, Toussaint L'Ouverture leads a slave uprising.

1807
After a century of huge profits, Britain and Denmark abolish the slave trade. The Dutch do the same in 1816, the French in 1818 and the Spanish in 1820. Slave ownership continues.

1863
Lincoln issues his Emancipation Proclamation during the American Civil War, though the president's concern is to save the Union, and 'loyal' states are permitted to keep their slaves.

In many respects it was the hard graft of these bonded labourers – employed in hacking out terraces from stony hillsides to cultivate corn, wine and olives, and in digging out mines, tunnels and foundations – that gave their ancient Greek masters the leisure they needed to bring their nascent studies in philosophy, art and mathematics to full flower.

Indeed, this strange and flawed paradox of freedom for some built on slavery for others was alive and well more than 2,000 years later at the foundation of the American republic. The USA was, after all, created by men seeking their personal and political liberty from the British colonial yoke. The noble words of the Declaration of Independence held as self-evident truths 'that all men are created equal; that they are endowed by the Creator with certain inalienable rights; that among these are life, liberty and the pursuit of happiness'. Yet there were at the time of its proclamation hundreds of thousands of black slaves labouring on the plantations of the American South, who would continue doing so for the best part of a century.

They or their forebears had been forcibly abducted from Africa and then shipped across the Atlantic – chained up like animals in cramped, fetid conditions, subjected en route to appalling cruelty, privation and disease – to lead lives of degradation and misery in the New World. Often they worked up to 20 hours a day, cutting cane and processing it into raw sugar; harvesting tobacco and drying it; hoeing, planting and picking cotton. If they did not die of exhaustion, their owners were at liberty to whip, shoot or lynch male slaves and rape the women with impunity.

Yet it would be mistaken to pretend that white Europeans alone were responsible for slavery. The same oppressive practices had been in evidence many centuries before among other great empires of the past, such as those of China or Egypt. In Africa slavery predated the arrival of the European traders, initially Portuguese and Spanish, but later spreading to other nationalities including the British, who saw in a westward expansion of the traffic a new export market and a ready source of profit. Stronger African tribes had long preyed on weaker ones, conquering and taking them prisoner; Arab traders plying the continent's long coastlines bought and sold these job-lots of human beings, finding markets in Africa

The history of civil rights

1943
Nelson Mandela joins the African National Congress, working as a lawyer and mounting a non-violent campaign against unjust laws early in the next decade.

1955
School segregation is declared unconstitutional; Martin Luther King organizes the Montgomery bus boycott and pioneers peaceful protest, culminating in the 1963 Birmingham campaign.

1963
King outlines his dream of brotherhood in an inspirational speech, as a quarter of a million people, both black and white, join a march on Washington for justice and jobs.

African slaves being taken on board for shipment to America in 1830. European sailors brought rum, cloth, guns and other goods to trading posts along the west coast of Africa in exchange for human beings. This cargo was sold to New World slave owners to work their crops.

and the Middle East. Some historians, however, insist on clear distinctions between Africa's indigenous slavery and the European-American 'chattel slavery' that replaced it from the seventeenth century.

When Europeans went to Africa in force, they did not create the slave trade, but they exploited it on a grand scale. Huge fortunes were made in the infamous 'Triangle of Trade' between Europe, West Africa and the Americas at the cost of countless lives, especially in the notorious 'Middle Passage' between Africa and the Americas. Many were simply thrown overboard in their shackles to drown or be eaten by sharks during epidemics and shortages; others were raped, beaten, starved or shot. It is estimated that between 1700 and 1807 British slavers alone transported 3 million Africans across the Atlantic, from the ports of Liverpool, Bristol and London. Most of the Africans taken overseas by European traders ended up on plantations in the Caribbean or Latin America; a smaller number were exported to the American South, increasing steadily as profits began to flow from the trade.

The US trade started in 1619 at Jamestown, Virginia, where a cargo of 20 African slaves was exchanged for food with a passing Dutch slaver. They were put to work harvesting tobacco alongside indentured white labourers, who were still paying off their passage to America. The town's merchants were in the midst of a tobacco boom, having already exported around ten tons of the stuff to Europe; in the coming decades more Africans were brought in – slowly at first, but their numbers rose as America's rural economy became steadily more dependent on their unpaid labour.

1964
Having eventually accepted armed struggle as an unavoidable necessity after the 1960 Sharpeville massacre, Mandela is jailed for life on a charge of sabotage.

1968
The day after telling his followers that he has 'seen the promised land', Martin Luther King is assassinated in Memphis, Tennessee, by James Earl Ray.

1990
Mandela is released after 27 years in jail. He goes on to win the Nobel Peace Prize and to become South Africa's very first elected president.

Right: Invoice of a 'Negro'
slave dealer dated 26 May
1835. The amounts give
a clear indication of the
financial gains from slavery.

Far right: Resistance in Haiti:
an illustration entitled 'Revolt
of the Negroes in San
Domingo' shows how African
slaves fought a desperate
battle for freedom, led by
Toussaint L'Ouverture.

At this point the Africans were called 'indentured servants' – the word 'slave' did not turn up in local statutes until some 40 years later, and then mainly as a term in legal or contractual usage. Southerners continued to designate slaves euphemistically as servants. By the 1680s, in any case, they had become an essential component of the Southern rural economy and slavery obtained legal recognition. Africans were not the only victims, for Native Americans were enslaved, too. In 1730 between a quarter and a half of the slaves in North and South Carolina were of Cherokee, Creek or other tribal extractions. Native Americans began to interbreed with Africans, sometimes by coercion in slave camps, sometimes voluntarily after escaping. There was a three-to-one imbalance of men over women among the Africans, while the male Native American population had been ravaged by war and disease. In 1790 the first national census showed more than three-quarters of a million Africans resident in the USA – almost one-fifth of the population – of whom almost 60,000 were 'free Negroes' and the rest slaves. The largest concentration was in Virginia, which had almost 300,000, the smallest in New England, where the count came in at just 157.

In the late eighteenth century, however, a rising tide of moral revulsion in Britain built up into an organized campaign, inspired and led by religious non-conformists, notably Quakers, as well as Protestants. Tireless abolitionists such as Thomas Clarkson (1760–1846), William Wilberforce (1759–1833) and Granville Sharp (1735–1813) documented the evils of the trade in detail and doggedly pursued humanitarian objectives inside and outside parliament. They organized mass petitions and canvassed political support through the Campaign for the Abolition of the Slave Trade, until at last the British traffic in slaves – though not yet the ownership of them – was outlawed across all its territories in 1807.

This new law came into force more than three decades after the American Declaration of Independence in 1776, and almost two decades after the outbreak of the French Revolution in 1789. While the French Revolution is ironically regarded today as having held back the abolitionist cause in Britain, its anti-authoritarian ideals helped to inspire courageous struggles against slavery elsewhere. This occurred most famously in the military campaigns of the rebel general Toussaint L'Ouverture

(1746–1803) on the island of Haiti, then known as Santo Domingo or Saint Domingue. Born into slavery, Toussaint rose to become a daring and effective military leader after joining an uprising in 1791, the year of the American Bill of Rights. Against the odds he organized successful armed resistance against both British and Spanish expeditions, enabling Haiti to declare its independence in 1804, until his capture and incarceration by Napoleon.

Thereafter slavery was re-established on the island for a time. But the whole history of the West Indies around the end of the eighteenth century and the start of the nineteenth is peppered with slave skirmishes, wars and revolts, extending across Jamaica, Grenada, St Lucia, Surinam, Dominica and Barbados. Sometimes the rebels were new arrivals, who did not yet know the extent of their oppressors' power; in other cases they were tough bands of armed runaways, nicknamed Maroons, who hid out in remote and inhospitable inland regions and fought back fiercely against recapture.

Britain made slow progress in persuading other European countries to ban the trade. While the Danes were moved to abolish in the same year as Britain, the Dutch waited until 1816, the French followed suit two years later, and the Spanish did not join in until 1820. Even so, by 1833 slavery was abolished outright in all British possessions, albeit on a phased, gradual basis designed to avoid destroying the privileged livelihoods of powerful vested interests overseas. The humanitarian case against slavery had been bolstered since the 1820s by economics: a growing faith in the doctrine of free trade as the engine of future prosperity, coupled with the knowledge that British taxpayers were subsidizing West Indian planters, conspired against it at the political level. France and Holland waited another 15 years to end the practice. Yet the US trade continued to flourish in the wake of Andrew Jackson's 1830 Indian Removal Act, which forcibly ejected five Indian nations from their rich agricultural homelands in the South to less fertile territory out West. Some 3 million hectares (25 million acres) of prime agricultural land were opened up to cultivation: 'King Cotton', tended by the plantation owners' African slaves, was the favoured inheritor.

The USA did not, of course, remain untouched by abolitionist fervour. One of the most celebrated instances arose from the

EMANCIPATOR—*EXTRA.*

NEW-YORK, SEPTEMBER 2, 1839.

American Anti-Slavery Almanac for 1840.

The seven cuts following, are selected from thirteen, which may be found in the Anti-Slavery Almanac for 1840. They represent well-authenticated facts, and illustrate in various ways, the cruelties daily inflicted upon three millions of native born Americans, by their fellow-countrymen! A brief explanation follows each cut.

The peculiar "Domestic Institutions of our Southern brethren."

Selling a Mother from her Child.

Mothers with young Children at work in the field.

A Woman chained to a Girl, and a Man in irons at work in the field.

"They can't take care of themselves"; explained in an interesting article.

Hunting Slaves with dogs and guns. A Slave drowned by the logs.

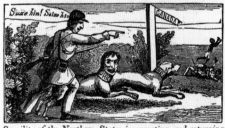

Servility of the Northern States in arresting and returning fugitive Slaves.

marriage of Fanny Kemble (1809–93), a renowned British actress and passionate abolitionist, to Pierce Butler (1806–67), wealthy descendant of a Georgia coastal plantation family that owned more than 700 slaves. Starting as an elegant dance of old-fashioned courtship, the 'fairytale romance' between the spirited Kemble and the rich, infatuated Butler degenerated into a fiery battle of wills over the moral foundations of Butler's wealth, ending in divorce. Their acrimony became the basis for Margaret Mitchell's legendary 1930s novel *Gone With the Wind*, and thence the massively popular film of the same title, starring Clark Gable and Vivien Leigh.

Well before the Butlers came to their mid-century marital impasse in the South, however, dedicated campaigners were hard at work in the North. In the 1820s abolitionist sentiment welled up from a strong evangelical Christian revival, which condemned the practice of slavery as sinful; from the next decade the calls for compulsory emancipation became steadily more vehement. For campaigners such as Theodore Weld (1803–95), who wrote two anti-slavery bestsellers, as for the brothers Arthur (1786–1865) and Lewis Tappan (1788–1863) and William Lloyd Garrison (1805–79), the issue became an all-out crusade, backed by the polemical writings of J G Whittier (1807–92) and the oratory of Wendell Phillips (1811–84). John Quincy Adams (1767–1848) presented his famous anti-slavery petitions to Congress in 1831, followed by the foundation of the American Anti-Slavery Society in 1833, which bombarded the South with abolitionist literature as political lobbying gathered pace.

Not all of those who fought slavery at this time were privileged, educated or white. For some the only available form of resistance was through violence. In 1800 Gabriel Prosser (1775–1800) planned an armed uprising by a thousand blacks, intending to attack the city of Richmond, Virginia, though it was washed out by a massive thunderstorm. In 1822 Denmark Vesey (c.1767–1822), a freed man and Methodist preacher, hatched a conspiracy to attack Charleston, Carolina, with an even larger force. But the plot was betrayed and Vesey was hanged along with 36 others. In 1831 Nat Turner (1800–31), a self-styled Baptist minister, led an uprising in Southampton County, Virginia, in which some 60 white men, women and children were slaughtered. Turner and 16 others were executed; thereafter several blacks unconnected with the massacre were murdered at random, their severed heads dumped at roadsides as a gruesome warning. News of slave uprisings in the West Indies continued to haunt the US slave owners, who were vastly outnumbered; they responded to the fear of insurrection with a new harshness.

Other blacks took a more circumspect path, such as Frederick Douglass (1817–95), who started life as a Southern slave. Transferred by his owner to Baltimore, he learnt to read and write, returning to teach fellow slaves and, later, engineering his escape to New York in 1838. Douglass became a prominent abolitionist, working with both Garrison and Abraham Lincoln (1809–65). He helped escaped Southern slaves who arrived in the North via the 'underground railway', lectured on the evils of slavery in Britain, encouraged transatlantic links in the abolitionist movement and championed women's rights. Douglass took the Declaration of Independence at its word, pointing out that it referred to *all* men, not just all white men, and treating it as a text for black liberation.

Yet the North–South divide was not always as clear-cut as the subsequent civil war might suggest. Solomon Northrup (1808–?) was a freed man who had been abducted in Washington in 1841 and held in captivity for another 12 years. He later recalled conditions at a slave pen in the nation's capital: 'It was like a farmer's barnyard in most respects, save it was so constructed that the outside world could never see the human cattle that were herded there. The building to which the yard was attached was two storeys high, and fronted one of the public streets of Washington. Its outside presented only the appearance of a quiet private residence. A stranger looking at it would never have dreamed of its execrable uses. Strange as it may seem, within plain sight of this same house, looking down from its commanding height upon it, was the Capitol. The voices of patriotic representatives boasting of freedom and equality, and the rattling of the poor slave's chains, almost commingled. A slave pen within the very shadow of the Capitol!'

Within a decade *Uncle Tom's Cabin*, the runaway bestseller of Harriet Beecher Stowe (1811–96) that was first published in serial parts in 1851–2, placed a new and powerful propaganda tool in the hands of abolitionist forces opposing slavery in the South. Some white abolitionists also proved willing to resort to direct action. John Brown (1800–59) was a veteran of the bloody ructions in Kansas between anti-slavery 'free-soilers' and pro-slavery elements who had rigged the state election. In 1859 he led a raid at Harpers Ferry, a federal armoury at the junction of the Potomac and Shenandoah Rivers where up to 90,000 weapons were stored. Brown was reported to have incited black workers to take up arms and liberate themselves, though the ensuing riot was swiftly put down. The fiery Brown later became an intimate of Frederick Douglass in Washington.

In 1860 Abraham Lincoln became US president. By then several Southern slavery states had already shown signs of going their own way, splitting the Democratic Party in two over its anti-slavery platform and fielding their own candidate in the election: Lincoln was the Republican beneficiary. The secessionist bandwagon, however, was now well and truly rolling. Early in 1861 Mississippi, Florida, Alabama, Georgia, Louisiana and Texas followed South Carolina into secession and four more states – Virginia, Arkansas, Tennessee and North Carolina – threatened to follow suit. By February Jefferson Davis was declared president of the Confederacy. The Civil War had begun, even though another four slave-owning states – Delaware, Kentucky, Maryland and Missouri – stuck with the Union. After a series of bloody battles, Lincoln's Emancipation Proclamation was issued in January 1863, freeing all slaves in the rebel states but still stopping short of total abolition. With black soldiers now fighting alongside whites on the Union side, many of them former slaves, the conflict lasted another two years and more, shedding yet more blood, to end in a Confederate surrender. Lincoln was assassinated less than a week later by an actor, John Wilkes Booth.

After the Civil War the euphoria felt by many black Americans at the end of slavery, albeit coupled with their anxiety and confusion about the future, drained away during a series of disappointments. The change in their civil status did not evoke a corresponding transformation of their social or economic

position, especially in the South, where vigilante groups and so-called 'Jim Crow' laws brought in new and more insidious forms of oppression. As industrialization began to encourage more northerly migration, picking up speed in the twentieth century, Southern blacks found themselves herded into squalid ghettoes, paying high rents to white landlords. Many had dreamed that the North would be a kind of paradise; quite patently, it was not. It was against this background, almost a century after the Civil War ended, that the black civil rights movement began to flex its muscles.

In Africa the story was naturally quite different. The growth of the slave trade and the colonization of Africa, arising from a series of imperial carve-ups that reached a frenzied peak in the closing years of the nineteenth century, were distinct processes, although interrelated on several levels. Leaving aside the intriguing but contentious question of ancient Egyptian racial

slave monopoly in 1470. The Portuguese also pioneered the sea route to India in the late fifteenth century and were regular visitors to the coasts of southern Africa from the early 1500s.

Then, in 1652, the Dutch East India Company set up a supply station in Table Bay at the Cape of Good Hope. Five years later Dutch Boers (farmers) began to settle on land that for centuries had been used by local tribes – the San, known to the whites as 'Bushmen', and the Khoikhoi, who were dubbed 'Hottentots' – as pastoral ranges for their sheep and cattle. Referred to jointly as the Khoisan, these two peoples had cultures distinct from those of the region's older hunter-gatherers or the Bantu-speaking farmers who had brought animal husbandry, crop-cultivation and metalworking into the eastern coastal regions before spreading out to the interior.

The Dutch settlers grew wheat and grapes to make wine, importing slave labour from Madagascar, East Africa and the East Indies. Within 50 years Boers were trekking further afield, foraging beyond the nearer mountain ranges for fresh pastures where their hunting and herding went more or less unchecked. The Khoisan were initially decimated by imported diseases such as smallpox; many of the survivors had no other choice but to enter service with the colonists. Mixed-race relationships began to sketch a new social hierarchy, with the colonists at the top, an emerging Asian artisan class (the so-called 'Cape Malays') and a separate group of mixed-race 'coloureds', all of whom suffered varying degrees of discrimination. The number of slaves at the Cape had outstripped the European 'free burghers' resident there by the mid-century.

Later in the century, there were sporadic confrontations between Boers and the Khoisan, the Xhosa and the Bantu peoples, developing early in the next century into a spate of rival empire

origins, by the fifteenth century, there were flourishing black African kingdoms elsewhere in the continent. These included the iron-working empire of Kongo, spread across what is now Angola and the Democratic Republic of Congo and the city states of Ife-Ife, Oyo and Benin, the latter renowned for its delicate bronzes, in Nigeria. Africa was far from 'primitive', but it served the interests of the slavers to portray the Africans as little more than animals. As one former American slave later recalled of the slave pens in Colombia, they were 'worse than hog-holes'.

The first white European settlement in Africa relevant to this history was established in 1570 by the Portuguese in present-day Angola. A Portuguese navigator had visited the kingdom of Kongo around 1483; the Portuguese were the first Europeans to involve themselves directly in the trade, recording a slave transaction as early as 1441, while the Spanish endorsed their neighbour's African

building by other African tribal groups. Political manoeuvring among the Africans was both aggressive and defensive: the most feared leader of all was the Zulu nation-builder, Shaka (c.1787–1828), a ruthless general who formed a standing army of 40,000 and made pitiless war on his neighbours until his assassination in 1828. At the same time Britain's annexation of the Cape in 1806, following an earlier incursion in 1795, provoked a Boer exodus, culminating in the 'Great Trek' of 1835–43. As thousands of *voortrekkers* set off by oxcart to found new republics in Natal, Transvaal and the Orange Free State, the dislocation of Africans in the Highveld by indigenous African conflict promoted the enduring Boer myth of an 'empty land', which they continued to claim, long afterwards, had been uninhabited until their arrival.

Yet it was the West Africans who had borne the brunt of the slave trade throughout the eighteenth century. They were snatched in their millions from their villages by other Africans working alongside Arab or European slavers. Roped or yoked together with forked wooden branches, they were force-marched across country or packed into canoes for the journey to coastal collecting stations where European sailing ships bobbed at anchor awaiting their human cargo. The slaves often faced a long wait in grim slave forts, such as Gorée Island of Senegal, crammed together in stinking cells without windows or proper ventilation. Though their captors did their best to keep such valuable commodities in marketable condition, many died. Once a deal had been struck, they were herded below decks on to rough wooden pallets that caused terrible abrasions as the ships pitched and rolled across the high seas on a voyage that could take six to eight weeks, or longer if winds were unfavourable. Sickness was rife, often affecting the white crews almost as badly as the slaves.

continent's ancient patterns of indigenous tribal settlement, following only the logic of colonial greed. To this day a glance at the map of Africa reveals a number of unnaturally straight boundaries, obviously drawn with the edge of a ruler.

Back in South Africa the Zulu wars with the British brought an African victory in 1879 at Isandlwana, with the loss of some 2,000 Zulu *impis*, and a courageous defence by a hugely outnumbered British force at Rorke's Drift that was eventually immortalized in the film *Zulu*. Other changes were afoot that had nothing to do with military heroics on either side: in the mid-1880s gold was discovered in abundance at Witwatersrand, prompting a gradual but inexorable shift of black workers from agricultural to industrial labour. But a few months before the century drew to a close, war swept across the country anew as the Boers attacked the British. They besieged Mafeking and Ladysmith and sparked an unequal conflict in which the much smaller force of Boer volunteers fought with skill and cunning until they were forced to surrender. The British, meanwhile, introduced a sinister innovation into the conduct of war – the concentration camp, where many Boers died of sickness.

When the Boer War ended in mid-1902, African hopes for new civil and political rights were cruelly dashed. The issue was left to a future self-governing white authority. Afrikaner nationalism had solidified into a hard and purposeful agenda, and the British quickly gave up trying to anglicize the Boers, instead seeking their collaboration to maintain order. The limits of African ownership were defined in 1913 through tribal reserves, later called homelands, which eventually comprised a paltry 13 per cent of the country's land. Black rental or purchase agreements outside these areas then became illegal. Pass laws followed in ten years, ensuring strict urban segregation and a ready supply of cheap African labour.

The colonial 'Scramble for Africa' came later. In 1870 King Leopold II of Belgium (1835–1909) set up a private venture to colonize Kongo. Then, 15 years later, having commissioned British explorer Henry Stanley (1841–1904) to help him establish his writ across the Congo River basin, he proclaimed himself leader of the Congo Free State and set about the brutal business of exploiting the country for all it was worth. Bursting with military conceit and economic rapacity, the European powers were starting to vie for the top spot in a new imperial pecking order. The British, still busy with the 'Great Game' in the Far East, were well aware of the attractions of carving fresh hunks off Africa. In the 1880s and 1890s, they won new possessions to East and West, and the French did likewise, with a second round of grabs and swaps during the first 15 years of the new century. Lines were scored across a map that bore no relation whatever to the

A few months before the end of World War I in 1918, Nelson Rolihlahla Mandela was born near Umtata in the Transkei. He was the son of the chief counsellor to a tribal paramount chief, who was later to become his guardian. His birth came just six years after the founding of the African National Congress, an organization in which he was to play a key role as a radical lawyer, campaigner and, eventually, the world's best-known political prisoner. He was a symbol of unflinching resistance to oppression and a supreme example of patient personal endurance throughout the years in jail, many of them in the grim fastness of Robben Island, a former leper colony and asylum for the insane.

A world away, at the other end of the old slave routes, another decade elapsed before the birth of Martin Luther King (1929–68). Born into the black middle class, he was to become the passionate advocate of black civil rights in the USA, hailed as 'an American Gandhi' on account of his firm religious principles and his deep faith in the value of non-violent direct action as a tool of political change.

The situations of these two men were superficially different. Mandela spoke out in his own land on behalf of his oppressed countrymen, who had been denied their freedom by white settlers who had prised the country away from them. King championed millions of downtrodden American blacks whose forebears had been torn from their ancestral homes and transported across the ocean to live as slaves in an alien land. He insisted on their right to be treated as equal citizens in a country that had taken a leading role in their uprooting. Their methods and rhetoric were different, yet their objectives were in essence the same. Both had been influenced by the black churches as well as by modern liberationist thinking. And both rose magnificently above the temptation to heap hate or blame on the whites, seeking racial reconciliation and harmony instead.

For Mandela, who spent his childhood in a mud-walled hut called a *rondavel*, the struggle began after his schooling at a strict Wesleyan college. He enrolled at university to study for a BA and became a student representative, but was suspended after taking part in a protest boycott. Moving to Johannesburg, he worked at Crow Mines, where the workers were segregated along tribal lines, later gaining his legal qualifications via a correspondence course. A fashionable fellow and man about town, the young Mandela learnt to box and was a fan of the musician Victor Silvester.

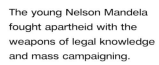

The young Nelson Mandela fought apartheid with the weapons of legal knowledge and mass campaigning.

Taken up by the ANC leader Walter Sisulu (1912–2003) in his early twenties, Mandela joined the movement's youth league. He met Oliver Tambo (1917–93), later to become ANC president, and together they established a legal practice – by all accounts the first black law firm in Africa. Their work concentrated on racial injustice. After 1948, when the Afrikaner National Party won an election on the strength of the hardline race policy known as apartheid, the ANC was determined to transform itself into an effective political force. In 1949 it adopted the youth league's programme of action, which advocated boycotts, strikes and civil disobedience as well as non-cooperation as weapons of resistance.

In 1952 Mandela coordinated the ANC's Campaign for the Defiance of Unjust Laws, travelling the country to gain support for a programme of mass disobedience. Mandela was arrested, but the courts handed down a suspended sentence after finding that he and his fellow defendants had consistently urged followers to stick with peaceful methods. Throughout the latter half of the 1950s, however, he was subjected to mounting official harassment, including demands that he and Tambo relocate their urban practice to 'the back of beyond' under racial zoning laws.

As Mandela focused on labour exploitation, the pass laws, the new Bantustan policy and the segregation of universities, he was drawn into a huge treason trial, which later collapsed. After the Sharpeville massacre of 1960, the ANC was banned; a year later, convinced that all other possibilities had been exhausted, Mandela and other ANC leaders set up a new group, Umkhonto we Sizwe, to prepare for armed struggle. Having slipped out of the country illegally to publicize the fight for black freedom abroad, he was arrested and put on trial on his return. Refusing to accept the authority of a white-controlled judiciary and a parliament that gave him no voice, Mandela declared at the outset: 'I detest racialism, because I regard it as a barbaric thing, whether it comes from a black man or a white man.' He was jailed for five years, later extended to life imprisonment on a second conviction for sabotage.

In the USA Martin Luther King grew up in the midst of racial segregation. In Atlanta, where he was born, blacks were barred from white schools, parks, swimming pools and lunch counters; when travelling by bus they entered at the back, whites at the front, and they stayed standing in case a white person might want to sit. King's parents were affluent, for his father was the self-made son of a share-cropper and could afford to sponsor his son's academic progress through university, theological seminary and postgraduate studies in Boston. King started out wanting to become a doctor or lawyer. He studied sociology; his enrolment as a pastor in Montgomery, Alabama – once known as 'the cradle of the Confederacy' – was to repay a sense of obligation to the black churches before then returning to academia.

King never made it back to full-time theological study. In 1954 the US Supreme Court declared school segregation unconstitutional. This was in the wake of determined efforts by Northern white liberals and educated blacks in the National Association for the Advancement of Colored Peoples (NAACP) to invoke the principles of the Declaration of Independence and the Constitution in defence of poor Southern blacks facing daily attacks and harassment. King set up his banner on the integrationist wing of the liberation movement, in contrast to the Nation of Islam of the African nationalists of Elijah Muhammad (1897–1975), such as Malcolm X (1925–65), who advocated racial separatism and claimed that the white man was the devil incarnate. King initially dismissed the nationalists as 'black supremacists' and did his best to avoid them.

Starting with the Montgomery bus boycott in 1955, launched on the arrest of Rosa Parks for refusing to give up her seat to a white man, King was pitched into a whirl of non-violent activism. He set up the Southern Christian Leadership Conference in 1957, bypassing the NAACP's cautious constitutional approach; Southern activists went on to organize lunch-counter sit-ins in 1960, the 'freedom rides' and the failed Albany movement of

1961. Then came the widely supported Birmingham campaign of 1963, ending in the arrest of 4,000 people, many of them children, after police beat protestors in the street, turning fire-hoses and dogs on them. The nation was aghast.

These efforts culminated dramatically that year in a march on Washington by a quarter of a million people, and it was

here that King delivered his famous 'I have a dream ...' speech, setting forth his passionate vision that 'the sons of former slaves and the sons of former slave-owners will be able to sit down together at the table of brotherhood.' Two weeks later white racists bombed a Baptist church in Birmingham, killing four black girls. King was griefstricken.

The exclusion of blacks in the Deep South from lunch counters, parks and swimming pools was the target of Martin Luther King's campaigning.

1968

Martin Luther King assassinated

4 April 1968. The Rev. Martin Luther King has spent thirteen years campaigning for black civil rights. Drawing inspiration from Gandhi's techniques of non-violent resistance, he won the Nobel Peace Prize for his campaigns against segregation and unemployment. But the price of progress has been more racist violence across the South, including murder: now he himself is a target. The question is, who wants him dead?

Evening

3 April. King arrives in Memphis, Tennessee, in a thunderstorm and checks into the Lorraine Motel. It has been an eventful day – a bomb scare held up his flight from Atlanta, Georgia – and he has an engagement at the Mason Temple, a modern church where 15,000 black people heard him speak a fortnight ago on behalf of the city's striking black sanitation workers.

Thinking that the downpour will keep supporters away, King sends two colleagues, Jesse Jackson and Ralph Abernathy, in his place. He feels that his time will be better spent on planning tactics for the next march, due in four days. This march is in support of 1,300 strikers laid off while white colleagues remain on full pay, who have been striking for 64 days. A march in Memphis a week ago turned ugly and was broken up by police using tear-gas; now the authorities have slapped a ban on further demonstrations.

King's reputation is on the line. He faces challenges from more militant groups, such as the Black Panthers, so it is essential that he makes this protest work. It will also be a curtain-raiser for his next national campaign – a Poor People's March on Washington. He needs to match that triumphant first march on Washington nearly five years ago, when a quarter of a million people turned out to hear his dream of brotherhood.

A call comes through. Abernathy tells him 2,000 people are waiting, clapping and cheering. King can hardly ignore this summons. He goes to the Mason Temple and tells those who have congregated that difficult days ahead do not matter, 'Because I've been to the mountaintop. And I don't mind. Like anybody, I would like to live a long life. Longevity has its place. But I'm not concerned about that now.' He has 'seen the promised land'; as a people, 'we will get there'. He works on until 5 a.m.

15:15   **4 April.** Across the road from King's motel, a tall man with slicked-back hair in a dark suit and tie pulls up in a white '66 Mustang. He climbs the stairs to the second floor of a cheap rooming house and asks if he can rent a room. Sure – $8.50. He gives his name as John Willard, but his real name is James Earl Ray – a white racist with a long criminal record. Ray goes out later to buy a pair of binoculars.

15:30   Ray is back in his room with the binoculars and a long package retrieved from his car, wrapped in a bedspread. King has now heard that the court order banning the march has been overturned and he confers with local black leaders to impress on them that the protest must go off peacefully. Still fatigued, he closes his blinds and rests in preparation for a dinner date with Pastor Billy Kyles from the Temple, later in the day.

18:00   Billy Kyles arrived half an hour ago in order to chivvy his guests along. He and King step out of the room onto the balcony. Across the road, having been locked in the bathroom for an hour, Ray cradles his rifle. King and Kyles emerge at street level.

At one minute past six a single shot is heard and King falls, struck in the neck.

Ray hastily exits the bathroom, gathers his possessions and flees, tossing the gun into the yard of an amusement arcade as he hurries to his car. Abernathy weeps as the ambulance arrives, but there is nothing they can do. By 7.05 p.m. King is pronounced dead. Riots erupt across 130 US cities; many suspect FBI involvement. Ray is caught later in London and jailed for life, but the question remains: did he act alone?

Above left: Martin Luther King delivers his famous 'I have a dream' speech in front of the Lincoln Memorial during the Freedom March on Washington in 1963.

Above right: Coretta Scott King sits surrounded by family at the funeral of her husband, Martin Luther King, in April 1968. King was assassinated with one shot by James Earl Ray outside a Memphis motel.

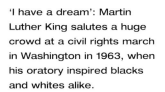

'I have a dream': Martin Luther King salutes a huge crowd at a civil rights march in Washington in 1963, when his oratory inspired blacks and whites alike.

Though he kept up his campaigning for a racially integrated USA, attacking poverty at home and the Vietnam War abroad, he began to treat the more militant views of African nationalists, as well as the Black Panthers, with a guarded respect.

In April 1968 King was shot dead in Memphis, Tennessee, by a white assassin, James Earl Ray, a known racist and criminal. Nelson Mandela lived on through another 22 years of imprisonment, repeatedly refusing government offers to release him and thereby rid itself of such a potent symbol of the African struggle. He was eventually freed in 1990 to worldwide acclaim, becoming ANC president in 1991, was awarded the Nobel Peace Prize in 1993, and took office as South Africa's first elected state president in 1994. He served five years in that role before then retiring to his birthplace at Qunu in the Transkei.

One cause, divergent fates. Today the USA is a different place, as demographic changes make the whites a minority. Times are better for the blacks, though they remain vulnerable to economic downturn. After the decolonizations of the 1950s and 1960s, the dire state of modern Africa – stricken with Aids, war, famine and a depressing number of corrupt, incompetent or oppressive black leaders, sometimes all three – can no longer be blamed on the heritage of slavery and colonialism. The politics of Western aid have not helped much, nor has a more sophisticated Western exploitation of their fragile economies. Where next for the black liberators?

1990

Nelson Mandela walks free

11 February 1990. Nelson Mandela spent a total of 27 years in South African jails, serving ten years in the grim penal stronghold of Robben Island. The true reason why he was locked away was his staunch campaigning for the ANC from the 1940s; in prison, he became a worldwide symbol of African resistance, refusing all offers of release until he felt the battle had been won.

04:30 Nelson Mandela wakes in a private cottage in the grounds of Victor Verster Prison about 48 km (30 miles) outside Cape Town, close to the affluent white suburb of Paarl. He starts his day, as always, with physical exercises. They keep him in good shape, but they are more than just a prisoner's sanity-saving routine. As a young man, Mandela was a more than passable boxer, and he kept the habit of self-discipline.

05:00 The two prison officers who have guarded him for 20 years enter with a bundle of newspapers and bring him breakfast – cereal and milk. Outside the gates, journalists and well-wishers begin to gather. Mandela puts on his glasses and begins reading with the quiet attentiveness of a trained lawyer, pausing to tear out articles, until the prison doctor arrives for his last prison examination.

07:30 Brigadier Keulder, the governor, arrives with the release papers. Both men sign, Mandela receives his copy, Keulder walks out. Mandela smiles to himself. After secret talks with the new South African premier, F W de Klerk, he is now satisfied. His long, patient, strategic waiting game is over: at 71, he is no longer a prisoner.

De Klerk is from the National Party, which devised apartheid; as education minister he upheld it. But he has seen that there is only one way to end the country's spiral of violence: lift the ban on the ANC, release its leading figurehead, and seek 'a new and just constitutional dispensation in which every inhabitant will enjoy equal rights, treatment and opportunity'.

Later, three ANC representatives are admitted to discuss how this extraordinary symbolic moment will be played on the outside. It is vital that everyone in South

Africa is left in no doubt that Mandela is not selling out but carrying on the fight for justice. They start drafting speeches.

09:30 With only half an hour to go until the scheduled release, some 30 dignitaries due to escort Mandela to the gate still have not arrived. Most importantly, Mandela's wife, Winnie, is stuck in Johannesburg trying to get a flight, and without her Mandela will not budge. He reads quietly in the cottage. Five minutes before ten o'clock and the crowd outside is now huge, rippling with excitement. A chant begins, rising to a roar as the white Nissan car belonging to Mandela's guard James Gregory drives up. But it dies away as the crowd realizes there is a hold-up. Helicopters circle overhead; nerves are getting frayed. As the delays continue throughout the morning into the afternoon, the crowd grows restless. Mandela takes lunch and then a nap.

15:00 A convoy of eight black limousines sweeps into the jail. Winnie is here, along with the rest of Mandela's escort. After a last-minute scare over a possible assassination attempt by one of the guards, all are disarmed. Then, just before four in the afternoon,

Mandela approaches the gate to shouts of 'He's walking! He's walking to freedom!' and steps outside. He raises a clenched fist in the long-banned ANC salute.

18:30 The 50,000 people waiting at Grand Parade in Cape Town were expecting Mandela half an hour ago; now they are starting to drift away. Then he appears. In a storm of flashbulbs, he declares that apartheid has no future, reminds them that the armed struggle was a purely defensive response, and ends by saying that 'a democratic and free society' is an ideal which, if necessary, he is prepared to die for.

Above left: Nelson Mandela behind bars became a worldwide symbol of the black liberation struggle, refusing offers of release until his own political aims were achievable.

Above right: Mandela gives the ANC salute with his then wife, Winnie, on his release from jail in 1990.

The Atlantic has been a source of fascination to voyagers from the time of the Vikings in their long ships to the well-heeled passengers on Concorde. Its challenges have included navigation by sail and steam, the exploration of new lands and sending messages across by radio and satellite.

[AD **1000**] : [**1974**]

ACROSS THE ATLANTIC

Beside the vast breadth of the Pacific Ocean, the Atlantic might today look like a relatively easy proposition to cross – no more than three hours and 20 minutes on Concorde, for as long as that elegant *tour de force* of supersonic engineering remains in service. Shaped a little like an hourglass, the Atlantic is less than 2,900 km (1,800 miles) across between Liberia and Brazil, as West Africa bellies out into the ocean towards a facing bulge on South America's eastern coast – though the distance expands to some 4,830 km (3,000 miles) if you travel from Norfolk, Virginia, to Gibraltar and the old Pillars of Hercules.

The Pacific, in contrast, is 17,700 km (11,000 miles) wide at the Equator, covers almost a third of the globe, and has a surface area of 166 million square km (64 million square miles). Even a modern jet flight across this vast expanse – travelling from Los Angeles to Peking – takes around 16 hours, longer with refuelling stops.

The Pacific is a zone of spectacular seismic instability, studded with some 300 active volcanoes in a 'ring of fire' stretching up from Tonga in the South Pacific, through Indonesia and the Philippines, up to Japan, and turning west via the Aleutian Islands to run all the way down the western coasts of North and South America. Earthquakes, eruptions, typhoons and tsunamis wreak havoc on its shores, making a mockery of the implied tranquillity of its name. The Atlantic, too, can unleash mighty storms and hurricanes, though their

The history of the Atlantic

1000
Leif Eriksen sails from Iceland to America and sets up a Viking settlement on the east coast, named Vinland after the wild vines growing there.

1492
Christopher Columbus sets sail from Spain with three vessels, travelling via Tenerife, hoping to open a westward passage to the Indies. He fails but hears of land farther west.

1497
Amerigo Vespucci makes his first voyage to the continent that bears his name, as Vasco da Gama finds a way to India round Africa and John Cabot reaches Newfoundland.

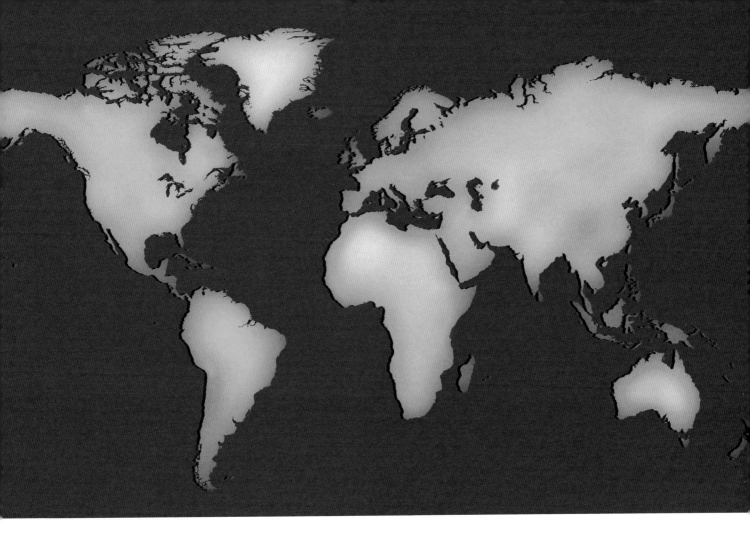

violence is perhaps less frequent, and less destructive of human life, than those that roar so frequently across the Pacific. Yet disparity of breadth between these two great oceans is in one sense deceptive, since the Atlantic runs 16,000 km (10,000 miles) from north to south, while its surface area of 106 million square km (41 million square miles), covering one fifth of the earth, makes it the world's second-largest ocean.

Above left: A view of the Strait of Gibraltar, joining the Mediterranean Sea and the Atlantic Ocean.

Above right: A map of the world shows the shortest distance across the Atlantic, from Liberia to Brazil.

1511
Hernán Cortés is the first of several Spanish conquistadores to arrive in America, conquering parts of Mexico; he is followed by Pizarro, De Soto, De Vaca and others.

1587
At Roanoke Island, where Sir Richard Grenville leaves the first English settlement on American soil, Virginia Dare is the first English child to be born in the continent.

1605
Port Royal becomes the first permanent French settlement in America, from where Samuel de Champlain journeys up the St Lawrence River to the site of Quebec.

Leif Eriksen in his boat just off the coast of Vinland, where the Vikings found salmon and wild grapes.

Their respective histories of navigation are very different. In the Pacific the ancient Polynesians took to the open ocean in voyaging canoes, covering immense distances with apparent ease. They set up their enigmatic statues on Easter Island – the loneliest inhabited island on earth at the time of its discovery by Europeans – situated 3,700 km (2,300 miles) from the coast of Chile to the east and another 4,000 km (2,500 miles) from Tahiti in the northwest. Even its closest neighbour, tiny Pitcairn Island, lies 2,250 km (1,400 miles) due west. The Polynesians lived in a world of water and they skimmed across the Pacific like natural amphibians, threading their way from island to island, leaving a patchwork of cultures across this far-flung scatter of habitable terrain. In China, meanwhile, the sailing junk developed from about 1,500 BC and spread to other parts of Asia, including Korea and Japan. The western reaches of the Pacific were explored by the Arabs and the Indians. Only much later did European sailing ships arrive, penetrating beyond India to open up new colonial possessions in the Far East: the Dutch in Java, the Spanish in the Philippines, the British in Hong Kong.

Europe started from a set of different principles, beginning with the reed boats of ancient Egypt, though these were designed originally for calm sailing on the smooth waters of the Nile. Then came more resilient vessels constructed from planks with ribbed hulls, better able to withstand the battering of the waves. These enabled the thriving maritime culture of the Mediterranean. By the first millennium BC, early European navigators began to pilot vessels of both types beyond Gibraltar, out on to the deep ocean, but it would be another 1,500 years at least before anyone ventured a crossing. When that moment came it was not the intrepid traders and warriors of the South who made the journey, but the hardy denizens of the far North – the Vikings – whose long ships were built to withstand harsher conditions in lands where cold and ice rendered navigation impossible for months on end.

The history of the Atlantic

1620
The *Mayflower* sets sail from Plymouth, in southern England, bearing religious non-conformists seeking freedom of worship in the New World.

1819
Savannah is often cited as the first vessel to have crossed the Atlantic under steam; others believe the Dutch vessel Curaçao has a stronger claim.

1858
A company backed by entrepreneur Cyrus Field and Samuel Morse, inventor of the telegraphic coding system, lays the first successful transatlantic cable.

The ocean's name derives from the Atlas Mountains of North Africa, though some insist it was named after the fabled island of Atlantis, believed by the ancient Greeks to have sunk below the waves more than 9,000 years before their time. The Atlantic inspired wonder and fear in Europeans for centuries. The Celts spoke of Hy Brazil, an island that appeared in the mist at sunset, as a paradise on earth where men and women lived perfect lives. Another legendary island was St Brendan's, reputedly found by a sixth-century Irish monk, and placed on early charts halfway to Zipangu, Japan, with no sign yet of the American continent. The Portuguese subscribed to a belief in Antilia, shown on a Genoese chart of 1450; it was a mythic island of seven cities, supposedly founded by a bishop from Oporto after the Moors invaded Spain. Along with the fanciful or often fearsome creatures employed to embellish medieval maps where an imperfect knowledge ran out and cartographic fantasy took over, there was, until the discovery that the world was round, the fear of simply sailing over the edge.

Viking exploration of the Atlantic began from the colony established in Greenland in AD 986 by Erik the Red (c.950–1001), an exiled Icelander. As with many discoveries, it seems to have begun by accident. According to the Greenland Saga, one Bjarni Herjolfsson and his crew were blown off course while sailing for Greenland in thick fog. They spied a wooded country of low hills, but did not go ashore. Instead they followed the coast for two days, then headed northeast for another three. This time they found an island, mountainous and surmounted by a glacier. Again, Bjarni refused to land. On his return to Scandinavia, Bjarni landed in Greenland before moving on to Norway. Having heard his traveller's tales, Eric the Red's son Leif (970–1020) resolved to buy his ship, mustered a crew of adventurous souls and set off to explore these new lands.

First, they came to a land of ice with a rocky shoreline. Leif named it Helluland (probably Baffin Island); next, they found a flat and wooded country with white sandy beaches, which they named Markland (now thought to be northern Labrador). Sailing on again, they entered a sound by a north-facing headland where they were beached as the tide went out, but rowed on up a river at its return to a lake. Here they found salmon and harvested grapes from wild vines, which gave the settlement its name, Vinland, though its location remains

1901
Guglielmo Marconi receives the first radio transmission across the ocean, a spark transmission of the letter 'S' in Morse, in Newfoundland.

1912
The Titanic hits an iceberg and goes to the bottom on her maiden voyage to New York with the loss of 1,500 passengers. She had been considered unsinkable.

1962
The Telstar satellite enables the first transatlantic television transmission from the USA to be picked up at the Radome, in Pleumeur-Bodou, France.

149

disputed, as does the authenticity of the so-called Kensington Rune Stone allegedly found in Minnesota in 1898.

Leif returned to Greenland the following year, laden with timber and grapes; further Viking voyages followed. The next was led by Leif's brother Thorvald (c.975–1003), whose men attacked and killed a group of natives, though Thorvald was struck by an arrow during a counterattack and later died. This set a pattern for later expeditions, as local people, whom the Vikings nicknamed skraelings (wretches) sought to trade and then steal weapons. The final chronicled expedition to Vinland was led by Leif Eriksen's cunning and strong-minded daughter, Freydis, who flirted, lied, bribed and murdered throughout her journey for personal gain. When her actions were discovered on her return to Greenland, she was cast out.

The Viking settlement in North America may not have lasted long, but it was to be some time before anyone else from the Atlantic's eastern margins was to try again. The navigator traditionally credited with 'discovering' the New World was, of course, Christopher Columbus (1451–1506), or Cristoforo Colombo in his native Italy and Cristóbal Colón to the Spanish, who eventually gained Spanish support for his attempt to find a new route to the Indies, sailing due west. Born in Genoa, a city renowned for the enterprise and daring of its navigators, Columbus found his métier early in life – some accounts say as early as 14, claiming that he had travelled as far as the coast of Guinea by the age of 16, though others place his maritime initiation five years later. Whatever, arriving in Portugal between 1471 and 1474, he tried in vain to interest the Portuguese king in his idea of a westward passage to India. Moving to Spain around the end of 1485 to try his luck anew, he faced further obstacles: his proposal was rejected by an ecclesiastical commission, while the Spanish king, Ferdinand (1452–1516), was preoccupied with the expulsion of the Moors. His brother Bartolomeo (1451–1506) had no greater success at the courts of England and France, but the tide turned after the fall of Granada, the Moors' last stronghold in Spain, early in 1492. The Spanish queen, Isabella (1451–1504), was persuaded to take an interest, and she in turn influenced her husband.

So, on 3 August, Columbus set forth in three vessels – the *Santa Maria*, *Pinta* and *Niña*. On the seventieth day, 36 days out from Tenerife, they sighted land: an island in the Bahamas, now called Watling's Island, which was then inhabited by Arawaks.

Columbus claimed it for the Spanish Crown under the name San Salvador. They went on to Cuba, which Columbus dubbed Juana, and to Hispaniola, later known as Santo Domingo and then Haiti. There was evidence of gold on the latter island, so a force of about 60 men was left behind there. This was the first Spanish colony in the New World, christened La Nadividad on Christmas Day. But before sailing for home, Columbus learnt of the prospect of much more gold on Yamaye (Jamaica); he also heard that the mainland was some ten days' journey by canoe

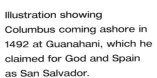

Illustration showing Columbus coming ashore in 1492 at Guanahani, which he claimed for God and Spain as San Salvador.

to Spain as prisoners. After a first sighting of Dominica and a tour round Jamaica, Columbus headed on for Haiti, where he found the fort at La Nadividad burnt out and the colonists massacred. A new settlement was established along the coast, and named Isabella after the Spanish queen, together with a new fort in the interior called San Tomas. As Columbus set off for five months, hoping to discover the coast of China or the Moluccas, conditions deteriorated at the colony. There was fighting with the Indians, and grievances began to fester among the colonists against the absent Columbus; on his return, he imposed harsh penalties on the Arawaks, while voices were raised against him in Spain.

A third and a fourth expedition followed after Columbus returned to Spain, garbed as a penitent, to make his peace with his royal patrons. On the third journey he named the island of Trinidad and came upon the mouth of the Orinoco River, which he believed would lead to the Earthly Paradise of Christian lore. As his health worsened the colony on Haiti split into two camps, and eventually Columbus and his two brothers were sent back to Spain in chains after a visit by a representative of the Spanish Crown. Though his property was restored to him and the stain lifted from his name, he was not reinstated as governor, arguably a role for which he was ill-suited. By the time of his fourth trip, a new governor was installed in Haiti, accompanied by 2,500 Spaniards; Columbus himself had now proposed a search for a western route to Jerusalem. He lost two of his four ships in storms and limped back to Jamaica to await rescue, returning to Spain and dying the following year, in 1506.

Historical research may have scotched the old story that he died in obscure poverty, but it is certainly the name of another Italian-born navigator, Amerigo Vespucci (1451–1512),

beyond that. Firm in his belief that this must be the coast of Eastern Asia, he suffered the loss of the *Santa Maria*, but returned to Spain in March 1493 to be greeted with much honour.

By September of that year, Columbus was on his way back, this time with a larger fleet, consisting of three big sailing ships, 13 caravels and some 1,500 men. His first objective was some smaller islands south of Hispaniola, then inhabited by the fierce, seagoing Caribs, who were said to practise cannibalism. He planned to enslave and convert them, later sending a number of them back a Florentine who made three voyages in search of a western passage to Asia, starting in 1497, that is commemorated in the name of the new continent – America. That was also the year when the Portuguese seafarer Vasco da Gama (c.1469–1525) set off on his successful voyage to discover the sea route to India, sailing south along the west coast of Africa and rounding the southern tip to enter the Indian Ocean, thus succeeding where all the westward-leading geographical speculations of Columbus had failed.

Nevertheless, the explorations of Columbus initiated a westward thrust across the Atlantic under sail that by the end of the sixteenth century had begun to transform the continent. In his seaborne wake followed the Spanish conquistadores, who made incursions into the North as well as the South – men such as Hernán Cortés (1485–1547), who participated in the conquest of Cuba in 1511 before moving on to Mexico with a force of 600 men. He had his ships burned to forestall retreat and entered what is now Mexico City in 1519, where he commanded the arrest and execution of the Aztec emperor Montezuma. Forced to withdraw in the face of fierce Aztec resistance, he later defeated them and opened the way to the conquest of Mexico in 1521, seizing large areas of land and people for himself and his soldiers. Farther south another great civilization, the Inca of Peru, was overthrown when Francisco Pizarro (c.1475–1541), having scouted the Peruvian coast in 1528, returned in 1532 and captured their emperor, Atahualpa, with a small force of about 180 men. The Spanish demanded a vast ransom in gold and silver, but put Atahualpa to death when they heard of the approach of a large Inca army. Pizarro went on to found the city of Lima.

Another famous conquistador was Hernando de Soto (c.1500–42), who landed in Florida in 1539, more than a quarter of a century after it had been explored by Juan Ponce de León (1460–1520), one of Columbus's captains. De Soto's expedition was well supplied with soldiers, guns, ammunition, horses and hunting dogs. He set off with his army on a 6,450 km (4,000 mile) trek through the southeastern part of North America, exploring Kentucky, Tennessee, Illinois, Indiana and Missouri in search of a wealthy Indian kingdom reputed to lie farther to the west. Villages were pillaged, women raped and men chained

Conquistadores, such as Hernando de Soto in the sixteenth century, explored the New World in search of gold. In this 1868 illustration, de Soto is shown discovering the Mississippi River.

like pack animals, with many dying from new diseases imported by the Spanish, before the attempt to colonize the North was abandoned four years later.

Less typical was Cabeza de Vaca (c.1490–1557), who in 1527 left Spain on a 300-strong expedition to Florida. Plagued by malaria, dysentery and native attacks, the Spanish fled inland on barges, two of which were wrecked on an island in Louisiana; all but 15 succumbed to starvation, exposure and an outbreak of cannibalism. De Vaca and three others spent six years in Louisiana before wandering through Texas, New Mexico and Arizona, where they were initiated into shamanistic tribal healing practices and found in 1536 by Spanish slavers in north Mexico. De Vaca wrote the earliest account of Native American cultures; he is a rare early example of a European in some sense 'colonized' by the indigenous cultures.

Naturally, the Spanish were not alone in casting covetous eyes on the vast new land in the West. In 1497 John Cabot (1450–c.1500), a British seafarer leaving Bristol on the *Matthew*, in company with one other small British vessel, sighted land after 52 days at sea – this was a place that would in future be known as Nova Scotia. In his captain's chest Cabot carried a parchment sealed by Henry VII of England (1457–1509), charging him to 'to subdue, occupy, and possesse' and 'to be holden and bounden to Henry of all the fruits, profits, gaines, and commodities to pay unto him in wares or money a fifth part of the capital gaine so gotten'. Cabot went ashore with his sons and a small band of sailors, hoping to take on fresh water and supplies; having set up a cross and a royal standard at the foot of Sugarloaf Mountain, on the tip of Cape Breton Island, Cabot then went back to his ship, weighed anchor and set a course for home.

By 1522 the French had proof of the riches to be gained in America thanks to the seizure by a French corsair of a Spanish ship sailing from St Vincent, its hold stuffed with precious cargo. Accordingly, some two or three years later, the French king, François I (1494–1547), dispatched another Italian navigator, Giovanni da Verrazzano (c.1480–1527), to investigate farther on an expedition that was also backed by eager Italian merchants and bankers based in Lyons. Sailing from Madeira, da Verrazzano made landfall at Cape Fear, turned south and doubled back, sending a boat ashore to speak with the natives, whom he described thus: 'These people go altogether naked except only that they cover their privy parts with certain skins of beasts like unto martens, which they fasten onto a narrow girdle made of grass, very artfully wrought, hanged about with tails of divers other beasts, which round about their bodies hang dangling down to their knees. Some of them wear garlands of birds' feathers. The people are of a color russet, and not much unlike the Saracens; their hair black, thick, and not very long, which they tie together in a knot behind, and wear it like a tail.'

Da Verrazzano went on to explore the east coast extensively. Having reached the outer banks of Carolina, he mistook the water of the sound beyond for the Pacific, thus introducing a mapmakers' inaccuracy known as the 'Sea of Verrazzano' that endured for a century. He visited New York harbour and Maine, encountering the Wampanoag, who impressed him favourably, and the Abenaki, who did not, showering the French visitors with arrows and flashing their bare behinds; eventually he reached Newfoundland. Verrazzano made two more transatlantic

Left: Under Elizabeth I, the Virgin Queen, Sir Walter Raleigh explored the coast of North America, naming it Virginia for his sovereign, but his efforts to colonize the new territory failed.

Right: Pilgrim Fathers: some 120 Puritans came ashore at New Plymouth in 1620, in search of food and religious freedom.

trips, reaching Brazil on his second outing despite threats of mutiny; on his third visit he went ashore, probably at Guadeloupe, only to be captured, slaughtered and devoured by Caribs under the horrified eyes of his brother, who was anchored too far offshore to help.

These early pioneers were followed by Jacques Cartier (1491–1557), commissioned in 1534 by the French king 'to discover certain islands and lands where it is said that a great quantity of gold, and other precious things, are to be found.' He winged across the Atlantic in double-quick time – just 20 days – and on his second trip, in 1535, sailed into Canada, forging on up the St Lawrence River to reach the sites of present-day Quebec and Montreal. Later in the century came Sir Humphrey Gilbert (1537–83), who reached Newfoundland but lost three of his

ships, returning only with the *Squirrel* and the *Golden Hind*; the following year, in 1584, Sir Walter Raleigh (1552–1618), who never set foot in America, sent two captains, Philip Amidas (1550–1618) and Arthur Barlow, on a voyage in 1584 that led to the founding of Virginia, named after England's 'Virgin Queen', Elizabeth I (1533–1603).

The first English settlement was set up by Sir Richard Grenville (c.1541–91), a cousin of Raleigh, who dropped off 108 people at Roanoke Island in 1586 before returning to England with the first consignment of tobacco. Feuding among themselves and with the local people, they were reduced to living on roots and oysters, and were returned to England by Sir Francis Drake (c.1543–96) at their own request. A second group of 116, arriving in the following year, had mysteriously

vanished by the time their leader sailed back from England with supplies, delayed by the battle with the Spanish Armada. The only clue was the word 'Croatoan' (the name of another island near by) carved on a tree but no trace was found there either. It was at Roanoke, often called 'the lost colony', that the first English child was born on American soil: Virginia Dare, born 18 August 1587.

By the early seventeenth century, more lasting settlements were appearing. The French base at Port Royal, in the Annapolis basin of modern eastern Canada – which was used to launch expeditions up the St Lawrence by Samuel de Champlain (1567–1635), the 'father of Quebec' – predated the foundation of the English settlement at Jamestown, Virginia, by two years, though it took another eight decades for the French to get round to founding Louisiana in 1682. In 1620 the *Mayflower* sailed from Plymouth, its freight of religious non-conformists seeking freedom of worship in what was to become known as New England. Within a few decades the 'Triangle of Trade' (see page 125) was beginning to accumulate serious fortunes farther south, as the slave ships sold off their human cargo at Jamestown and headed back to England or the Netherlands, laden with sugar, tobacco and cotton. Furs were exported farther north. Meanwhile, the booming trade with India of the British East India Company transported tea and spices to America, along with European luxuries such as brandy and, of course, guns, ammunition and soldiers. In South America the large-scale importation of slaves, mainly from Angola, began soon after the conquest.

Thus the sparse and scattered sails of the early arrivals, bobbing like discarded white snippets on the vast, grey expanse of the Atlantic, swelled to a teeming procession of canvas. The numbers coming in to North America were pushed up in the seventeenth century by England's use of transportation as a penalty for convicts, which became an official policy by the early years of the eighteenth century – between 30,000 and 50,000 English convicts are estimated to have been transported west across the ocean thereafter. At the same time the rapid build-up in the number of immigrants arriving on the eastern seaboard created a growing hunger for land, and the settlers began to look farther west. After the War of Independence, this pressure grew to a point where the pent-up drive to expand beyond the Mississippi became unstoppable.

Yet the means employed to ply between America and Europe did not start to undergo a major change until 1819, when the steamship *Savannah* put out from the city of the same name in Georgia, bound for Liverpool. *Savannah* had a steam engine but was rigged for sail; the engine was scarcely used in the crossing, with estimates varying from 80 hours in 27 days to just eight hours in 21 days. Others hand the accolade of the first crossing under steam to a British-built, Dutch-owned steamship, *Curaçao*. Built of wood at Dover, the 438-ton vessel, originally called Calpe, was 50 m (134 feet) long and powered by two 50 hp engines, though like *Savannah* it was fully rigged for sail. The voyage began at Hellevotsluis, near Rotterdam, on 26 April 1827 and ended at Paramaribo, Surinam, on 24 May, before the ship continued to the Dutch possession from which its new name had been taken. It spent 11 days of its journey under engine power on its outward trip, as the boiler leaked and the paddles had to be changed frequently; on the return journey, the record improved. *Curaçao* is credited with inaugurating the first regular intercontinental steam mail service, serving also as a warship until 1848.

The age of steam brought a new dimension to transatlantic traffic. In 1840 the Cunard Line was founded in Britain, using four small steamships to run a mail service, though each had room for only 115 passengers and no steerage. The displacement of sail by steam took decades, but the era of mass migration from Europe to the USA, which included many hundreds of thousands of Irish people fleeing the potato famine as well

as numerous emigrants from Eastern Europe, coincided with the emergence of regular, reliable steam services. The transatlantic route was the largest shipping market of the late nineteenth century; most Europeans emigrating overseas before World War I were heading for the USA. Between 1850 and 1914, some 70 per cent of all US immigrants arrived via the port of New York, and half of them travelled by the four largest European lines: Britain's Cunard and White Star lines and the two big German lines, Norddeutscher Lloyd and the Hamburg-America Packet Company.

In May 1911, just four weeks after Britain's first airship went down at Aldershot, the pride of the White Star Line, SS *Titanic*, was launched from a shipyard at Belfast. Within less than a year, this reputedly unsinkable passenger ship – equipped with 16 watertight compartments and, with its sister ship the SS *Olympic*, then the largest vessels afloat – ploughed into an iceberg on its maiden voyage and sank. More than 1,500 of its 2,340 passengers and crew were lost. While the managing director of White Star got away by lifeboat, only 20 of the 180 Irish passengers were saved and many others were shoved back into icy seas as they tried to claw their way aboard. The tragedy was blamed on an inadequate number of lifeboats; Captain Smith, who went down with the ship, was posthumously found guilty of negligence when it emerged that the ship had been going full speed ahead in spite of iceberg warnings.

Well before 1912, however, others were seeking new ways to convey not just people but messages across the ocean at greater speed. The steam mails were one method, a big improvement on sailing ships, which were always more vulnerable to vagaries of wind and weather, but still relatively slow. It took the creative mind of an inventive Italian, Guglielmo Marconi (1874–1937), to achieve what until then had been deemed impossible: to bounce

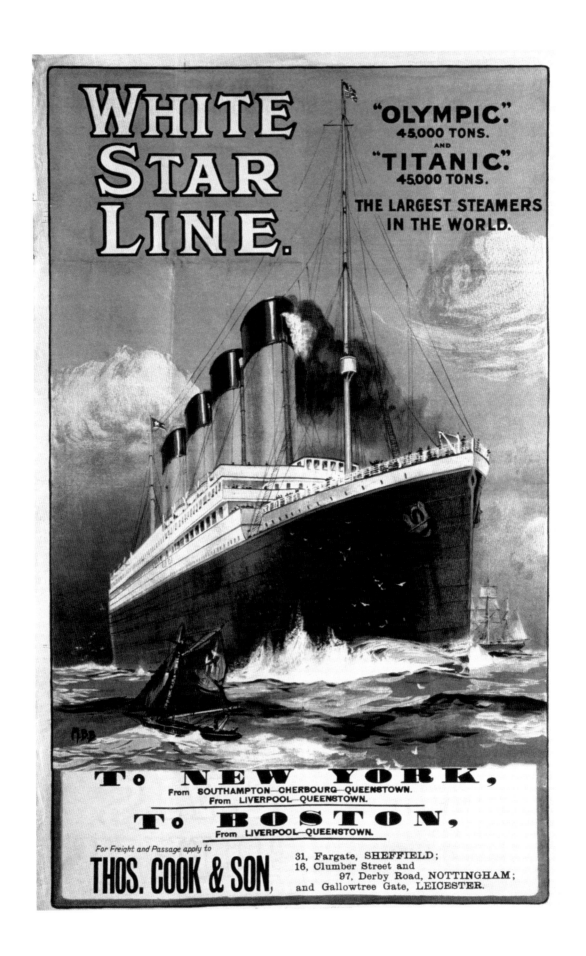

a radio signal over the earth's curvature from one side of the ocean to the other. In December 1901 Marconi succeeded in sending the first transatlantic wireless transmission – a spark-signal consisting of three dots, representing 'S' in Morse Code – from Poldhu in Cornwall to St John's in Newfoundland, Canada. It was an extraordinary achievement, with immediate benefits to the maritime world, the letter 'S' being the first letter in the standard distress signal, SOS, and it was swiftly adopted by ships at sea to improve their chances of survival.

In fact, Marconi's epoch-making transmission fell almost exactly 50 years after the first undersea cable came into service across the 14 miles of sea between Dover and Calais. The first successful transatlantic cable – an immensely more ambitious undertaking, covering a distance of more than 2,575 km (1,600 miles) – came in 1858. The venture's promoters were an American entrepreneur, Cyrus Field (1819–92), and his countryman Samuel Morse (1791–1872), who in 1830 had invented both the electrical telegraph and the signalling alphabet that bears his name. Field conceived the possibility of extending a telegraph cable connecting Nova Scotia, already linked up with New York, to St John's in Newfoundland and thence across the Atlantic to Ireland.

A company was floated and help solicited from the governments on both sides of the ocean, though Congress almost scuppered the proposal, objecting that both ends would be located in British territory. The first practical attempt, in 1857, involved two specially fitted warships – Britain's *Agamemnon* and the US *Niagara* – but the cable, weighing in at nearly a ton per mile, snapped in two and the broken tip sank out of sight. A second effort ended in much the same way; this time the snapped end sank two miles down. But a third brought success, defying the close approach of a frolicking whale as the cable paid out and a magnetic compass defect caused by the metallic cable itself. Effusive telegrams were exchanged, followed by a 100-gun salute and a torchlight procession in New York. But the cable ceased to work that day. It took two further attempts, using heavier cable and a larger ship, the *Great Eastern*, before the continents were reliably connected by not one but two transoceanic cables.

While these breakthroughs in communications brought the USA and Britain closer, as well as improving the safety of maritime traffic, the Atlantic became deadlier than ever to

shipping during the two world wars owing to the attacks by German U-boats. In 1917 400 Allied ships a month were being sent to the bottom; in 1942 the Allied tonnage sunk by U-boats reached more than 6.2 million in that year's total loss of 7.8 million, while the cost in lost lives was grievous.

Yet the age of flight sent bold new pioneers out across the waters. The Englishmen John Alcock (1892–1919) and Arthur Whitten-Brown (1886–1948) made the first nonstop airborne crossing in 1919, from Newfoundland to Clifden, Ireland; the American Charles Lindbergh (1902–74) won worldwide celebrity for the first solo nonstop crossing, flying from New York to Paris in 1927; Amelia Earhart (1898–1937) became the first woman to accomplish that feat five years later, setting a new record flight time across the Atlantic of 13 hours 30 minutes before moving on to the challenge of the Pacific. By 1969 the era of jet travel brought the awesome launch of both the 747 and Concorde, the latter achieving its fastest New York–London crossing in 1996 in just two hours, 52 minutes 59 seconds.

As for the advance of communications, the first transatlantic transmission of a television signal was received in 1962 at the Radome, in Pleumeur-Bodou, France, from a station in Andover, Maine, via the Telstar satellite, demonstrating the huge potential of satellite systems to make possible communications between other continents worldwide.

As the once awesome horizons of the Atlantic shrank, it became customary for Americans to refer to the saltwater between the USA and Europe as 'The Pond' – an expression of cultural amity with Britain as much as a reference to the sense of reduced distance arising from shorter travel times. Sadly, it looks as if The Pond is now widening again: in October 2003 Concorde is due for retirement, and the *Queen Elizabeth II*, the luxury liner that has for 34 years plied to and fro across the Atlantic, will cease to operate that route in January 2004. Even so, we have come a long way since the days of Leif Eriksen.

Charles Lindbergh's monoplane *Spirit of St Louis* flies triumphantly over the Eiffel Tower and the Seine in 1927.

1901

Marconi bounces Atlantic signal

12 December 1901. Guglielmo Marconi started experimenting with radio waves in 1894 at his home in Bologna. By the end of 1895, he had sent a signal more than 1.5 km (1 mile), opening the way for wireless telegraphy, and he moved to England to set up a company in association with the Post Office. Six years on he is trying to get a signal across the ocean.

11:30

11 December. Five days ago Marconi and his assistants, Kemp and Paget, arrived in St Johns, Newfoundland, by ship from Liverpool. The press has been kept at bay with a cover story about tests for a new ship-to-shore station. So here they are in this draughty old hospital – they have a stove, fortunately, but not much else in the way of furniture – hoping to pick up a spark transmission from Poldhu, Cornwall, 3,380 km (2,100 miles) away on the far side of the Atlantic, created by making a high-voltage spark jump the narrow gap between two spherical electrodes.

In England they should now be starting to transmit the letter 'S' in Morse – three sparks for three dots – using the powerful 25-kilowatt alternator he has persuaded his board to invest in. At the receiving end Marconi has his own refinements in place, improving on the old spark 'detector' used to show signals by pioneering physicist Heinrich Hertz. Starting with iron filings in a glass tube, Marconi now uses mercury in his 'coherer-detector'. And he has his patented transformer-tuning system to cut interference – syntony, he calls it.

The issue that's worrying him most is the antenna – everything depends on that. And Marconi has had some bad setbacks in this area. Originally he had two inverted cones of wires rigged up, 46 m (150 feet) high and 61 m (200 feet) in diameter, one at Poldhu and the other at Cape Cod, Massachusetts. Then, back in September, the Poldhu array collapsed in a gale and the same thing happened later at Cape Cod. There is now a temporary rig at Poldhu, which is less than ideal. However, at the receiving end of this all-important experiment – the one Marconi is banking on to convince a sceptical world of the real potential of wireless telegraphy – he is relying on two hydrogen balloons and half-a-dozen kites to hold the aerial wire aloft. And these cold winter winds, buffeting in off the Atlantic, blow strong in St Johns.

15:30 By now the team in Cornwall has been briefed to stop transmitting – the time is seven o'clock in the evening there. If all has gone according to plan, they must now have been transmitting at regular intervals for four hours. Still, it's not surprising if they have picked nothing up in St John's: first, the blustery weather set the kites and balloons dancing like crazy things, so Kemp and Paget had to wrestle to keep the aerial in place; then a particularly strong blast snapped a cable and blew a balloon clean away. Try again tomorrow.

12:30 **12 December.** They fix the aerial wire to a kite, abandoning the balloon, and Marconi puts aside his tuned receiver. Instead he wires his detector and an earphone between the aerial and the buried metal plates used as an earth. They listen, straining like bats. At last Marconi hears something – three clicks of a letter 'S'?. 'Do you hear anything, Mr. Kemp?,' he murmurs. Yes: a few faint sequences, fading into the background noise. Marconi's diary records 'Sigs. at 12.30, 1.10 and 2.20', and more the next day. The farthest he has sent a signal until now is 362 km (225 miles): what they are hearing now emanates from more than 3,218 km (2,000 miles) distant, or one-twelfth of the earth's circumference. Only later is it understood how signals reflect off the ionosphere. On 15 December the *New York Times* heralds 'the most wonderful scientific development in modern times'.

Above left: After Newfoundland, Marconi had a wireless station at South Wellfleet, Massachusetts, which sent a message from President Theodore Roosevelt to Edward VII.

Above right: Not just flying a kite, as Marconi's team tries to get the aerial aloft on Signal Hill, Newfoundland.

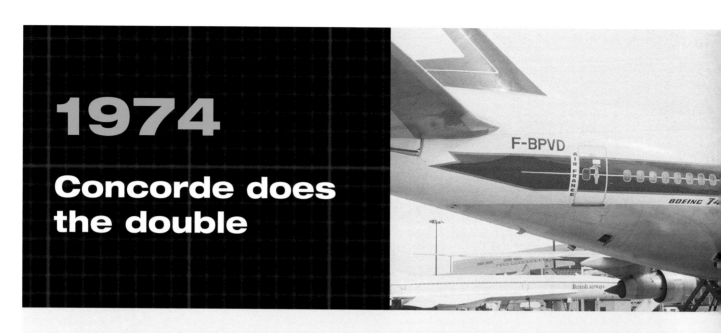

1974

Concorde does the double

F-BPVD

17 June 1974. This was a time when Concorde had to prove it was something more than an absurd white elephant and a waste of taxpayers' money. For 27 years it has successfully carried passengers at supersonic speeds. Yet the terrible sight of an Air France Concorde bursting into flames on take-off in July 2000 and crashing, killing all 109 people on board and four on the ground, was a warning that its high-flying career might be coming to an end.

06:30 As the ground crew at Boston Airport run through the preflight checks, there is no doubt anyone's mind that this aircraft is a magnificent specimen of aeronautical engineering. The hundreds of millions of pounds spent by the British and French governments since they sealed their development pact in 1962; the countless hours of design and testing by France's Aerospatiale and British Aerospace; the hold-your-breath test flights in 1969 – it all looks worthwhile in the early morning light as the engineers cast their eyes over the sleek lines of this most elegant of all flying machines. This may well be the most beautiful aeroplane ever built, as clean and simple in its basic shape as a boy's paper dart perfected by technology.

So never mind the media mockery: Concorde is special in so many ways, from its ingenious, needle-pointed dropnose to its swept-back wings. Nearly 26 m (84 feet) long, with a 61 m

(202 feet) wingspan and four Olympus 593 Mark 610 turbojet engines from Rolls-Royce-Snecma, each yielding 38,000 pounds of thrust. Concorde cruises at 18,000 m (60,000 feet), where they say you can actually see the darkness of space through the top of the cabin windows. It has a maximum speed of 2,400 km/h (1,490 mph) and a cruising speed of 2,180 km/h (1,354 mph) – more than twice as fast as any passenger jet in the air. And today, Concorde is going to show the world what it can do.

08:22 Weighing in at 79,000 kg (173,500 pounds) empty, Concorde is one of the heaviest planes ever built, but you would hardly guess as this model, sporting the livery of Air France, speeds down the runway at 402 km/h (250 mph). The engines have a different pitch, and it is a truly dazzling sight as the silvery-white machine lifts gracefully into the air, soaring skyward. Within minutes it reaches

Mach 1 and breaks the sound barrier, the boom rolling away in its slipstream unheard by the flying crew – though the prospect of it provoked some spirited opposition among Bostonians. Soon they are at Mach 2, 18 km (11 miles) above the ocean, setting a direct course for Paris.

At precisely the same moment, on the opposite side of the Atlantic, an Air France Boeing 747 – the new workhorse adopted by most commercial airlines – leaves Paris Orly Airport. It is Boston-bound, and the hope of the pilots is to get there before Concorde has time to land in France, refuel and fly straight back. But the 747 is a mere 995 km (620 miles) into its run when it passes Concorde coming the other way, clocking 3,862 km (2,400 miles) already. Concorde lands safely but has to wait while almost 20,000 gallons of aviation fuel are pumped into its tanks. It is 68 minutes before it can take off again, still heading west.

15:47 A plane touches down in Boston, cheered by hundreds of spectators, an echo of the air races from aviation's golden age. Concorde lands 11 minutes ahead of the 747, having flown twice the distance *and* stopped to refuel. The outgoing flight took three hours 10 minutes, the return flight three hours 7 minutes. After

this striking demonstration, British Airways launches passenger flights to Bahrain in 1976, and services to the USA later that year. High fuel costs and 'green' objections prompt other airlines to cancel orders, however, and production ceases in 1979 with just 16 built. Though Concorde becomes a badge of status for rich travellers, British Airways and Air France will ground their fleets at the end of October 2003 in the face of rising maintenance costs, and the planes will become museum pieces.

Above left: Boeing 747, Air France's passenger plane, was no match for Concorde's speed.

Above right: The Franco-British Supersonic Concorde touches down at Logan International Airport after making its first transatlantic round trip from Boston to Paris and back.

Less than two and a half centuries old, American democracy has had a turbulent history. From George Washington, who drove the British out of Boston in 1776, to John F Kennedy's military build-up in Vietnam before his assassination in 1963, many presidents had prominent roles on the world stage.

[1776] : [2003]

US PRESIDENTS

It is often said that the United States of America is a young nation. Having stated its claim to independence on 4 July 1776, its first president did not take office until the year of the French Revolution in 1789. Thus, as a nation, it is still less than two and a half centuries old. Whichever of these dates is used, the USA remains a newcomer when ranked alongside countries whose history and civilization can be traced back thousands of years.

Given the fact that a nation's identity is rooted in its historical past, the relative youth of the USA cannot but affect its vision of its place in the world, its unfolding relationships with other countries, and its attitudes towards the men who have occupied its highest political office.

Yet even before the trauma of 9/11 in 2001 and the attack on New York's Twin Towers, treated by many US commentators as

a 'loss of innocence', a national lifespan of more than 200 years could scarcely have been termed as infancy. Not even childhood, really. So is the USA now a teenager? A young adult? Within sight of early middle age? It is very difficult to say, especially given that the pace of change between succeeding generations has accelerated since the nineteenth century – not just in the USA, but all over the industrialized world. What might

A history of the US presidency

1789–97
Leader of the Continental army during the War of Independence, George Washington becomes the first US president. He has estates in Virginia and eventually owns more than 300 slaves.

1801–09
Inspired by French Revolutionary ideas, the wealthy Thomas Jefferson drafted the Declaration of Independence. Later he fathers three children by a slave.

1829–37
Andrew Jackson once killed a man in a duel for insulting his wife; as president he resists entrenched privilege and wants government jobs rotated on merit.

more profitably be argued is that this rich, powerful country – the one superpower left standing after the Cold War (though some now predict its decline in the face of the rising economic powers of Asia) – has manifested many of the typical strengths and weaknesses of youth during its two centuries of nationhood.

The strengths include a willingness to try out new ideas and get things done; a restless, adventurous spirit of change

A solemn moment as the Founding Fathers append their signatures to the Declaration of Independence in this painting by John Trumbull.

1861–5
Having grown up in the wilderness, Abraham Lincoln becomes an icon of US self-improvement. He leads the Union to victory in the Civil War but is later assassinated at a theatre.

1901–09
Theodore Roosevelt was a hero of the Spanish-American War. As US president he settles labour disputes, launches trust-busting suits and wins the Nobel Peace Prize.

1913–21
Woodrow Wilson is a former political science professor who persuades Congress to enter World War I, drafting a postwar blueprint for the League of Nations.

and self-reinvention, springing from adaptable pioneer genes; an idealism relatively untouched by the weariness, inertia and cynicism that can afflict older, more conservative nations. One of the historic constants of the USA's self-image has been the welcome accorded to immigrants fleeing poverty or persecution, offering a fresh start in an open society where individual freedom is cherished and defended with eagle-eyed vigilance under the safeguards of the nation's founding charters. For countless newcomers, unhappy histories in the Old World, sometimes stretching back for generations, could be forgotten when the Statue of Liberty came into view. What mattered here, after all, was the future: their future.

For the USA's supporters, this open-heartedness has repeatedly been matched by a willingness to come to the aid of other nations in trouble or to rebuild them after wars, though critics often detect some element of underlying economic and political self-interest in these acts. Openness in public life means that Americans can usually find out what their leaders and corporations have been up to, even if it takes time. Openness also implies trust. Then there is the USA's love of freedom, innovation and fun, often welcomed by other countries with open arms – from cars and comics and cola to bubblegum, burgers and theme parks; from the Broadway musical to the golden age of Hollywood. Such things were not always seen as harbingers of 'cultural imperialism'. Thus if the old association of youth and idealism still holds true, the USA should still remain closer to its youthful ideals than other nations.

Many of its weaknesses, meanwhile, might equally be seen by its detractors as typical of youth: a clumsiness in its dealings with others and a lack of subtlety or diplomacy; a readiness to charge in without thinking; and a lack of understanding of the needs of a larger world community. The country's refusal to sign up to worldwide anti-pollution targets, while producing one quarter of the world's carbon emissions, has caused widespread resentment and anxiety. A nonstop media feast appears, paradoxically, to leave many Americans hermetically sealed inside their myths. It is easy, in any case, for them to feel that the world has already pitched up on their shores.

Additionally, there is the US tendency to see life as a Darwinian struggle, in spite of the relative comfort that many of its citizens enjoy. This was reflected in, or perhaps arises from, the destruction of the Native American culture (now much lamented). In more recent times the extensive US influence at work within international institutions – the United Nations, the World Trade Organisation, the International Monetary Fund and the World Bank – has alienated many, especially in poorer countries.

The USA's sense of manifest destiny is such that rival systems have been portrayed by some politicians as not just wrong, but evil.

Coca-Cola-ization? A young man stencils a Coca-Cola logo on the side of a building in Tegucigalpa, Honduras, where US marines intervened in a 1903 revolution.

A history of the US presidency

1933–45
Franklin D Roosevelt launches the New Deal to combat unemployment. He takes on big business before leading the USA into World War II after Pearl Harbour.

1945–53
Taking office just before the end of the war, Harry S Truman immediately faces a tough decision – whether or not to drop the atom bomb on Japan to end the Pacific conflict.

1953–61
Commander of the US wartime armies in Europe and head of NATO, Dwight Eisenhower is more of a peacemaker in office. He ends the Korean War.

1961–3
Youthful and glamorous, John F Kennedy has a gilded reputation at the onset of his presidency, but is shaken by events abroad and scandal at home before his assassination in Dallas.

1961–74
Richard Nixon enjoys foreign-policy successes and a landslide re-election in the year of the Watergate break-in, which later forces his resignation.

2001–present
George W Bush, son of a previous incumbent, has a baptism of fire with the 9/11 attack on the World Trade Centre. He tries to fight terrorism by conventional military means.

Think of Ronald Reagan's stigmatization of the Soviet bloc as the 'Evil Empire' or George W Bush's 'Axis of Evil', though it might be argued that the demonization of enemies is a very old human story, and far from unique to the USA. To Islamic fundamentalists, after all, the USA has been and still is 'the Great Satan'.

Against such indications, both positive and negative, we must weigh a hard-won reserve of bitter or chastening experience. This includes a bloody civil war fought in the nineteenth century to eradicate the homegrown evils of slavery, and a courageous participation in the two world wars of the twentieth century, both begun in faraway Europe. Then there was the disaster of Vietnam, where US soldiers were

driven back by peasants using homemade pipe guns, until the USA itself inadvertently helped arm them with modern weapons through its policy of 'fortified hamlets', supposedly to protect them from the Viet Cong guerrillas.

To these sobering episodes must be added others. There was the Great Crash of 1929 and the Great Depression of the 1930s, when the US faith in capitalism was rocked to its foundations. Then there were the Prohibition years (1919–33), designed to reduce the nation's consumption of alcohol, and the accompanying rise of murderous gangsters to positions of great wealth and political influence. Then in the Nixon era (1968–74) came the trauma of finding out that its

In Vietnam, US soldiers found themselves on the wrong side of the parapet as world, and in some quarters domestic, opinion turned sharply against the war.

conflicting trends at any one time. Its diversity is often poorly perceived by the outside world – almost as often as the world's diversity seems to remain a closed book to many decent and kind-hearted Americans, who feel that 'the American Way' is the only way, confirmed by the number of foreigners wanting to live there.

Whatever point the USA is deemed to have reached in its developmental cycle, however, there is no question about its belief in the honesty and goodwill of its founding fathers, and a glance at its history reveals just how deep this belief runs.

Take the famous, probably apocryphal, story of the boyhood of George Washington (1732–99). The lively young sprig who grew up to be first president of the USA was reported by an early biographer, Mason Weems, to have tested a new hatchet by cutting down a fine cherry tree belonging to his father. When asked why this prized specimen had fallen, the young George fought back the natural temptation to deny the deed: 'Looking at his father with the sweet face of youth brightened with the inexpressible charm of all-conquering truth, he bravely cried out, "I cannot tell a lie. I did cut it with my hatchet."' It scarcely matters whether the story is true or not; what matters is the meaning it has carried for generations of Americans. It is an ideal of innocence. In the springtime of his years, the first president was possessed of an 'all-conquering truth'; and so, by extension, was America, the lusty newborn that entered the family of nations under his adult guidance.

Born in Westmoreland, Virginia County, to a prosperous family of planters of English stock, Washington was shaped to the life of the eighteenth-century landed gentry. At home he studied mathematics and the classics, land surveying and the 'rules of civility'; aged just 16, he was commissioned to carry out a survey for Lord Fairfax and, a year later, laid out the town of

'open' and democratically accountable political system was not as foolproof as had once been thought. In recent years the increase in gun crime and several shocking massacres have left some Americans questioning the US constitutional right to bear arms. And lately the internet mania and ensuing telecoms crash exposed massive corporate fraud, again shaking the USA's faith in capitalism and sending the economy into a tailspin.

Attempts made to come to terms with these shocks have sometimes verged on confessional self-flagellation. They might therefore count as signposts on the rocky road to maturity. Yet the 'young nation' analysis holds good only up to a point, since like all complex, industrialized societies, the USA has many competing and

Belhaven, Virginia. But at the age of 21, he was drawn into the colonial rivalry between England and France. Having played a major part in instigating the French and Indian War (1754–60), he rose quickly to the rank of colonel and commander of the Virginia militia, maturing from a military novice into a seasoned and capable officer after just five years of service.

On leaving the army in 1758, he entered politics in Virginia. He became steadily more hostile to British colonial policies, not least because substantial land grants that he had obtained from the British were revoked. In 1775 he was chosen as commander-in-chief of America's Continental army, training up 14,000 recruits into a disciplined fighting force. The tide of Washington's war rose and fell as he drove the British out of Boston in 1776, ensuring his place in the national pantheon, then lost New York through a strategic blunder; he won at Trenton, New Jersey, but suffered a double setback in Pennsylvania. As the conflict shifted

south in 1780, Washington remained in command, coordinating newly arrived French troops with American forces, and honed his political skills in negotiations with Congress.

He went on to engineer the Constitutional Convention in 1787; by the time he was sworn in as the USA's first president in April 1789 – the unanimous choice of the electoral college – he had proved himself a strong war leader and effective political figurehead. Washington knew that the government of the new republic would set precedents, professing a 'devout wish' that these should be 'fixed on true principles'. Though there is no cause to doubt the sincerity of his devotion in the political sphere, in the last decade his image as a man of unassailable virtue has had to be revised in the light of claims that he fathered a child with a black woman, Venus Ford.

Like all well-to-do Virginia planters, Washington was a slave owner. Having inherited ten slaves indirectly from his father, he

had acquired at least 20 more by the time he was married. By 1760 he personally owned 49 black slaves, increasing the number to 87 in 1770, 216 in 1786 and 317 by 1799. If slave ownership was typical of all large Southern estates at the time, so, at first, was Washington's treatment of his slaves. On occasion he would punish them or threaten to reduce house servants to the status of a 'common hoe Negro'. As commander of the Continental army, he purged the ranks of black soldiers, in defiance of those on the American side who argued a military gain to their cause from their presence. He was convinced that arming them would pose a long-term threat to slave ownership, especially if the British followed suit.

Later in life Washington showed signs of developing more enlightened views. In 1778 he wanted to sell his slaves and buy government securities, but felt that he could not if it meant splitting families. By 1784 Washington had agreed in principle

Above left: The famous 'Boston Tea Party', when colonists dressed as Indians dumped imported tea overboard, was a protest against British economic exploitation.

Above right: Lounging at ease in a chair, a buyer at a slave auction casts an appraising eye over the human chattels on offer.

to a land-purchase scheme to help emancipate the blacks, but the following year he resisted a petition calling for gradual emancipation. He insisted he did not wish 'to hold these unhappy people in slavery', adding that 'no man living wishes more sincerely than I do to see the abolition of it.' Yet the reality of emancipation would, he believed, 'be productive of much inconvenience and mischief'. Some say he freed his slaves in a charitable last testament, others that their liberation came on the death of his widow, Martha. As for the claims about his mixed-race descendants, such illicit relationships were then quite common, but not the sort of thing to which the leader of a new nation would admit.

Thomas Jefferson (1743–1826) was another giant of America's early years. Born in Albemarle County, Virginia, Jefferson drafted the clarion prose of the Declaration of Independence when he was still in his early thirties, distilling the ideals of the American Revolution into forthright and unforgettable words in a single night. Trained as a lawyer, Jefferson was drawn to French Revolutionary ideals after being posted as secretary to France in 1785; as secretary of state under George Washington, he led the pro-French Democratic-Republican faction in opposition to the Federalists under the pro-British treasury secretary, Alexander Hamilton (1757–1804). Jefferson upheld self-determination for individual states against the centralizing thrust of federalism. He drafted a bill for religious freedom, enacted in 1786; after resigning from office in 1793, he went on to become the USA's third president, serving from 1801–1809.

A staunch advocate of liberty, Jefferson wrote in a private letter the year before taking office, 'I have sworn upon the altar of God eternal hostility against every form of tyranny over the mind of man.' During his two terms he cut military spending, slashed budgets, eliminated the tax on whisky and also slimmed down the national debt. Later, he was successful in keeping the USA out of the Napoleonic wars, though less so in preventing British and French interference with US merchant shipping.

Like Washington, Jefferson was a Southerner born to wealth and privilege, inheriting a high social status on his mother's side and some 616 hectares (5,000 acres) from his planter father's estates. He built a magnificent hilltop palace, Monticello, revealing how strong was the influence of European civilization on his tastes and ideals; down the hill he had slaves working in a nail factory. He, too, had a lasting relationship with a slave, Sally Hemings, producing three children. This awkward fact, proven beyond doubt by DNA testing during recent years, produced a cold *frisson* in US minds, representing a lethal short-circuit between the noble early ideals of liberty and the reality of exploitation.

For some Americans the interracial peccadilloes of the founding fathers reflect gross inequalities of power, raising thorny retrospective issues of race and gender and thereby hinting at moral cracks running through the whole edifice of US democracy. White America has always found the notion of interracial desire difficult and dangerous; even today it can be a no-go area for Hollywood producers who normally stop at nothing in their urge for a quick buck. Another school interprets such early racial crossovers in the broader perspective of relationship and family, some even finding a compensating image of black belonging. Either way, the sexual misuse of slaves shows that these men were not gods. American myths are still close enough in time to be caught in the unforgiving searchlight of modern historical research.

As the presidency evolved from the founding ideals into a functional institution, different kinds of president began to emerge. There was a line of so-called 'log-cabin' presidents, from far humbler backgrounds than Washington or Jefferson. The fifth US president, James Monroe (1738–1831), praised as 'so honest that if you turned his soul inside out, you would not

The Declaration of Independence enshrined the rights of citizens to 'life, liberty and the pursuit of happiness' – but such freedoms were denied to blacks for another century.

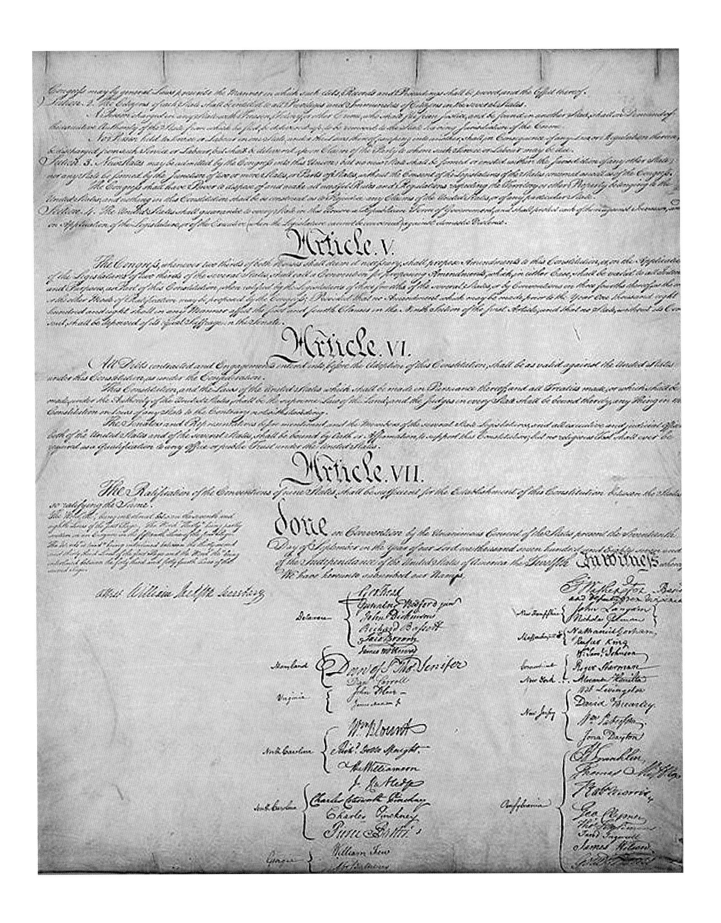

find a spot on it', articulated the so-called Monroe Doctrine that many regard as the historic basis for American isolationism. It took the form of a warning to European powers not to meddle in the affairs of the continent by helping Spain recover former colonial possessions. It was also, unwittingly or not, an early draft for the enduring conception of an American sphere of influence abroad – of 'our hemisphere'.

After Monroe came Andrew Jackson (1767–1845), the seventh US president, a Carolina-born backwoodsman who trained as a lawyer and made enough to build a mansion with attendant slaves near Nashville, Tennessee. Jackson was jealous of his honour and had once killed a man who insulted his wife. Yet he was the closest yet to election by popular acclaim, and the first to hold it a presidential duty to act as the direct representative of the people. Jackson sought abolition of those fledgling institutions that he judged undemocratic, such as the electoral college, and resisted the encroachments of patronage. He believed government jobs should be rotated on merit alone. During his tenure party politics polarized and began to assume something like their present shape as the Democratic Republicans – the Democrats – gave him their support, while the National Republicans made common cause against his hands-on leadership style.

His protégé and successor, Martin Van Buren (1782–1862), was of modest Dutch origins – in Jackson's eyes 'a true man with no guile'. Unfortunately, Van Buren's attempts to finish off his predecessor's battle with the Second Bank of the United States, a private corporation enjoying a *de facto* government monopoly, backfired badly. A wave of land speculation in the West was unleashed by state banks following Second Bank's demise, bringing on a financial panic in 1837 and precipitating the first severe economic slump since independence. The depression dragged on for five years, with hundreds of banks and businesses going bust and thousands forfeiting their property.

Abraham Lincoln (1809–65), the sixteenth president, has been widely feted by historians as the incorruptible Yankee who brought Southern slavery to an end, but the truth is slightly more complex. Lincoln was the self-made son of a Kentucky frontiersman, in other words, a Southerner, who spent part of his boyhood in the rough wilderness of Indiana, where the woods were still believed to be haunted by wolves and bears. He split fence rails on a farm and kept a store in Illinois until he mastered the law,

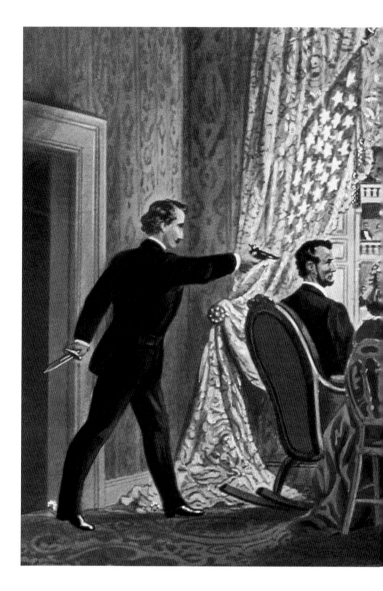

thereafter joining the state legislature and working for eight years in circuit courts. His earnest and arduous struggle for self-improvement has ever since enshrined a key American value: the common man who pulls himself up by sheer guts and grit.

Despite losing a Senate election in 1858, Lincoln made such a strong impression as a campaigner that he was chosen as the Republican candidate for the presidency in 1860. His battle with the South was joined, initially, on a legal condemnation of southern secession plans, rather than on the immorality of slavery. And though responsible for the Emancipation Proclamation of 1863, Lincoln was also enough of a realist to restrict its application to the 11 rebel states, whereas the four slavery states that had thrown in their hand with the Union were, for the time being, exempt. Yet there

can be no doubt of Lincoln's greatness of spirit. His dedication of the military cemetery at Gettysburg, the scene of one of the climactic battles of the Civil War, captures this spirit: 'We here highly resolve that these dead shall not have died in vain – that this nation, under God, shall have a new birth of freedom – and that government of the people, by the people, for the people, shall not perish from the earth.' Words and deeds are all too often ill-matched in politics; here, for once, they were not.

Not long after, in 1865, Lincoln was shot dead by an actor, John Wilkes Booth, who had somehow got it into his head that the president was assisting the South. And so there entered into US politics another factor that, although by no means unique to the USA, has become closely identified with

it: a woeful tradition of presidential and political assassinations. So far the USA has lost a total of four presidents out of 43 to the assassin's bullet – a casualty rate of just under ten per cent. This probably compares quite well with the bloody chronicles of intrigue and murder that distinguish some of the old ruling dynasties of Europe, but Lincoln's shooting certainly left an ugly stain on the unfolding history of American politics that was to be repeated in later years.

The next presidential murder victim was another self-made man, James Garfield (1831–81), who, like Lincoln, combined strong principles with hardheaded political acuity. Having made a strong start as a Republican leader, Garfield was shot down by an attorney with thwarted political ambitions. Some mention is also due to his predecessor, Grover Cleveland (1837–1908), the only US president to have served two terms with a four-year gap in between. The son of a Presbyterian minister based in New Jersey, Cleveland had plain tastes and set his face against special treatment for any economic group. He forced the railroad companies to surrender more than 9.8 million hectares (80 million acres) of land held under federal grant; conversely, he refused federal aid to farmers on the grounds that it would weaken national character and sent in troops against strikers.

James Garfield was succeeded by Theodore Roosevelt (1858–1919), a New Yorker who was at the time the youngest president to have taken office. Though his background was rich and metropolitan, Roosevelt's vision of the presidency was inclusive. He emerged as a hero of the Spanish-American War, graduating from his role as Republican state governor of New York to the presidency in 1901. Roosevelt saw the president as a 'steward of the people'. He arbitrated labour disputes, launched trust-busting suits to break monopolies, and enlarged the national

stock of public land to include some mighty forests in the West. He pushed through the Panama Canal project, sought a wider international role for the USA, and won the Nobel Peace Prize for his intercession in the Russo-Japanese war.

During World War I the occupant of the White House was Woodrow Wilson (1856–1924), twenty-eighth in America's line of presidential succession. Wilson was a reforming Democrat who cast himself in Roosevelt's mould. Virginia-born, this son of a Presbyterian minister made his name first as a professor of political science, then went on to win the presidency in 1913. Much preoccupied later with the USA's international role and the construction of a new world order, Wilson followed Roosevelt's lead at home by taking action against unfair business practices, placing limits on working hours and outlawing child labour. Voted in for a second term on the strength of having kept the USA out of the worldwide conflict, by 1917 he felt impelled to 'make the world safe for democracy' – a phrase much mocked by the USA's detractors later, but wholly sincere at the time of its utterance – and sought the blessing of Congress to join the Allied war effort. In 1918 Wilson proposed a League of Nations as the culminating idea in his 14 Points, a postwar blueprint drawn up, in part, to counter communism. But Wilson's hopes that the

candidate in 1928, Hoover enjoyed a brief honeymoon until the Crash of 1929; his answer was to cut taxes and commission public works, leaving relief largely to voluntary, local efforts that had a limited impact on the misery of the Depression.

Franklin D Roosevelt (1882–1945) was a distant cousin of Theodore. After contracting polio in his late thirties, he took up the Democratic struggle against the Depression on his election to the first of four terms in 1932. With unemployment at 13 million, Roosevelt launched the 'New Deal', a national recovery programme geared to farmers, small businessmen and the industrial jobless, and took the US dollar off the gold standard. His measures aroused hostility from big business, which sought to limit their impact through the Supreme Court; Roosevelt responded to this by extending the constitutional scope of government control over the economy, introducing higher taxes for the rich along with new welfare and social-security programmes. He countered US isolationism by fostering new alliances; when the Japanese attack at Pearl Harbour confounded his efforts to keep the USA out of World War II, he committed the country unstintingly to the struggle against fascism and backed the development of the atomic bomb.

When Roosevelt died suddenly of a cerebral haemorrhage, it fell to Harry S Truman (1884–1972) to make the momentous and controversial decision on whether to use the atomic bomb. Hiroshima and Nagasaki paid the terrible price. At home Truman pursued full employment and industrial peace, enhancing social-security programmes and backing slum clearances; abroad he presided over the Berlin Airlift, flying food to the beleaguered Germans during Russia's 1948 blockade of Berlin's western sector, and instigated the Marshall Plan to rebuild postwar Europe's shattered industrial infrastructure. Under the leadership of Truman,

Treaty of Versailles would adopt his design in its totality were dashed as the European nations settled down to squabble over territory and German war reparations.

The Great Crash was the great challenge of Herbert Hoover (1874–1964), the thirtieth US president. An engineer and son of a Quaker blacksmith, he distinguished himself through rescue work in the Chinese Boxer Uprising of 1900 and the evacuation of more than 100,000 Americans from Europe at the outbreak of World War I. His coordination of wartime food programmes for the Allies and postwar shipments to central Europe and Soviet Russia cemented his reputation. Adopted as a Republican

US troop ships disembark men and equipment for the invasion of Inchon, South Korea, September 1950.

the USA sharply upped the stakes in the ideological war against communism; in 1950 it entered the Korean War after the communist North attacked the South. By the time the conflict ended three years later, two million people were dead.

Truman's successor was Dwight Eisenhower (1890–1969). Campaigning in 1952 under the 'I Like Ike' campaign banner, he was riding high on his wartime record as commander of the US liberation armies in Europe and his elevation to supreme commander of NATO when he swept into office. A Texas-born Republican, Eisenhower sought to contain the risks of a Cold War turning hot – in the new world of nuclear terror, conflict with Russia could mean Armageddon. He negotiated a Korean truce in 1953, just a few months after the death of Stalin; within weeks Russia announced it had broken the US monopoly on thermonuclear weapons by making its own hydrogen bomb. In Geneva two years later, at the first East-West conference since the war, 'Ike' urged exchanges of plans and aerial photographs to promote security; he also backed the 'atoms for peace' scheme, loaning uranium to other countries for civil use, and at home he made a start on the hard task of desegregation.

After Eisenhower came John F Kennedy (1917–63), the thirty-fifth president, sworn in on a cold January day in 1961. JFK, as he was snappily known to his fellow citizens, arrived at the White House in a swirl of glamour and expectation. He was a vigorous, handsome Democrat who, at 43, had become the youngest president in US history. Wealthy in his own right thanks to the Prohibition fortune accumulated by his unscrupulous senator father, the new incumbent was married to an heiress of aristocratic composure. The USA wove a fairytale around them as Jacqueline set about remodelling the

White House into 'Camelot', a place fit for kings and queens. Yet the words of Allan Jay Lerner's lyric, from the hit musical of that name, were prophetic: this was indeed 'one brief shining moment', and its brightness began to fade well before Kennedy's assassination barely a thousand days into his administration. How did it all go so wrong?

In 1961 Kennedy was eager to push various liberal reforms, including civil rights and desegregation, while US benevolence

would extend overseas through the newly formed Peace Corps. Then trouble erupted on a Caribbean island fewer than 320 km (200 miles) south of Miami, Florida. Cuba was a former Spanish colony where, until the 1959 coup led by Fidel Castro (b.1927), the US Mafia had had a free hand to run offshore casinos and prostitution rackets. Three months into his presidency, Kennedy was embroiled in the Bay of Pigs fiasco, a failed invasion by Cuban exiles trained with CIA connivance. Sharp exchanges followed with the Russian premier, Nikita Khrushchev, but far worse came 18 months later, when Khrushchev sent nuclear missiles to Cuba in response to US blockade and threats of invasion, bringing the world to the brink of nuclear war.

In 1962 Kennedy signalled US resistance to 'communist aggression' by starting the military build-up in Laos and South Vietnam that led to a bloody, chaotic war soon after his demise.

1963

JFK shot dead in Dallas

22 November 1963. President John F Kennedy is touring Texas with vice-president Lyndon B Johnson and state governor John Connally. Kennedy spent the night in Fort Worth; next stop, Dallas. Friends have warned him that the place is a right-wing hothouse, what with the John Birch Society and the Dixiecrats, as well as staunchly Republican – but JFK has made up his mind.

11:37 The presidential party lands in Air Force One at Love Field Airport, 11 km (7 miles) northwest of Dallas's downtown business centre. A last-minute route revision for the motorcade: when they reach Dealey Plaza, instead of heading straight on down Main Street towards the Stemmons Freeway, they will turn right into Houston Street and swing left again into Elm Street. This will take them past the Texas School Book Depository, a tall, oldish brick warehouse on the far right-hand corner, and within sight of the 'Grassy Knoll' farther ahead on the right. Then they are on their way, the president seated in the back of an open-topped limousine with Jackie Kennedy to his left.

12:29 Kennedy waves and smiles at the crowds as the limousine rounds the corner into Elm Street and passes the depository. Suddenly, at 30 seconds past the half-hour,

there is a sharp crack and Kennedy's hands jerk to his throat – he's been hit in the neck. As Connally turns, he is struck in the back, suffering further injuries to his chest, wrist and thigh. Another shot hits the president in the head, blowing away part of the back of his skull and spattering the motorcycle escorts behind with blood and brains. Jackie screams, kneeling half-upright as she leans across in a desperate effort to stem her husband's bleeding; in the same instant security man Clint Hill hurls himself on to the car in a vain reflex to shield the president.

12:32 Responding to a police message, patrolman Marrion Baker draws his gun and races up the stairs of the book depository with building supervisor Roy Truly. In the second-floor lunch room, they spot a slight, dark-haired man later identified as Lee Harvey Oswald, chairman of a pro-Castro group called Fair Play for Cuba. He seems calm, though it is

only 90 seconds since the fatal shot was fired, while a later search of the sixth floor uncovers a half-eaten chicken dinner, a brown paper sack, three shell casings and a 6.5 mm Mannlicher-Carcano rifle. Baker and Truly thunder on up as Oswald buys a cola and saunters out via the Elm Street exit. The presidential car is tearing along Stemmons Freeway to Parkland Memorial Hospital 6.4 km (4 miles) away.

13:00 At Parkland, President Kennedy is pronounced dead; an official statement follows half an hour later. Oswald, who took a bus along Elm Street and then a cab to his rooming house, arrives back at the very time Kennedy is declared dead. He leaves again four minutes later. Within 15 minutes police officer J D Tippit is shot dead almost a mile away. Then, at 1.40 p.m., six blocks from the scene of this second shooting, Oswald is seen entering the Texas Theatre by a suspicious shoe-store manager, who calls the police. Ten minutes later he is under arrest.

19:00 Oswald is charged with Tippit's murder and paraded for the press. Two days later he is shot down by small-time hoodlum Jack

Ruby during a jail move. Before his death Oswald said cryptically, 'I'm just the patsy'. Yet he remains the focal point for the Warren Commission's 'lone nut' theory, which determines that he acted alone and fired three shots, missing with the second. Hence the bizarre ballistic trajectory imputed to the 'magic bullet', which would have to have passed through two people and inflicted seven wounds. Conspiracy theories sprout like boils from all parts of the evidence – ballistic, forensic, audiovisual – and many conclude there had to be more than one gunman, usually placing a second shooter in front of Kennedy on the Grassy Knoll. The Mafia and the CIA are both suspected, but nothing is proved, nor has been since.

Above left: President John F Kennedy, First Lady Jacqueline Kennedy, and Texas Governor John Connally ride in a motorcade in Dallas, Texas, 22 November 1963.

Above right: Prime suspect Lee Harvey Oswald is paraded for the press.

This was the year when Marilyn Monroe, the iconic blonde who once trilled 'Happy Birthday, Mr President' and had, it was suggested, shared his bed, was found dead of an overdose. The US space effort was crowned with success as John Glenn orbited the earth three times. On a cheer-leading visit to Germany in 1963, Kennedy included the whole 'free world' in his famous 'Ich bin ein Berliner' remark; later, he saw his hopes for civil rights hit a high note in Martin Luther King's 'I have a dream' address in Washington. Within a few months,

however, Kennedy was dead – shot when in an open-topped limousine in Dallas by Lee Harvey Oswald, an ex-marine, Soviet defector and Cuba activist, who was then, shortly afterwards, assassinated in his turn. Conspiracy theories have proliferated ever since.

Kennedy's untimely death left his lugubrious Texan vice-president, Lyndon B Johnson (1908–73), in charge. Re-elected a year later, Johnson faced race riots and student unrest at home as bodybags were being airlifted back from Vietnam in

Not quite Mount Rushmore: four ex-presidents – Ronald Reagan, Jimmy Carter, Gerald Ford and Richard Nixon – line up beside the then incumbent George Bush for the dedication of a presidential library.

of Watergate and its scandalous aftermath brought threats of impeachment as the *Washington Post* pieced the details together in an investigative *tour de force*. Nixon's political stock seemed irretrievably damaged, but after resigning in 1974 he rehabilitated himself as an elder statesman; some US commentators then began to revise his reputation upwards as Kennedy's sank lower.

Since then the roll records dull-but-decent Gerald Ford (b.1913); Jimmy Carter (b.1924), an earnest Democratic peacemaker; the right-wing Republican populist and ex-film actor Ronald Reagan (b.1911), who deregulated business and pursued visions of the Star Wars defence initiative; and two members of a Texan dynasty, George Bush (b.1924) and his son George W Bush (b.1946), Republicans both, whose family made its money in oil. Both went to war in the Middle East, in the latter's case apparently not for oil but because of alleged 'weapons of mass destruction' in Iraq, still undiscovered at the time of writing.

Between the Bushes came Bill Clinton (b.1946), one of the sharpest presidential thinkers, if not always the frankest. It was Clinton, perhaps, who best summed up the paradoxes of his country back in 1997: 'We were born with a declaration of independence which asserted that we were all created equal and a constitution that enshrined slavery. We fought a bloody civil war to abolish slavery but we remained unequal in law for another century. We advanced across the continent in the name of freedom, yet in doing so we pushed the Native Americans off their land. We welcome immigrants but each new wave felt the sting of discrimination.'

growing numbers. With US strategy in Southeast Asia unravelling, achievements in space and progress on civil rights were pushed into the shade. It then fell to Johnson's Republican successor, Richard Nixon (1913–94), elected in 1969, to sort out the mess in Vietnam and to calm the domestic ferment. Nixon was a gifted politician, but also secretive and obsessive, his saturnine looks conferring none of the glib Kennedy charm, and his reputation was badly besmirched by the Watergate break-in. The botched cover-up

1974

'Tricky Dick' Nixon resigns

8 August 1974. Richard Nixon, facing impeachment since a Supreme Court ruling on 27 July overruled his attempt to withhold tapes from the Watergate trial on the pretext of 'executive privilege', has spent more than a week crawling over the chain of events that has led him to this hopeless predicament. The Watergate break-in, it seems, has done for him at last.

Morning Nixon shaves in the bathroom mirror. Today of all days he needs to cut it fine. Even when he was younger, his stubble played badly on television – not so much five o'clock shadow as the try-it-again-at-midday variety. That, and his tendency to sweat under the studio lights. Today his brooding face, baggy and shadowed with fatigue, cannot banish from his slightly puffy eyes the leaden stare of abject, self-inflicted defeat. Today he has to do what no serving president has ever done – resign. Quit. And one thing Richard Nixon never has been, in his entire life, is a quitter.

If a week is a long time in politics, as a seasoned British politician once observed, two years must be close to an eternity. No question about it – 1972 looked set to be a crowning year for a man of his ambition, tenacity and hard work. Check the record: it is almost exactly two years since he pulled the last US ground troops out of Vietnam, which had scarred the presidency of his predecessor and turned the USA upside down. In February that year he had been to China to meet Prime Minister Chou and Chairman Mao, urging them to join the USA on 'a long march together' towards world peace. In May he met with Brezhnev. Then, in October, he signed a strategic arms limitation treaty with the Russians. And in November, to cap it all, he was re-elected in a landslide victory, blowing his Democratic rival George McGovern clean out of the water.

But 1972 was also the year when five guys were caught breaking into the Democratic National Committee's offices in Washington to plant bugs: Watergate. Jim McCord – ex-CIA, Republican security coordinator for the Committee to Re-elect Nixon – was one of them. Hunt and Liddy were there, too. In 1973 John Mitchell quit as Republican campaign manager; John Dean, White House counsel, then started playing a dangerous game of ball with the investigators.

At the end of April, Dean was fired and Ehrlichman and Haldeman quit. In August 1973 Butterfield blew the gaff about the tape machines that were hidden in his office; in August 1974 the president was forced to release tapes revealing how he aborted the FBI inquiry six days after the break-in. And all the while those *Washington Post* bloodhounds, Woodward and Bernstein, were all over him like a pack of dogs scenting blood – presidential blood. His blood. Why didn't he just trust his record to win the damned election for him?

Evening Nixon delivers his televised resignation speech. He says: 'From the discussions I have had with Congressional and other leaders, I have concluded that because of the Watergate matter I might not have the support of the Congress that I would consider necessary to back the very difficult decisions and carry out the duties of this office in the way the interests of the Nation would require. I have never been a quitter. To leave office before my term is completed is abhorrent to every instinct in my body. But as President, I must put the interest of America first.' He quits the next day.

A month later his former vice-president, Gerald Ford, who takes office directly after his resignation, pardons Nixon 'for all offenses against the United States which he … has committed or may have committed or taken part in during the period from January 20, 1969, through August 9, 1974.' Nixon has been in politics since 1947. Always tried to play a long game; always had an eye to the future. But now – game over, it seems.

Above left: Still hoping to convince – Nixon speaks of Watergate on television in 1973, in an effort to restore public trust.

Above right: Millions of Americans had their faith in the presidency badly dented by Watergate, but the scepticism did not last.

The concept of the atom goes back to the ancient Greeks, but it was not until the nineteenth century that scientists began to unpick its strange secrets. They unwittingly unleashed a terrible new power, which would lead to human disasters from the Hiroshima bomb to the Chernobyl meltdown.

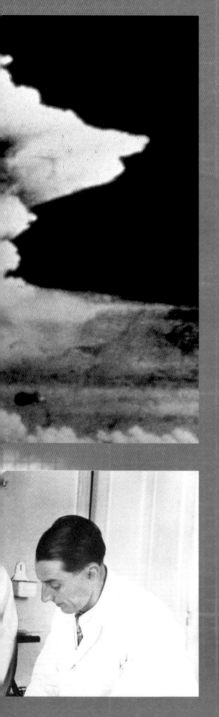

[1803] : [1999]

ATOMIC POWER

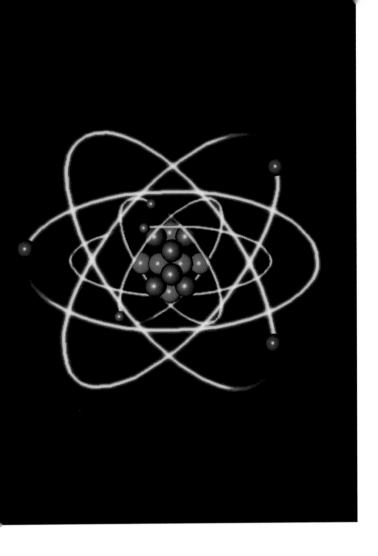

There is something that is pleasantly old-fashioned about our picture of the atom, especially now that theoretical physics has moved on to dizzying concepts such as superstrings and ten- or even 11-dimensional universes, sliding over one another like vast, interacting ripples across an infinite ocean of space.

The magnified structure of an atom, that orderly orbit of electrons whizzing round a larger nucleus, is somehow reassuring in that it seems to reflect the structure of our solar system – an echo at a physical level of the old alchemists' belief in a spiritual law of 'as above, so below'. The finely balanced forces of attraction, repulsion and neutrality that hold it all together bring us back to gravity – or back to earth with a bump,

if you like – with electrons weaving an illusion of solidity round the empty space enclosed within their orbital shells. To the layman atomic structure evokes the idea of a bunch of cheerfully rotating billiard balls, behaving in the sensible, predictable, scientific ways that Sir Isaac Newton (1642–1727) himself might have recognized with a bit of fresh theoretical input and a little extra cogitation.

The history of the atom

1803
Meteorologist John Dalton notes that compounds of elements combine in fixed weight ratios and deduces that atoms of one element have the same mass.

1895
Wilhelm Röntgen discovers a new type of emanation in experiments with cathodes: X-Rays. A year later, Henri Becquerel identifies radioactivity in uranium ore by darkening a sealed photographic plate.

1897
J J Thompson is involved in related breakthroughs, deducing the existence of a light electron and measuring the electron charge-to-mass ratio by deflecting cathode rays.

To recall how astonishing this subatomic universe must first have appeared, we need to cast our minds back at least three-quarters of a century to the days of the pioneers, those who groped their way into the hidden recesses of invisible particles that defied Newtonian logic. And to some, how mysteriously beautiful. After the false starts and the blind alleys, the patient grind of laboratory experiment and the intuitive flashes of the

Above left: Atomic structure is not so like the solar system as it appears to be.

Above right: Albert Einstein (standing, second right) and Marie Curie (seated, second right) amongst a group of scientists at a conference in Brussels, *c.*1911.

1898
Pierre and Marie Curie separate radioactive elements radium and polonium. Ernest Rutherford discovers alpha and beta radiation and four years later publishes a theory of radioactive decay with Frederick Soddy.

1905
Albert Einstein publishes his special theory of relativity, an equation showing that energy equals mass multiplied by the speed of light, squared. Two years on Rutherford deduces the existence of an atomic nucleus.

1919
Rutherford is reported to have 'split the atom', six years after Niels Bohr introduced the 'quantum theory' of electronic orbits and inferred that radioactive emission comes from the atomic nucleus.

theoreticians, these seekers understood that what had always been presumed 'solid', and by implication inert, was in fact almost unimaginably dynamic. They entered a secret matrix of powerful, compressed energies that utterly confounded attempts to measure or define the world in material terms. Indeed, the 'building blocks of matter' were not blocks at all, as matter turned out to be capable of spontaneously transmuting itself from one state to another like electrified jelly.

You only have to rejig the famous equation of Albert Einstein (1879–1955) – $E=mc^2$ – to get some idea of just how great the implied energy of the atom is. This formula, first published in 1905, can be rewritten as $m=\dfrac{E}{c^2}$. To arrive at a mathematical statement about the relationship between matter (m) and energy, we divide the energy (E) by the speed of light (c) – 280,000 km (176,000 miles) per second – multiplied by the speed of light again. Put another way, 1 kg of matter yields 90,000 trillion joules of energy, and it takes just under 100 joules to lift a 10 kg suitcase off the ground. This means that 1 kg of matter has enough latent energy to raise the same suitcase 900 trillion times, or to raise a single suitcase weighing 900 trillion times as much – the Creator's personal luggage, perhaps? Or it could raise itself 9,000 trillion times. The disparity between 'matter' and 'energy' is therefore truly jawdropping.

Even at the time when they were pursuing their scientific work, chasing dreams of discovery, a Nobel Prize and worldwide fame, the pioneers saw that matter was an awesome storehouse of energy. As one of them observed in a 1936 lecture: 'There is no doubt that subatomic energy is available all around us, and that one day man will release and control its almost infinite power.

We cannot prevent him from doing so and can only hope that he will not use it exclusively in blowing up his next-door neighbour'. Many of them saw the power as offering huge benefits to humankind, transforming human life and industry at a profound level.

Within less than a decade of these hopeful but ironic words, on 6 August 1945, the USA dropped the first atom bomb on Hiroshima. It was nicknamed 'Little Boy' – a gross misnomer, as it actually weighed nearly four tons – and detonated with an explosive force equivalent to 12,500 tons of TNT about half a kilometre (one third of a mile) off the ground, right above a hospital courtyard. The blast flattened the city like a monstrous hammer, leaving only a few ghostly concrete shells standing, and also sparked a massive firestorm. Eyewitness accounts from survivors tell a tale of horror and pity unique in the annals of human suffering. By the end of 1945, the death toll had reached 140,000, rising to 200,000 after five years thanks to the long-term effects of radiation. The atom's energy, released from its bonds, had proved to have undreamed-of destructive potential.

Albert Einstein in 1931. When reflecting on the atomic bomb in later life, he wished that he had been a watch-maker.

The history of the atom

1932
James Chadwick discovers a second component of the atomic nucleus – the neutron – and Werner Heisenberg infers that the nucleus consists of neutrons and protons bound together.

1939
Albert Einstein, with Hungarian emigrés Leo Szilard and Edward Teller, writes to President Roosevelt to alert him to the feasibility of an atomic bomb. Rudolf Peierls and Otto Frisch sketch the 'critical mass' principle.

1940
Nazi Germany tries to buy heavy water – one possible ingredient of an atom bomb – from Norsk Hydro in Norway; later, the Wehrmacht invades Norway and captures the plant, but their plans are confounded.

The top-secret Manhattan Project, run by Robert Oppenheimer and General Leslie Groves, is set up to design atom bombs. A year later Enrico Fermi creates the first self-sustaining fission reaction.

1945
After the Trinity test in New Mexico detonates in a flash equivalent to more than 18,500 tons of TNT, two different designs of bomb are dropped on Hiroshima and Nagasaki, killing some 150,000 outright.

1953
Russia tests its first thermonuclear weapon – the hydrogen bomb – one year after the USA explodes a prototype at Eniwetok. Britain, France and China follow suit; later India, Pakistan and Israel claim the capability.

It had all started from that most basic and definitively human of motives: curiosity. The way the pioneers proceeded was the way Western science has often proceeded – bash things together, break them apart; analyse the ensuing phenomena to figure out how the original object was constructed. Of course, it was fiendishly difficult, too, simply because atoms are so small. This early 'atom-bashing' led eventually to controlled fission – splitting – and this became the basis for designing bombs. Yet before that could happen, a special kind of fusion was required. Not of the atom itself, nor indeed of its subatomic particles – rather, it was the dedicated efforts of groups of talented physicists, scattered across Britain, Germany, France, Denmark, Italy, the USA and Japan, which had to be combined. Some of the key figures in the US programme were Hungarian or German Jews who had fled the Nazi onslaught in the early 1930s; they used different but complementary approaches that had to merge into one before the nuclear puzzle could be solved.

The original concept of the atom goes back to the ancient Greeks. Leucippus and Democritus in the fifth century BC, and Epicurus in the fourth, suggested that the world was composed of particles so minute as to be incapable of further division. This was a philosophical rather than scientific statement, asserting that atoms existed simply because, logically, they must. Such notions were opposed by Aristotle (384–322 BC) and, later, by the Church, though there remained a strong undercurrent in Renaissance thinking that inclined towards Greek atomism. One supporter was the Dominican friar Giordano Bruno (1548–1600), who in 1588 declared: 'The division of natural things has a limit; an indivisible something exists. The division of natural things attains the smallest and last parts which are not perceptible by the aid of human instruments.' The unfortunate Bruno was later burned as a heretic after espousing the theories of Nicolaus Copernicus (1473–1543), though Pierre Gassendi (1592–1655) fared better in the next century, disseminating atomistic theory more widely and absolving it from the lingering taint of atheism.

Related ideas were developed in the seventeenth century by Robert Boyle (1627–91), the wealthy, Irish-born alchemist and natural philosopher whose name is remembered in Boyle's Law – the principle that the volume of a gas varies in inverse proportion to the pressure on it. Boyle developed another

theory that he dubbed 'Corpuscular Philosophy'. Though there is no substantive difference between Boyle's 'corpuscles' and the older Greek concept of atoms, Boyle insisted that he had not been influenced by the Greeks. Either way, his theory sought to account for natural phenomena through the position and movement of the corpuscles; it influenced both John Locke (1632–1704) and Sir Isaac Newton, and Boyle helped found the Royal Society in 1660.

It was not until the early nineteenth century, however, that John Dalton (1766–1844), a meteorologist and the discoverer of colour-blindness, came up with an atomic theory closer to modern conceptions. In 1803 Dalton noted that oxygen and

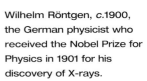

Wilhelm Röntgen, *c.*1900, the German physicist who received the Nobel Prize for Physics in 1901 for his discovery of X-rays.

during experiments with cathodes. This was christened the X-ray, a find that brought him a Nobel Prize in 1901. A year later, in 1896, the French scientist Henri Becquerel (1852–1908) discovered radioactivity on observing that uranium could darken a photographic plate sealed in black paper, though at first he thought the process was activated by the sun. The next year brought another breakthrough, this time by J J Thompson (1856–1940) of the Cavendish laboratory in Cambridge. He discovered the electron, also while experimenting with cathodes, and described it in terms of Boyle's coinage as a 'negative corpuscle'. Two years later Ernest Rutherford (1871–1937), the bluff, kindly New Zealander who was to become the father of British experimental nuclear physics, identified two distinct types of radiation emanating from radium. One consisted of positively charged particles, which he dubbed alpha particles; the second emission, more penetrating and less easy to explain, became known as the beta-ray.

At the turn of the century, Britain's Frederick Soddy (1877–1965) noted the process of the spontaneous breakdown of radioactive materials into variant forms, which he christened isotopes; two years later, in 1902, he and Rutherford published a joint paper setting out their theory of radioactive decay. Nobel Prizes followed in 1903 and 1904 – first a Physics prize, jointly awarded to Becquerel and to Pierre Curie (1859–1906) and Marie Curie (1867–1934) for the discovery of radioactivity; then a Chemistry prize to Rutherford for his finding that alpha radiation carried a strong positive charge. Then, in 1905, Albert Einstein published his special theory of relativity. This groundbreaking new equation revolutionized scientific thought and ultimately transformed the very way that human beings view the nature of material reality.

carbon combined into two types of compound, one of which had exactly twice the ratio of oxygen to carbon by weight as the other. Observing that various elements would combine in fixed weight ratios, or exact multiples thereof, Dalton concluded that all atoms of a given element must be identical because they had the same mass, while elements differed from one another because their atomic masses were different. Compounds consisted of atoms of diverse elements bonded in fixed ratios, while chemical reactions involved an orderly rearrangement of such combinations.

Towards the end of the nineteenth century, Wilhelm Röntgen (1845–1923) in Germany discovered a new and strange emanation

Above: Ernest Rutherford, the father of experimental nuclear physics, in 1932, flanked by Cambridge colleagues.

Above right: Computing fission – this early sequence calculator used more than 12 million steps to give a step-by-step picture of how an atom 'splits' in the same way as a drop of water.

Two years later, however, Rutherford developed a new experiment in Manchester that went straight to the heart of the matter. Working with Hans Geiger (1882–1945), inventor of the Geiger Counter, and an 18-year-old undergraduate called Ernest Marsden (1888–1970), he fired alpha particles at a corner-shaped array shielded with gold foil. Rutherford deduced from the resultant scattering of particles that the 'greatest part of the atom' must be concentrated in a minute nucleus. Later on, he said, 'It was quite the most incredible event that has ever happened to me in my life ... almost as incredible as if you fired a 15-inch shell at a piece of tissue paper and it came back and hit you.'

Even after this remarkable discovery, there was a long way to go to understand the inner mysteries of atomic structure. Another key contributor to the joint effort was the brilliant, intuitive Danish scientist Niels Bohr (1885–1962), a theoretical physicist who ushered in the new field of quantum theory, leading on to quantum mechanics. He developed an early insight that the

radioactive properties of elements originated in the nucleus, while their chemical characteristics depended on the electrons. In 1913 he argued that electrons were held in 'stationary states' – stable orbits that prevented them from spiralling in towards the much larger nucleus or spinning off elsewhere. Later still, he found that when atoms are heated, taking in more energy, the orbiting electrons would 'jump' to new stationary states in discontinuous leaps, finding new paths of circulation round the nucleus, farther out from the centre, before jumping back into place on cooling. Bohr won his Nobel Prize in 1922, one year after Einstein.

In 1919 it was Rutherford who made headlines as excited journalists broke the news that the New Zealander had 'split the atom'. Strictly speaking, what he had done was to bombard nitrogen atoms with alpha particles, thus dislodging a hydrogen nucleus (or proton) and leaving behind a new atom – an isotope of oxygen. What this meant to science was a whole new technique for getting inside the atom, instead of simply bouncing radiation off it or calibrating what emerged naturally through radioactive

decay. However, Rutherford's one great blind spot was his adamant refusal to concede that the atomic nucleus could ever be a source of usable energy. It was to be almost 20 years before another, quite different, experiment achieved what became known to the worldwide nuclear physics community as 'binary fission'. This was carried out in Germany by Otto Hahn (1879–1968) and Franz Strassman (1902–80) and interpreted in Norway by their departed Austrian-Jewish colleagues, Lise Meitner (1878–1968) and Otto Frisch (1904–79).

More experiments and hypotheses followed after World War I. These included the theory of Erwin Schrödinger (1887–1961) in 1926 that matter at the atomic level behaves just like waves. Also, Werner Heisenberg (1901–76) developed an even more startling suggestion in the following year that there were limits to how precisely any atomic event could be defined, postulating that the precise position and momentum of a particle could not be specified simultaneously. This introduced indeterminacy into the atomic world, a concept still known today as Heisenberg's

Frédéric Joliot and his wife, Irène Joliot-Curie, shown in their laboratory. Both physicists, they shared a Nobel Prize in 1935, on the trail of the neutron.

Uncertainty Principle. Form became fuzzy. This was an insight that acted in the same way as a detonator, blowing apart the entire, painstaking edifice of post-Newtonian scientific determinism.

From early in that decade, experimenters such as Francis Aston (1877–1945) were using mass spectrography to study radioactive isotopes. There were cloud chambers to plot the visible tracks of ionizing radiation, invented by C T R Wilson (1869–1959) and Arthur H Compton (1892–1962). Then, in 1931, the cyclotron was devised by an American, Ernest O Lawrence (1901–58), to accelerate particles to very high speeds by means of enormous magnets, weighing hundreds or even thousands of tons. All won Nobel Prizes. Yet the next critical breakthrough in the structure of the atom did not come until 1932. Following on from experiments by the French husband-and-wife team of Frédéric Joliot (1900–58) and Irène Joliot-Curie (1897–1956) at Marie Curie's Radium Institute in Paris, Rutherford's assistant, James Chadwick (1891–1974), pursued an inspired hunch developed by Rutherford himself in 1930 and discovered a third elementary particle after the electron and the proton: the neutron.

Carrying no electrical charge, but with a mass that was almost equivalent to that of the protons within the nucleus, this particle could far more easily penetrate the powerful bonds holding the atom together than could the positively charged alpha particles mostly employed by researchers until then. Unlike alpha particles, neutrons were not repelled by the positive charge of protons clustered in the nucleus. This was to prove crucial in the development both of the nuclear bomb and, later, of civil nuclear power.

Only one year later, in 1933, Adolf Hitler became chancellor of Germany. The Nazis swiftly unveiled their first anti-Semitic measures under the bland-sounding Law for the Restoration of the Professional Civil Service. This decree banned 'non-Aryans' from government posts; it also covered state-employed academics, thus beginning a steady exodus of some of the most able and creative scientific minds in the country. Einstein, who had renounced German citizenship long before in 1896, got out early, showered with instant offers of employment by US academic institutions. His departure had been preceded by the Hungarians John Von Neumann (1903–57), a brilliant mathematician, and Eugene Wigner (1902–95), an able physicist, both of whom had also headed for the USA. They were joined by Hans Bethe (b.1906), a talented theoretical physicist, Edward Teller (b.1908), another prolific Hungarian, and Otto Frisch (1904–79). Leo Szilard (1898–1964) was also Hungarian, a shrewd, far-sighted idealist who had been inspired by the writings of H G Wells to believe that atomic power could be the saviour of humankind; he slipped away by train just in time. He landed up in London, where he was soon to hatch the idea of a nuclear chain reaction. He sealed it

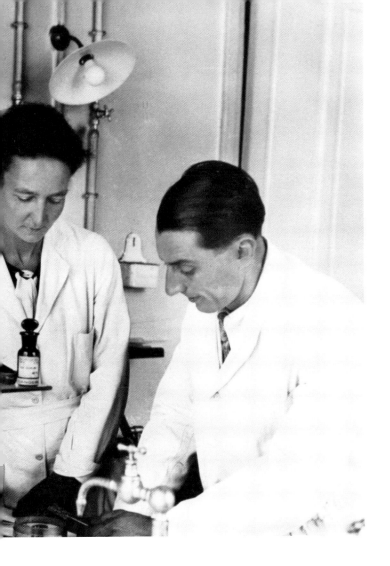

under a secret patent, apparently hoping more to protect it from misuse than to profit himself.

There were many others, too, but these men were the core group of immigrants who were to play key roles in developing the USA's nuclear bomb. Prominent among them was the triumvirate of Szilard, Teller and Wigner, jokingly nicknamed 'the Hungarian conspiracy' in their adoptive country. Yet as the Nazi Reich moved decisively in 1939 to annexe Austria, occupying part of Czechoslovakia and subduing the rest by military force before launching the *Blitzkrieg* against Poland that pitched the world into a new and terrible war, the time for joking seemed to have run out. Hitler had not spiked his atomic guns with the 1933 anti-Jewish decree; there were still plenty of capable scientists in Germany who were willing or could be strong-armed into working on a nuclear project for the Nazis – not least Werner Heisenberg.

In the USA it took much patient advocacy, especially by the ingenious Szilard, to persuade the US government of the military value of nuclear research. At that stage the war was still a European war, and though the Americans accepted that tapping the incredible energy of the nucleus might well have future military uses, it was not an urgent priority. Einstein himself was induced by Szilard to write a letter setting out the case for a research programme that was used as the basis for a presentation to the US president, Franklin D Roosevelt, by a politician of Einstein's acquaintance.

The US leader accepted that action was needed and set up a committee to investigate. But new delays followed as the committee's chairman, a lifelong bureaucrat, proved slow, inefficient and lacking in scientific perspicacity. Piffling amounts of money were allocated. The project was batted about between government agencies, getting nowhere, to the gradually mounting frustration of its promoters.

Several events helped quicken the pace. The first was Germany's attempt in early 1940 to buy heavy water from the Norwegians, who had the world's only large-scale facility for producing it at Norsk Hydro. A compound in which the two hydrogen atoms, bonded to one of oxygen in ordinary water, are replaced by deuterium, heavy water was seen by many physicists, along with carbon, as a promising experimental medium for neutron bombardment. The Germans, who had set up a secret project under Heisenberg, were still studying the explosive potential of natural uranium. The Norwegians rebuffed an approach from their German stockholder, I G Farben, to buy up their entire supply of heavy water, and were later scooped by the French – all of which became irrelevant when the Germans invaded Norway and captured the Vermork plant for their own use. But only for a time: the plant was blown up in a daring Norwegian commando raid early in 1943. It was rebuilt and restarted by the Germans, then bombed by British planes in November, until its last supplies of heavy water were sunk on a ferry in transit to Germany. This effectively ended German hopes for a bomb.

In the USA, scientific efforts were focused increasingly on the difficult and complex task of extracting Uranium 235, occurring naturally at a concentration of less than one per cent – a far more reactive isotope than the commoner and stabler Uranium 238. At around the same time, the concept of 'critical mass' emerged in Britain: a quantity of U-235 sufficient to set in motion a self-sustaining reaction. Otto Frisch drastically revised estimates of the weight of uranium needed in a bomb, dropping them from many tons to a pound or two, while the physicist Rudolf Peierls (1907–95) sketched a triggering mechanism that would supposedly work by jamming two hemispheres of U-235 together to kickstart the chain-reaction. the British physicist James Chadwick concluded gloomily that a bomb was not only possible – it was now inevitable.

The British had their own research committee by April 1940, albeit one still sceptical of its military value; US efforts were bolstered by the creation of a National Defense Research Council, though this, too, was initially dismissive. But the scientific quest for new fissionable materials carried on, and so there emerged another powerful isotope, Uranium 239. This took its place in the periodic table at 93 as neptunium and, bombarding this again in a laboratory, a chemist, Glenn Seaborg (b.1912), took transmutation a further stage to the even more deadly element 94 – plutonium. At the same time the Italian physicist Enrico Fermi (1901–54), a Nobel laureate who had emigrated to the USA with his Jewish wife, was working with 9 m (30 feet) 'piles' of interleaved uranium and graphite on a disused squash court in Chicago to prove critical mass in the world's first prototype reactor. Other researchers tried many methods to extract U-235, ranging from gas and heat diffusion to centrifuges and electromagnetism.

The Russians, who had been kept in the dark by Britain and the USA throughout, had started work in 1939, but their programme did not prosper – five years on there were just 20 scientists involved. In April 1941 the Japanese launched their own research study, though the Germans had by that time downgraded their nuclear programme, thanks in part to some notable bureaucratic bungling. The Japanese navy gave up less than two years later; other Japanese programmes limped on for another couple of years.

But the event that really galvanized US efforts was Japan's traumatic surprise attack on Pearl Harbour in December 1942. Not only did the destruction of the Pacific fleet suck the USA into the war against Germany and Italy as well as Japan; it also placed the nuclear project under military supervision, with millions of dollars at its disposal. The eventual cost of developing the bomb was projected at some $2 billion – a truly

colossal sum in those days – thus creating an infrastructure that grew in a few years to be estimated at roughly the same size as the entire US automobile industry.

In the absence of a determined espionage effort to gauge German progress, moreover, there was no reliable estimate of how far the Nazis might have got until the end of the war. This strange omission allowed apocalyptic speculation to proliferate on the part of the Allies like a deadly radiation leak. Robert Oppenheimer (1904–67), a rich, clever, inwardly self-doubting physicist with interests that ran from T S Eliot's poetry to Hindu philosophy, became scientific director; a hard-nosed career soldier, General Leslie Groves (1896–1970), seized the project by the scruff of its neck and demanded results.

These two became the driving force behind what was then known as the Manhattan Project. The skinny, chain-smoking

Oppenheimer had a strong scientific reputation and had flirted with left-wing politics before the war; consumed with fury at Germany's treatment of the Jews, he turned out to be a brilliant administrator and motivator of people. He and Groves were convinced that a dedicated central laboratory was essential to success, though they kept their plans carefully compartmentalized. They lighted on the desert location of Los Alamos, at the site of a boys' ranch-school on a 2,000 m (7,000 feet) mesa outside Santa Fe, where cheap barrack-blocks were hastily thrown up round the old school complex to prepare for the induction of the scientific team. By the end of the war, Los Alamos had swollen to the size of a town, housing 10,000 people. Two massive production facilities were located elsewhere, with huge diffusion and enrichment plants built at Oak Ridge in a remote area of Tennessee,

By the end of World War II, 10,000 people were employed in the Los Alamos National Laboratory. In the foreground is the old school at the nucleus of the site.

and three plutonium 'piles' at Hanford, overlooking the Columbia River in Washington State.

Coordinating the research was an enormously complex business, necessitating working on many fronts at once, while the rate of production of deadly nuclear materials was at first painfully slow. Security was always a source of anxiety, causing sparks to fly between the military and some of the scientists, who believed in an open exchange of ideas. They used codes to communicate about their work – 'tubealloy' for uranium; 'gadgets' for atomic bombs. But at last a plethora of design concepts was narrowed to just two: one worked by firing a uranium 'bullet' from a built-in gun to strike rings of U-235 lodged in the nose; the other employed hemispheres of plutonium, no bigger than an orange, sheathed in uranium and activated by an outer shell of high explosive to create vast inward compression on the core. These became Little Boy, to be dropped on Hiroshima, and Fat Man, the still more powerful weapon used at Nagasaki.

Left: Ground Zero: the Trinity atomic test was carried out at Jornada del Muerto – Dead Man's Trail – near Alamogordo. The bomb detonated with a force equivalent to 18,600 tons of TNT.

Right: Manhattan project leader Major General Leslie Groves (right) and Robert Oppenheimer inspect the remnants of the steel tower where the atomic bomb was tested. The intense heat of the bomb melted the tower, and seared the surrounding sands into jade-green glass.

The enormity of what the project created burst into full, fiery flower on a barren patch of desert in the Alamogordo bombing range, 320 km (200 miles) south of Los Alamos. The bomb was suspended on a steel tower at Ground Zero, ten miles from base camp, with camera bunkers to record the flash and scientific equipment packed into shelters closer in. The brilliant white double-flash of the detonation, which was too fast for the human eye to separate, was followed in milliseconds by a hemispheric fireball. Beautiful and terrifying, the shockwave shook the ground as if it were a dirty rug as the ball swelled to 600 m (2,000 feet) in diameter before rising and turning brilliant purple at the edges where it touched the clouds. The blast was compared by one scientist to 'opening a hot oven and the sun coming out like a sunrise'. Others ran a sweepstake on the explosive yield, Isidor I Rabi (1898–1988) coming closest to the actual equivalent: 18,600 tons of TNT, though more by luck than judgement. The more poetically-minded Oppenheimer reached for Hindu scriptures to do justice to the overwhelming impact, quoting

Moments after the detonation of the Trinity test, a tremendous flash of light and smoke rings fill the early morning sky.

the *Bhagavad Gita*: 'Now I am become Death, the destroyer of worlds.' This was no high-flown metaphor – it was literally true.

Yet the Trinity desert trial, which left a ring of sand fused into green glass on 16 July 1945, was as nothing beside the fateful decision to use the bomb on the teeming cities of Japan. A new president, Harry S Truman, had taken office on the death of Roosevelt, and arguments raged back and forth among a handful of top politicians about whether the bomb should be used at all. As Groves helped draw up lists of potential targets,

pleas when intercepted cables between Tokyo and Moscow disclosed Japanese peace overtures towards the Russians. With Stalin's forces already occupying parts of Eastern Europe, the leaders of Truman's administration were peering into a postwar future still half-hidden by the drifting smoke of war, trying to gauge the likely impact of a bomb on a completely new political world order. Some saw the grim inevitability of a new arms race; others calculated that dropping the bomb on Japan would serve a double purpose, ending the war quickly and warning off the Russians.

Then came the Potsdam Declaration by the Allied leaders – a non-negotiable list of terms for Japanese surrender. In the end, though, the question of Japan came down not to its refusal to surrender, but its refusal to do so unconditionally. This proud race, devoted to their emperor, was being asked not just to relinquish the old samurai code of never submitting, hardened further by wartime propaganda: seemingly they would also have to give up their most venerable symbols of national identity in the Allied quest to root out militarism. And on that slender pretext, bitterly controversial to this day, the decision was made. General Eisenhower was only one of those opposed on the US side. There remains something chilling about the mechanics of the final target selection – God might not play dice, as Einstein once said, yet it was as if the US war planners were not just electing to play God, but to play dice, too, with the lives of many thousands of Japanese non-combatants.

Japan's sinking of the US vessel *Indianapolis*, with a horrific loss of 500 men, drowned or devoured by sharks, gave a last vengeful spurt to US resolve: the ship had in fact just delivered key bomb components to the Pacific island of Tinian. Accordingly, Little Boy was loaded on to a B-29 bomber, a slender silver giant with 43 m (141 feet) wings, bearing the name of flight commander Paul Tibbets's mother jauntily painted on the fuselage: Enola Gay. The plane took off with a roar and the crew settled in for the six-hour flight to Hiroshima.

When the bomb went off, triggered by timers and barometric pressure, the plane was already more than 18 km (11 miles) away. But it bucked and creaked as if hitting heavy flak. A blinding flash filled the sky, then Tibbets looked back to see Hiroshima hidden by 'that awful cloud, boiling up, mushrooming and incredibly tall'; another crew member compared the scene to a 'pot of boiling black oil'. There was absolute silence immediately after the blast.

starting with 17 cities and excluding those already devastated by US incendiary raids, the morality of such a monstrous and unprecedented weapon was debated against the ticking clock of a bloody war in the Pacific.

One side held that the Japanese would never lay down arms, as their soldiers had shown in their kamikaze resistance against invading US marines on the Pacific Islands; another insisted that Japan should be given the chance to surrender, with proper foreknowledge of the USA's deadly new weapon, redoubling their

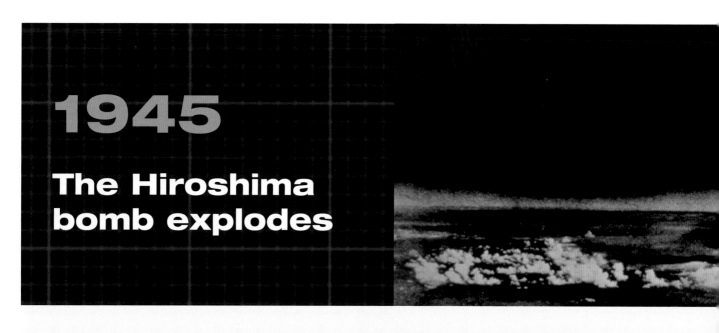

1945

The Hiroshima bomb explodes

6 August 1945. After the Trinity test in New Mexico, the USA knew that the atomic bomb worked. Two days before the Potsdam Declaration of 26 July, setting out Allied terms for a Japanese surrender, President Harry S Truman authorized its use. The top-secret research project had cost $2 billion: now the cost of the bomb would be counted in human lives.

14:00 **5 August.** General Curtis LeMay, head of 20th Bomber Command in the Far East, confirms that the mission will take place the next day. On Tinian Island, in the afternoon, Little Boy is dollied to a loading pit and hoisted in by hydraulic lift. Sheathed in blackened steel, the bomb weighs 4,400 kg (9,700 pounds) and resembles 'an elongated trash-can with fins'.

Equipped with radar, timers and a barometric pressure switch to arm the nuclear charge, Little Boy is manoeuvred into the bay of the B-29, held in place by a single shackle and sway braces. Paul Tibbets, a veteran of the first B-17 bombing mission in Europe, will lead this mission. He finds a signwriter to paint his mother's name, Enola Gay, in foot-high letters on the fuselage under the pilot's window.

00:00 **6 August.** Final briefing. Tibbets reminds his 11 crew members to use their polarized goggles. The forecast is moderate winds, skies clearing above the target at dawn. A minister asks the Almighty 'to be with those who brave the heights of the heavens and who carry the battle to our enemies'. The crew have breakfast – ham and eggs with pineapple fritters for Tibbets. Take off is at 2.45 a.m., so there is no chance of sleep.

The co-pilot starts the engines at 2.27 a.m. The plane is 6,800 kg (15,000 pounds) overweight but clears the two-mile runway, flying low over Saipan. Deke Parsons and Morris Jeppson crawl into the bay to complete the bomb assembly. Three hours later they rendezvous with their escort planes above Iwo Jima. By 8.50 a.m. they fly over Japanese territory at 9,500 m (31,000 feet), a short run from Hiroshima.

09:16 It is about 8.15 a.m. Hiroshima time when the bomb drops, detonating 580 m (1,900 feet) above the courtyard of Shima Hospital in a blinding flash. From the plane looking back, the city resembles 'lava

or molasses covering the whole city', flowing out into the foothills, fires breaking out everywhere.

On the ground this city of one third of a million people was going about its business – soldiers exercising beside Hiroshima Castle, schoolgirls dutifully clearing firebreaks; street cars and bicycles taking people to work. The flash lasts milliseconds, but the temperature at the centre reaches 5,400°C (9752°F). Birds are incinerated in mid-air, roof tiles bubble at 1,180 m (1,300 yards), telegraph poles flare like matches at 3,650 m (4,000 yards). The searing heat prints a giant photograph of the city: the outline of a man pulling a handcart left in unburned asphalt, another etched on the stone steps of a bank; shadows of trees.

A brief, terrible silence, as though the whole world were dead; darkness; then flame as the firestorm takes hold. Stunned survivors drag themselves along like sleepwalkers, their peeled skin looping down like rags. Faces so swollen that you cannot see eyes or mouths, or even tell the front of someone's head from the back. A woman with her jaw missing, tongue flapping, tries to call for help; a man with his feet blown off staggers on the stumps. Another balances his own eyeball in the palm of his hand.

As the parks catch fire, the rivers fill with burnt bodies like charred driftwood. A desperate thirst takes hold: drowned schoolgirls are found with grotesquely swollen, red faces submerged in the cistern where they tried to drink. The city fills with cries, moans, screams. Yet this vision of hell is just the beginning: by 1 September, 70,000 people will be dead and 130,000 wounded, a third of them severely. The eventual death toll is estimated at well in excess of 100,000 people.

Above left: Photographed in the slipstream of the *Enola Gay*, the Hiroshima mushroom cloud rises above the devastated city.

Above right: Hiroshima after the blast, which flattened thousands of buildings and consumed thousands of lives in a firestorm.

There followed scenes from hell: temperatures had reached 2,980°C (5,400°F), and victims near the blast were vaporized or incinerated into oven remnants; stunned survivors staggered along like sleepwalkers, their charred skins hanging off their flesh like rags. Wooden housing erupted in a ferocious firestorm, kindling parks and trees; rivers became choked with blackened corpses. The city had housed some 290,000 civilians and 43,000 soldiers; contemporary estimates within less than a month put the death toll at 70,000, the injured at 130,000. Some 70,000 buildings were damaged or destroyed. Then, three days later, at Nagasaki, Fat Man exploded with a force equivalent to 22,000 tons of TNT, killing 70,000 people by the end of 1945 and twice that over five years.

Small wonder that some scientists who had worked to develop this weapon felt they could never atone for what they had unleashed. Their one real hope of salvaging something from the destruction was to bring to fruition the old dream of using nuclear power to humankind's benefit. The arms race took off with a vengeance, however, working up to intercontinental ballistic missiles with warheads that were measured in multiple megatons – enough, according to one estimate, to kill the entire world population 12 times over by the end of the Cold War. Alongside this, the postwar civil power programme was pushed to supply cheap and plentiful electricity to improve the daily lives of citizens, power up new industries and speed further developments.

Even in its earliest days, there was a real duality of purpose. Britain's Sellafield, based in Cumbria and formerly known as Windscale, was started in 1947 and claims to be the world's first commercial nuclear power station. From the start the 'Windscale piles' were a source of plutonium for the British nuclear deterrent, tested in 1952, as well as serving civil purposes. In 1957 the confidence of nuclear engineers and the public at large was badly dented by a serious fire at Windscale, releasing some 400,000 curies of radioactivity, which led to the dumping of 2 million litres (3.5 million pints) of milk. Sellafield has continued to attract frequent controversy over leaks, faulty nuclear storage and alleged cancer-clusters developing near by.

There have been even worse disasters – Three-Mile Island in 1979, Tokaimura in 1999, and the daddy of them all, the Chernobyl meltdown of 1986, estimated by one international

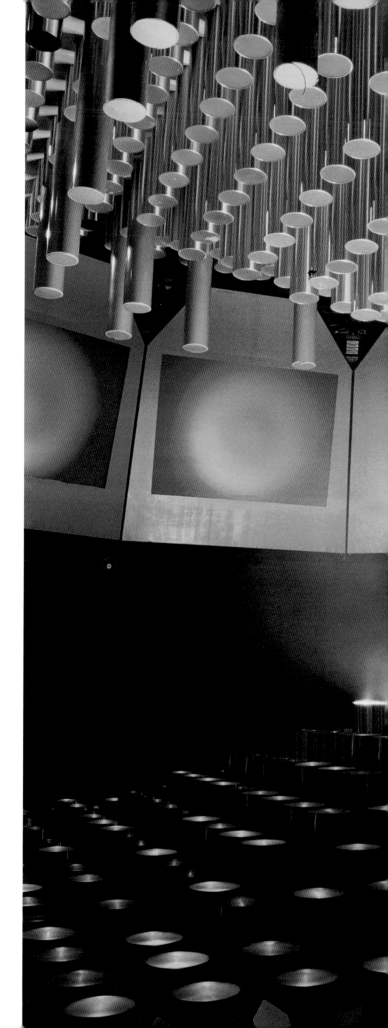

authority to have released 200 times as much radioactivity into the atmosphere as Hiroshima and Nagasaki combined. Many also believe civil nuclear programmes are storing up incalculable trouble for the future. The International Atomic Energy Agency, for instance, has forecast a worldwide accumulation of around a quarter of a million tons of spent fuel and high-level radioactive waste by 2015 – an amount highly unlikely to be consumed by nuclear reprocessing. While pressing ecological and economic concerns have now cut back nuclear power development in Western Europe, contractors still pitch for new work among the countries of the former Soviet bloc. Yet, according to one Western estimate, there are already 27 plants in operation across that region that can be classified as high risk.

Worse, the collapse of the Soviet Union in 1989 has sharpened fears that nuclear materials could fall into the hands of terrorist bombmakers, to say nothing of 'rogue' states such as Iraq or North Korea, or that nuclear power stations might present lethal targets to enemies in an unstable world. Of all those involved in the early theoretical triumphs of nuclear physics, the great Niels Bohr probably understood best the pact man had entered into on prising open the atom. He saw it as a complementary dialogue of hope and terror that required the invention of a new set of open international relationships, more like the old democracy of science. But minds of Bohr's class are rarely drawn to politics, and the politicians ignored him.

A mock-up of a nuclear reactor is displayed at Calder Hall Power Station's visitor centre in Sellafield, showing the uranium rods that power the reactor.

1986

Chernobyl meltdown

26 April 1986. In the late 1960s, the Soviet Union hoped to fill its domestic energy gap by building a string of RBMK-1000 nuclear reactors across its territories. One site chosen was 19 km (12 miles) north of Chernobyl, on the banks of the marshy Pripyat River in the Ukraine. By the mid-1980s four reactors were operational there, with two more being built – but the Soviet system had long concealed deadly flaws in both materials and construction.

01:00 **25 April.** As the May Day Holiday draws near – an important date in the Communist calendar – the weather is warm enough to suggest the promise of early summer. Thus it has been decided to close down Chernobyl's Reactor no. 4 in the expectation of low demand for power in the grid. On the orders of deputy chief engineer Anatoli Dyatlov, in charge during the absence of chief engineer Nikolai Fomin with a spinal injury, shift foreman Alexander Akimov starts to reduce power, but it must be done gradually to avoid closing the reactor down permanently.

8:00 A new shift comes on; by lunchtime the reactor has reached half-power and turbogenerator no. 7 can be switched off, in preparation for a test on turbine no. 8, scheduled by the plant's operator, Donenergo. But the test is postponed in the face of a last-minute demand from the power grid. The reactor is held at half-power.

16:00 The next shift arriving for work assumes the test has been completed. One operator asks another whether he should comply with a deleted section in his instructions and is told to go ahead. Meanwhile, Gennady Metlenko, from Donenergo, is waiting in a control room annexe with two assistants for Kiev's clearance on his test.

23:00 Kiev gives permission for turbine no. 8 to be disconnected. Dyatlov orders a reduction in reactor power from 1,700 to 700 MW, at which point the test can begin. At midnight the night-shift comes on. By now the emergency core-cooling system has been switched off; next to go off is the local automatic control system, governing the

number of control rods inserted into the reactor to dampen it. But there is a sudden and unexpected power dip to just 30 MW, caused by a build-up of iodine, which will take time to disperse. Normal practice would be to scrub the test and close the reactor down, but Dyatlov is itching to get on with it. He orders the withdrawal of more control rods, losing his temper when the decision is questioned by his juniors; power rises again to 200 MW, but the steam pressure in the separator drums is dropping to automatic shutdown levels. More control rods are withdrawn.

01:23 **26 April.** As emergency regulating valves to the turbine generator are shut off to allow the test to run again if need be, reactor power rises sharply. Suddenly a series of dull thuds rocks the building, but the control rods freeze in mid-air, no longer responding to the controls. Next, an explosion shakes the walls like an earthquake. The control room is plunged in darkness, leaving its dials illuminated only by emergency circuits. Now neither control rods nor emergency pumps to flood the reactor are working. The explosion has buckled concrete walls 1 m (3 feet) thick and blown a huge hole in the roof. The overseer notes with horror that the reactivity gauge has turned positive.

Desperate attempts are made to open the huge valves of the emergency cooling system by hand, but to no avail; workers who race to the top of the building gaze down into a molten inferno where the reactor used to be. Scalding water gushes from ruptured pipes, severely injuring workers, fires light up the night, and radioactive debris rains down like meteorites. The fire brigade arrives. Again and again, without protective clothing, firemen try to control the raging blaze below, but the roof melts beneath their feet. Many die in the aftermath, while sickness and birth defects afflict many more over a huge nuclear 'footprint'.

Above left: Terrible injuries were inflicted on Chernobyl's staff and on firemen, who were burned, scalded or exposed to lethal doses of radiation.

Above right: For workers who climbed to the top of the ruined reactor, it was like looking into a volcano.

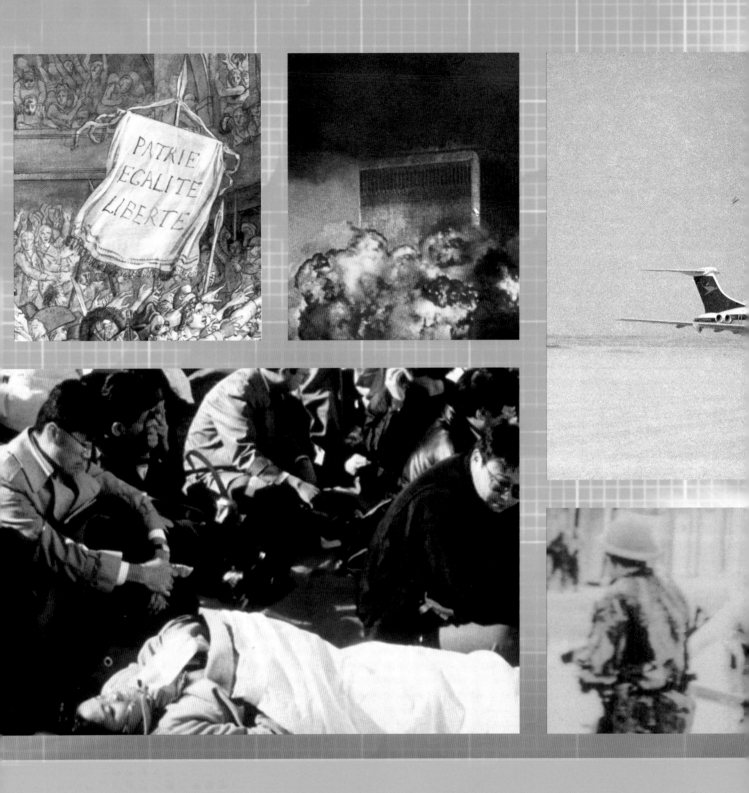

Terrorism has become an international plague, yet its violence is driven by fiercely held convictions. Its causes range widely, from the deep social inequalities underlying the French Revolution in 1789 to the anti-USA hostility that led to the destruction of the Twin Towers in Manhattan in 2001.

[1789] : [2001]

MODERN TERROR

Politics and violence, whether implied as threat or employed as method, have always been closely intertwined. The celebrated dictum of the early nineteenth-century Prussian soldier and military theorist Karl von Clausewitz (1780–1831) – 'War is the continuation of politics by other means' – was true not just of his own time but for many centuries. In the days of rival empires with big armies and bigger territorial ambitions, war was conducted on a fairly open basis and, in theory, on an equal footing.

In the gleam of polished steel, sunlight flashing on armour or on uniforms made splendid with gold piping, in the roar of cannon and musket, wreathed in the blue smoke of burnt powder, war was the martial twin of diplomacy. And while military conflict would always exact its toll of death and injury, both war and diplomacy were then treated in some sense as a game – a game of two halves: one played out in palace or chancellery, the other on the battlefield.

Rules of engagement were understood by both sides, outcomes determined by men and military resources, together with training, preparation and the quality of military leadership, from the top generals down through the whole chain of command. Accidents of weather, timing, supply or communication played their part, too. It was often said that a good general is a lucky general, but a good general would strive to minimize the effects of the unforeseen.

The history of terrorism

1867
The Fenians, their name recalling warrior heroes, plant the first Irish bombs on English soil and begin fundraising among Irish expatriates in the USA.

1881
Sophia Perovskaya, a leader of the Russian terrorist group the People's Will, is arrested and hanged following the assassination of Tsar Alexander II.

1919
The Irish Republican Army forms under the leadership of Michael Collins, taking over from the Volunteers, to harass British troops in rural areas by guerrilla attacks.

The qualities required were strategic vision, meticulous planning, boldness, and the ability to respond to changing situations with swift and decisive tactical improvisation. Napoleon and Wellington both displayed these attributes in securing their greatest victories. If they neglected them, as Napoleon did when he overreached himself by leading his armies into Russia, the result was defeat, or worse: the retreat from Moscow was a full-blown disaster.

First among equals?
The traditional art of war
in the West placed its
combatants on a similar
footing of implied power.

1945
Jewish terrorists strike against the British in Palestine, activity escalating in two years to a big hotel bombing, grenade attacks and murder. Arab terrorism rises sharply as the Jewish state is born, three years on.

1955
Greek Cypriots from EOKA begin a concerted terrorist campaign against the British, which continues until independence. In Algeria FLN terrorists attack French citizens in a struggle for independence.

1968
Palestinian PFLP terrorists carry out their first aircraft hijacking, holding 32 Jewish hostages in Algeria for five weeks. Two years later the Palestinians blow up three hijacked airliners in Jordan.

When diplomatic duelling reached an impasse, war would often follow. Diplomacy has been described as a form of chess, and chess is itself a stylization of war. Not for nothing is the chessboard arranged to represent the human types of medieval society: king and queen, plus castle; bishop, knight and pawns – the 'poor bloody infantry'. At its most basic level, war is no more than organized violence. Fear is bred by violence, especially in civilian populations; and when fear runs out of control, it easily slips over into terror. But the identification of terror as a specific political weapon – Terror with a capital 'T' – was heralded by the French Revolution. Edmund Burke (1729–97) first used the word 'terrorism' to describe the wholesale slaughter of the French aristocracy at the guillotine. Their executions were watched by the gloating *tricoteuses*, women who knitted while observing the spectacle, glorying in the sight of one noble head following another into the basket, leaving the prone torso to shower the scaffold with fountains of blood that ran down into the dust below.

It was a horrific spectacle, and yet it sprang from the logic of war and from the immemorial use of execution as the final sanction of royal authority. In France, as in other parts of Europe, the peasants had for centuries been 'terrorized' by war, seeing their homes burned, their fields laid waste and their food stocks plundered by passing armies marching to the tune of royal conquest. And they were powerless. These were people who had never had a voice in the counsels of power; the faceless, muddy victims who must somehow try to survive and restore the broken rhythms of agriculture after the armies had gone. In France the revolution began over bread shortages. The poor had seen bread snatched away before, whether it was taken to fill the

The history of terrorism

1970
Andreas Baader is freed from a West German jail during an attack by Ulrike Meinhof. Both are linked to the Red Army Faction and become notorious as the Baader-Meinhof Gang.

1972
Palestinian terrorists from Black September storm the Olympic Village in Munich, killing a total of 11 Israeli athletes. Five of the terrorists are killed during a bungled police rescue operation.

1979
Iranian radicals seize the US embassy in Teheran, taking 66 US diplomats hostage in a crisis that lasts more than 14 months and leads to an unsuccessful rescue attempt by US special forces.

The terror begins: Louis XVI is held captive by the General Assembly during the French Revolution as a violent crowd demands his execution.

bellies of soldiers or denied them by the greed, vanity and indifference that characterized all too many of the aristocratic landowners who controlled their farms and livelihoods.

Thus the French Revolution moved from the euphoria of liberation at the storming of the Bastille to the bloody elimination of an entire class. It was scarcely surprising that this left an ugly stain on the revolutionary cry of '*Liberté, Egalité, Fraternité!*' and sent a shudder through the ruling elites of Europe. In one sense the more ruthless tribunes of the Revolution – including educated men like the Jacobin leader, Maximilien Robespierre (1758–94) – were doing little more than apply the lessons they had learnt from the powers they had sworn themselves to topple. These powers had for centuries been able to back their authority with both the threat and the actuality of violence. The French Revolution extended those lessons into a systematic slaughter, and in doing so created a tyranny that many saw as no better than the one its leaders purported to oppose. It was the ancient logic of 'this could happen to you', well known to the Romans: a cruel and dictatorial logic, certainly, but in essence not new. Large-scale massacres to eliminate opponents, religious or political, were hardly unknown in European history in earlier times.

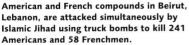

1983
American and French compounds in Beirut, Lebanon, are attacked simultaneously by Islamic Jihad using truck bombs to kill 241 Americans and 58 Frenchmen.

1984
More than five years after the death of British politician Airey Neave by car bomb, the IRA blows up the Grand Hotel in Brighton in an attempt to assassinate Conservative Prime Minister Margaret Thatcher.

2001
Al-Qa'eda terrorists hijack four planes and fly two of them into the Twin Towers of the World Trade Center in Manhattan, causing them to collapse with the loss of 3,000 lives. Another plane hits the Pentagon.

Modern massacre: chaos
follows a Sarin gas attack
in Tokyo in March 1995 by
the Japanese terrorist cult
Aum Shrinyiko.

What was new in the French Reign of Terror would not become fully apparent for another three-quarters of a century and more. For in its bloody convulsions, the possibility of a new way of waging war began to take shape, subsidiary but related to the overt agenda. This new approach would in time be defined by the word Burke had coined for the revolution's excesses: terrorism. Burke denounced the 'terrorist' revolutionaries of France as 'Hell-hounds', yet some forms of terrorism would come to be associated with genuine liberation movements long after his time. Unlike the old imperial battles, where contenders fought on a notional basis of equal power and status, if unevenly matched in practice, this method seemed to offer a chance of fighting back to the oppressed and downtrodden. It was adopted in situations where all the power – the army, the police, the judiciary, the money – was concentrated on one side while the other had none. By the time the noble families of France were dragged to the guillotine in carts, of course, it is true that the old roles had been reversed: it was the people who were in control now, or their tribunes. Sometimes it was just the mob.

Terrorism went on to become one of the great scourges of the twentieth century, killing or injuring thousands of innocent civilians as they were blown to bits by car bombs detonated without warning on busy streets, or hurled down from the sky in stricken airliners. Its practitioners developed an armoury of techniques: selective political assassination; the commission of acts of violence or public outrages to create a climate of fear that, they believed, would force the authorities into making concessions; kidnapping, hostage-taking, torture, murder, hijacking and sabotage. How effective these methods were remains a matter of heated historical debate. Governments like to say that they never negotiate with terrorists; but if terrorism can ever justifiably be defined as a form of war, then it is rare for wars to end without the combatants talking.

Besides, terrorists were able to introduce cunning new variants, such as Sinn Fein's 'ballot-box and bomb' strategy, empowering Irish nationalists to engage in conventional political discourse backed by the ever-present threat of violence. This two-pronged approach, based on a readily adjustable interplay between the two, suggests a shrewd but sinister reworking of Clausewitz, enabling the nationalists to trip up the authorities while allowing their elected political representatives to disown complicity in the violence. Another turn of the screw brought a different synthesis: state-sponsored terrorism, as employed by President Gaddafi of Libya (b.1942), among others, whereby the ruling regime of one country would attack another indirectly by supporting its terrorist enemies at home. The former Soviet Union was repeatedly accused of using this approach by the USA, while the CIA was guilty of fostering such methods in Latin America, even though political assassination was banned by an executive order in the mid-1970s. In Libya's case it meant bankrolling the IRA and supporting it with arms shipments. Yet Libya was not alone. Another development was so-called 'state terror', with its apparatus of disappearance, torture and murder. Ironically, this was probably closer to the terror of the French Revolution, but for the fact that it was also practised by rich, powerful right-wing elites against their defenceless peoples.

At the heart of terrorism lies an old conundrum, encapsulated in the observation that 'one man's terrorist is another man's freedom fighter'. That view is hotly disputed by those who argue that the random violence of modern terrorists against innocent civilians and non-combatants violates the most fundamental conventions of war. In any case, even this contentious paradox became blurred in time as terrorism became allied to gangsterism. Terrorists would often resort to other branches of crime – robbery or extortion – as a means to finance their proscribed organizations and illegal activities. On occasion this gave them an economic incentive to carry on almost irrespective of their original political aims. In addition, more and more tiny splinter groups and sects, working to increasingly deranged agendas, began to get in on the act. One example is the deadly lunacy of Japan's Aum Shrinyiko cult, which released nerve-gas on the Tokyo subway; another is the bizarre one-man war waged on the USA from a tiny cabin in the wilderness by the bespectacled, middle-aged anarchist known as the Unabomber.

Terrorism remains hard to pin down not only because it is necessarily highly secretive, but also because it is inherently variable in its nature, changing form in accordance with circumstances. What, for instance, is the difference between a 'terrorist' and a 'guerrilla'? Many would say that terrorism is an urban phenomenon, dependent for its effect on the rapid dissemination of violent outrages through the mass media, and usually evoking a police response. Whereas the guerrillas who fought, say, in the Cuban Revolution were predominantly rural and opposed mainly by the army. Is terrorism the province of those who have no other means to fight oppression? Or is it the preferred method of those whose ideological extremes mean they have no earthly chance of gaining significant support through normal democratic processes, which they despise anyway as a con-trick orchestrated by the covert controllers of society – the banks, big business, the arms industry? Could it be both?

Many historians, however, date the emergence of terrorism in a recognizably modern form to Russia in the second half of the nineteenth century. And the group credited with this dubious distinction was the People's Will, which was responsible for the assassination of the reformist Tsar Alexander II in 1881. As early as 1825, when the 'Iron Tsar' Nicholas I took the Russian imperial throne, there had been an attempted uprising by the Decembrists, a group of well-born army officers and intellectuals, many of them freemasons, who had come into contact with French revolutionary ideas and were bitterly opposed to the Tsarist autocracy. Some 3,000 soldiers were persuaded to refuse the oath of loyalty to the new Tsar and marched on Senate Square in St Petersburg, but their abortive rebellion was swiftly crushed. More than 120 Decembrists were arrested, stripped of their titles and exiled to Siberia, while five ringleaders were hanged.

When Karl Marx (1818–83) published *Das Kapital*, he supplied a context for the historical analysis of revolution and a quasi-scientific justification of its supposed inevitability. Gradually the early stirrings in Russia gave way to more overt revolutionary tendencies. Prominent among them were the ideas of Aleksandr Herzen (1812–70), who believed the native institutions of Russian peasant life would form the basis for cooperative socialism and an eventual transition to communism. Another influence was the revolutionary anarchist Mikhail Bakunin (1814–76), an aristocratic ex-soldier dubbed 'the apostle

of universal destruction' by his enemies. Bakunin expounded theories of permanent peasant revolt, the 'instinctive revolutionary' tendencies of bandits and brigands, and the formation of free communes without any centralized authority.

Herzen's 'Land and Liberty' slogan was later adopted by the *narodnichestvo* – the *narodniks*, or Populists – a group of idealistic students who from the 1860s tried but failed to evoke revolutionary sentiment among the rural peasantry. Among their ranks could be found Peter Tkachev (1844–86), sometimes described as a Russian Jacobin, who argued that revolutionaries must seize power before attempting to change society. The ideas

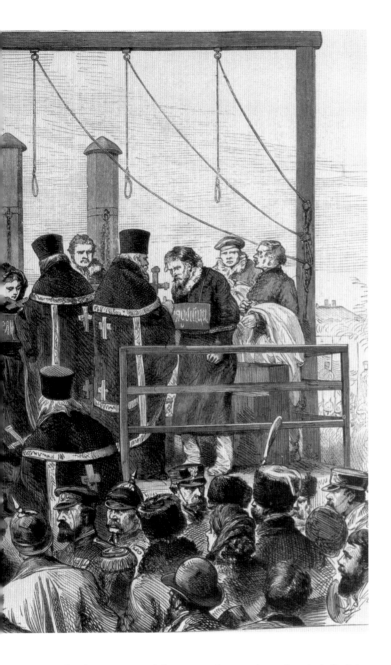

Five conspirators found guilty of the assassination of Tsar Alexander II in 1881 await execution by hanging.

of Bakunin, meanwhile, were taken up by a fanatical disciple, Sergei Nechayev (1847–82), who disseminated the anonymous *Catechism of a Revolutionist*, variously attributed to both men. This inflammatory document advocated the abandonment of all conventional morality; a cold, instrumental approach to fellow revolutionaries on the basis of their usefulness to the cause; and the infiltration of all society's institutions to foment unrest. It even proposed deliberately aggravating the burdens of the people to rouse their anger into an explosion and thus ignite a revolutionary flame that would burn down the citadels of power. Nechayev formed Narodnaya Rasprava, the People's

Vengeance, on terrorist lines, though it was quickly broken up by factional infighting and a wave of mass arrests.

By 1879 the disillusionment of the Populists culminated in a split that led to the formation of Narodnaya Volya, the People's Will. That year also saw a failed attempt on the life of Alexander II (1818–81) by a member of Zemlya i Volya, Land and Liberty, in the wake of other physical attacks on senior leaders in the police and military. All such actions were openly acknowledged, setting a pattern that continues to this day. Initially a violent action is carried out, with or without advance warning, then this is followed up by a claim of responsibility, often accompanied by a justification that may be riddled with political jargon and bolstered by a great deal of specious revolutionary rhetoric.

After the formation of the People's Will, supported by the more hardline elements in Land and Liberty, there followed an attempt to blow up the imperial train, directed by Sophie Perovskaya (1854–81), daughter of the governor general of St Petersburg, and a dynamite explosion at the Winter Palace. In 1881 Perovskaya was more successful in her campaign of violence against the autocracy: the Tsar was attacked and killed by terrorists from the People's Will, who threw a number of small bombs at his carriage on the very day he signed a new decree promising liberal reforms. The Tsar was mortally wounded and died a few hours later; his murderer was also killed outright, while Perovskaya and four others were hanged a month or so later. Though the assassination of Alexander II incurred a much harsher period of repression enforced by the Tsarist secret police, the Okhrana, the People's Will remained active for some time longer. But it was eventually

POBLACHT NA H EIREANN.

THE PROVISIONAL GOVERNMENT
OF THE
IRISH REPUBLIC
TO THE PEOPLE OF IRELAND.

IRISHMEN AND IRISHWOMEN: In the name of God and of the dead generations from which she receives her old tradition of nationhood, Ireland, through us, summons her children to her flag and strikes for her freedom.

Having organised and trained her manhood through her secret revolutionary organisation, the Irish Republican Brotherhood, and through her open military organisations, the Irish Volunteers and the Irish Citizen Army, having patiently perfected her discipline, having resolutely waited for the right moment to reveal itself, she now seizes that moment, and, supported by her exiled children in America and by gallant allies in Europe, but relying in the first on her own strength, she strikes in full confidence of victory.

We declare the right of the people of Ireland to the ownership of Ireland, and to the unfettered control of Irish destinies, to be sovereign and indefeasible. The long usurpation of that right by a foreign people and government has not extinguished the right, nor can it ever be extinguished except by the destruction of the Irish people. In every generation the Irish people have asserted their right to national freedom and sovereignty; six times during the past three hundred years they have asserted it in arms. Standing on that fundamental right and again asserting it in arms in the face of the world, we hereby proclaim the Irish Republic as a Sovereign Independent State, and we pledge our lives and the lives of our comrades-in-arms to the cause of its freedom, of its welfare, and of its exaltation among the nations.

The Irish Republic is entitled to, and hereby claims, the allegiance of every Irishman and Irishwoman. The Republic guarantees religious and civil liberty, equal rights and equal opportunities to all its citizens, and declares its resolve to pursue the happiness and prosperity of the whole nation and of all its parts, cherishing all the children of the nation equally, and oblivious of the differences carefully fostered by an alien government, which have divided a minority from the majority in the past.

Until our arms have brought the opportune moment for the establishment of a permanent National Government, representative of the whole people of Ireland and elected by the suffrages of all her men and women, the Provisional Government, hereby constituted, will administer the civil and military affairs of the Republic in trust for the people.

We place the cause of the Irish Republic under the protection of the Most High God, Whose blessing we invoke upon our arms, and we pray that no one who serves that cause will dishonour it by cowardice, inhumanity, or rapine. In this supreme hour the Irish nation must, by its valour and discipline and by the readiness of its children to sacrifice themselves for the common good, prove itself worthy of the august destiny to which it is called.

Signed on Behalf of the Provisional Government,

THOMAS J. CLARKE.

SEAN Mac DIARMADA.   THOMAS MacDONAGH.
P. H. PEARSE,   EAMONN CEANNT,
JAMES CONNOLLY.   JOSEPH PLUNKETT.

222

Nationalist aspirations:
the proclamation of the
Irish Republic, by the leaders
of the 1916 Easter Rising,
whose names are detailed
at the bottom.

crippled by the execution of five students implicated in a plot against Alexander's successor, Alexander III (1845–94) – including one Alexander Ilyich Ulyanov (1866–87), elder brother of the man better known to the world in later years by the name Vladimir Lenin.

After a long struggle (described in the Communism chapter), the October Revolution of 1917 brought Lenin and the Bolsheviks to power and plunged Russia into civil war. But the year before that, in a western outpost of Europe far from Russia, there had been another armed uprising of a different kind: the Easter Rising. On a Monday afternoon in 1916, some 100 Irish nationalists stormed the General Post Office in central Dublin and proclaimed the right of the Irish people to the ownership of Ireland and control over their own destinies after 'the long usurpation of that right by a foreign people and government'. The declaration read out by Padraig Pearse (1879–1916) referred, of course, to the British; the nationalists flew the flag of the IRB, an acronym that could be read in two ways: the Irish Republican Brotherhood or Irish Revolutionary Brotherhood.

The Irish leaders were quickly overwhelmed, arrested and shot, but this flashpoint marked the beginning of a lengthy terrorist struggle in which the objectives were not those of revolution – or not primarily – but rather those of national self-determination. This type of terrorism might be based on a desire to enforce secession, as with the Basque separatists of ETA. Alternatively, it might be to recover a lost homeland and punish past wrongs, as with the Armenian terrorist group ASALA. In the case of the latter, they took up arms 60 years after the Ottoman Turks deported hundreds of thousands of Armenians and massacred thousands more in 1915, when they felt that all avenues of conventional protest or redress had been exhausted.

Britain's presence in Ireland can be dated back to William the Conqueror (1027–87). Henry II (1133–89) invaded the country in the twelfth century with the blessing of the Pope, seizing baronial estates as well as rendering tribute of one penny per household to the Vatican. The conquest of large tracts of Ulster by England followed in the next century, though the Gaelic chieftains continued to fight English dominion for 400 years, including a claim to sovereignty by Henry VIII (1491–1547), and they finally drove the English out in 1641. Later in the seventeenth century, there was an invasion by Oliver Cromwell (1599–1658), with considerable savagery towards the Catholic Irish by English troops, then another by William of Orange (1650–1702). Having been invited to take the English throne, William sent the army in to Ireland; thereafter more Protestant Scots and English settled in the country, joining those who had arrived already at the Plantation, which began in the North in the early decades of the century. Between the agitation for Catholic emancipation led by Daniel O'Connell (1775–1847) in the 1820s and Charles Stewart Parnell's (1846–91) campaign for Home Rule in the 1880s came the Irish famine. This was caused by an imported potato blight from the USA, which led to the death by starvation of at least one million Irish people and the emigration of 1.5 million more.

Ireland's nationalist history is complex, but it begins with the Society of United Irishmen. They were inspired by events in France: like the Jacobins of Brittany and the Sons of Liberty in the USA, they started out with clubs and discussion groups. The members were mostly educated, middle-class Protestants – Belfast Presbyterians or Anglicans based in Dublin – and their society was born hard on the heels of the French Revolution in response to the pamphleteering of Wolfe Tone (1763–98).

Tone was the sworn enemy of Edmund Burke, who regarded Ireland's Protestant Ascendancy as an occupying force to keep the natives in order. In 1791 Tone argued that the interests of the Protestant Irish commercial middle class were identical with those of the Catholic peasantry, since they shared a common interest and a 'common enemy'. A little over half a century later, a more radical, working-class Catholic movement arose, first in the USA then in Ireland – the Fenians, so called after the *Fianna*, legendary Irish warriors. The Irish Fenians established links with the Irish expatriates in the USA, starting a long tradition of American fundraising and IRA support through Noraid, and planted the first Irish bombs on English soil in 1867.

Yet nationalism in Ireland developed in several different strands. One of these was constitutional nationalism, which opposes violence and is represented in recent Northern Irish history by the Catholic-supported SDLP. Another is so-called 'physical-force' republicanism, distantly derived from the United Irishmen. There are also newer strains of radical republicanism, wholly secular in approach, which see social revolution as well as the 'armed struggle' as an essential precondition of political change. On the Protestant side an early agrarian secret society known as the Peep O' Day Boys, which had fought pitched battles with the Catholic Defenders during land disputes, formed the Orange Order in Armagh in 1795. Thus were the hard, uncompromising lines of sectarian rivalry laid down. In time both sides were to resort to terrorism, resulting in a complex, three-way choreography of politics and violence embroiling all Ireland. This vicious, smouldering war, flaring up time and again over many decades, eventually came to involve the Ulster police and the British army, as well as numerous paramilitary

Londonderry, 1972: British troops hurdle a barbed wire barricade after coming under attack from Catholic demonstrators who had defied a government ban on marches for a second successive day.

IRA's name came into currency in 1919, subsuming the earlier designation of Volunteers. Led by Michael Collins, it was conceived as a rural guerrilla force of 'flying columns', each 20 or 30 strong, to launch hit-and-run attacks on the Royal Irish Constabulary, later to be reinforced by the notoriously violent British regiment dubbed the Black and Tans. After Partition in 1920 there were sectarian assaults on Catholics in the Northern cities of Derry and Belfast for three years running, in the wake of nationalist victories in local elections, while the IRA continued to oppose the 'Free State' in the South.

By the 1930s, economic depression provoked non-sectarian rioting in Belfast in response to unemployment and harsh poor laws. But the two communities were driven apart again as unionist propaganda stirred fresh hostility to 'papists', who continued to suffer gross discrimination by unionist employers. After World War II, during the 1950s, the IRA took nationalist election victories in the North as a cue from the Catholic community for an armed campaign on the border; the 1960s injected revolutionary currents into Republican thinking. After the Northern civil rights campaign was formed in 1967, loyalist vigilante groups proliferated and rioting spread. Strategic and political disagreements fissured the IRA, which split into 'official' and 'provisional' wings.

Then, in 1972, came Bloody Sunday. British troops fired on marchers in Londonderry, leaving 13 people dead: seven were teenagers. This new round of Ireland's 'Troubles' set off a wave of bombings by the 'Provos', first against commercial targets in Northern Ireland, later aimed at civilians across mainland Britain.

groups. On the nationalist side there was the IRA, Provisional IRA, Irish National Liberation Army and others; for the loyalists there was the Ulster Defence Association, Ulster Volunteer Force and Ulster Freedom Fighters.

The emergence of the Irish Republican Army after the Easter Rising, with its ensuing history of splits and regroupings, is a labyrinthine story. Yet the IRA co-existed from the start with the political entity of Sinn Fein – 'Ourselves Alone' – and from the start it was never clear which of the two was calling the shots. The

Four members of Italy's Red Brigades leave a Turin courtroom in chains in 1970, facing charges of kidnapping and terrorism.

As loyalist violence escalated, political initiatives faltered. It was a long, bloody period of confrontation, marked by mounting savagery and breakaway factions on both sides. There were 'dirty protests' by Republicans held in prison, where cells were smeared with excrement; the deaths of IRA hunger-strikers in the Maze Prison enshrined Bobby Sands as a Republican martyr; allegations of a 'shoot-to-kill' policy operated by the British fanned the flames. The chaos and violence began to subside, and then somewhat fitfully, only with the Anglo-Irish intergovernmental agreement of the 1980s; now politics gradually took centre-stage again and Sinn Fein came to the fore.

By the late 1960s, in any case, an upsurge of student radicalism in universities in Europe, coupled with strong opposition to the Vietnam War, had drawn a new crop of eager young recruits to terrorism, operating from the early 1970s across a wider international arena. They were driven by fashionable revolutionary politics and by an implacable hatred of 'US imperialism'. From this period of student unrest sprang various national groups. There was West Germany's Red Army Faction, or the Baader-Meinhof Gang; in Italy the Red Brigades and the fascistic Nuclei Armati; Action Directe in France; Britain's Angry Brigade; Rode Hulp in the Netherlands. This is to mention just a few, though the same people would often invent new names to confuse the authorities when claiming responsibility for some outrage. In countries with a fascist past – Germany, Italy and Spain – the upsurge of left-wing terrorism evoked outbreaks of terrorist activity on the right, characterized by less frequent but often more destructive bombing attacks aimed at maximizing chaos and disorder. Even Japan sprouted its own terrorist underground: the Japanese Red Army.

All the leftist groups saw themselves as the vanguard of an international struggle against capitalism, NATO or 'the military-industrial complex'. Their targets and methods varied, from attacks on embassies and government buildings to robberies, street gun-battles, bombings, kidnappings and assassinations. The Baader-Meinhof Gang, founded in 1970, ran amok for several years, robbing banks and abducting people, planting bombs in West Germany and beyond. Some of its members trained in Jordan with the Marxist Popular Front for the Liberation of Palestine (PFLP); others were in contact with the infamous 'Carlos the Jackal', real name Ilich Ramirez Sanchez (b.1949). The terrorist son of a Venezuelan millionaire, Sanchez by 1976

was wanted in Britain and France for his part in the Hague embassy siege and for holding OPEC ministers hostage.

By the time the Gang's original leaders, Andreas Baader (1943–77) and Ulrike Meinhof (1934–76), were caught in 1972, they had blown up four US servicemen and assassinated a police officer, and caused serious injuries to 36 others. One member, Holger Meins (1941–74), died on hunger strike before they came to trial; after the rest were sentenced, following a delay in opening the proceedings and a long court case, Ulrike Meinhof hanged herself in 1976. Baader shot himself in the back of the head with a smuggled gun, hoping to make his death look like an official 'execution'. Others remained at large and

were still active. In 1975, Baader-Meinhof terrorists seized the German embassy in Stockholm in an attempt to force the German authorities to release their leaders. In 1976 another member, Wilfried Böse, took part in the hijack of an Air France flight from Tel Aviv, which ended in the violent deaths of all the hijackers when Israeli commandos stormed the plane, using guns and stun-grenades, at Entebbe Airport in Uganda.

The most high-profile operation by Italy's Red Brigades was the kidnap and murder of Christian Democrat politician Aldo Moro (1916–78), snatched in 1978 after he took the Communist Party into a coalition government and held pending the release of jailed terrorists. Moro's dead body was found in the boot of a car.

1970

Hijack crisis in Jordan

12 September 1970. Palestinian terrorists have hijacked three jets – British, US and Swiss – and landed them in Jordan pending demands for the release of prisoners in Switzerland, Germany and Israel. Another hijacked plane, a Pan Am jumbo, was blown up in Egypt, while the attempted hijack of an Israeli jet ended with the capture in London of female terrorist Leila Khaled. More than 300 hostages are still sweating it out in the desert.

05:00 **12 September.** It is now 48 hours since the original expiry deadline of an ultimatum delivered by the Popular Front for the Liberation of Palestine to Western governments. That ultimatum set conditions for the release of hostages held at Dawson's Field, in Zarga, Jordan, depending on their nationalities. Britons are to be released in exchange for Leila Khaled, the Palestinian terrorist captured at Heathrow following a failed attempt to hijack an El Al jet, who has not yet been charged; the Swiss and Germans go free on the release of six recently convicted terrorists from their jails; the Americans will be swapped for 50 Palestinian fighters – *fedayeen* – imprisoned in Israel. Failing this, the Marxist Popular Front for the Liberation of Palestine (PFLP) threatens that it will start killing. The British government, under Prime Minister Edward Heath, decides to treat the demands as independently negotiable.

At the time when the 72-hour ultimatum was wired by PFLP representative Abu Omar, the day after three airliners were hijacked on 6 September, there were two planes on the tarmac at the disused RAF airstrip in Jordan – now dubbed 'Liberation Airport' by the terrorists. The third plane was blown up in Cairo, moments after the passengers and crew were allowed off. But the terrorists have since upped the stakes with yet another hijack, three days after they seized the first trio of planes in mid-air: this time their target was a British VC-10 with 65 passengers on board. The aim was to increase pressure on the British, who have since managed to secure a postponement of the deadline. With US support Britain is negotiating through the International Red Cross in Berne, Switzerland, and its own channels in Amman, in spite of a formal pledge not to negotiate with hijackers under the terms of the 1963 Tokyo International Convention.

15:00 The situation is precarious on the ground in Jordan. The terrorists have wired all three planes to explode, and the airstrip is in turn surrounded by the Jordanian army. After cautious initial support for the Palestinian cause, King Hussein of Jordan now sees the growing power of the Palestinians as a threat to his regime – they are trying to establish control in parts of the country. At Dawson's Field the terrorists decide to underline their demands with a show of force. The hostages are taken off and 255 of them are released, though 56 others are retained and transferred to a secret location. Then all three planes are blown up in a fiery, apocalyptic spectacle relayed round the world by television cameras. Black smoke billows out over the desert.

19:00 **13 September.** The BBC World Service broadcasts in Arabic that the British government will swap Khaled for the hostages. The Israelis are furious: they have been shut out of the talks and are convinced that such an act of apparent capitulation will only encourage more terrorism. Eight days later a message from King Hussein reveals that he wants the Israelis to bomb Syrian forces entering Jordan in support of the Palestinians, but they do not intervene directly. At the end of the month, Khaled is flown out to Beirut, along with six others from European prisons, and the last of the hostages are released.

Above left: Leila Khaled, one of two hijackers of an El Al flight in 1970, smiles after returning to her guerrilla base in Jordan.

Above right: Terrorists blow up one of three hijacked planes after removing the hostages. The terrorists agreed to free all hostages except for a group of Israelis who would be freed only when their demands were met.

Masked terror: a member of the Black September gang that stormed the Olympic Village in 1972 keeps watch, while another listens to a plea from an IOC member.

Italy especially was plagued with terrorist activity throughout the 1970s, culminating in 1980 with the detonation of a massive suitcase bomb at Bologna station. The blast killed 84 people and injured hundreds more; the pretext was the trial of eight neofascists for planting a smaller device in the same location some six years earlier, which had claimed a dozen innocent lives. Action Directe, emerging in France in 1979, started with machine-gun attacks on French government buildings, spraying bullets round the streets, before switching to diplomatic assassination in support of the Palestinians after Israel's invasion of Lebanon. Then they changed tack yet again, to collaborate on European bombing campaigns with expatriate Italian terrorists and an indigenous cell in Belgium.

What worried the authorities most at the time was not just the violence unleashed by these groups and the attendant public anxiety, nor the saturation coverage generated in the media. It was also the prima facie evidence of an emerging worldwide terrorist network. In fact, the retrospective consensus seems to be that most such terrorist collaborations were ad hoc and opportunistic. Yet it was only too easy for intelligence agencies, confronted with the endlessly reiterated ambitions of terrorist propaganda to spark off a world revolution, and the mystique of secrecy with which the terrorists surrounded themselves, to imagine a common operational agenda behind the revolutionary rhetoric. Soviet Russia was one suspected culprit, yet the role of the Palestinians in feeding that belief was pivotal.

The first major terrorist publicity coup for the Palestinian cause came in 1970, when three jets – one British, one US, one Swiss – were hijacked and blown up (empty) in the Jordanian desert at a disused RAF airstrip dubbed 'Liberation Airport' by the hijackers. On the same day another attempted hijack of an El Al flight by Palestinians ended in failure as the crew

overpowered the hijackers, killing one and handing over the other to British police on touching down at Heathrow Airport. She was Leila Khaled (b.1944). And when she was flown out to Beirut less than three weeks later, in exchange for the 56 hostages still being held in Jordan, she became – wrapped in her *kefiyeh* headdress – an international symbol of the new 'liberation chic' as well as a new feminist icon.

Such images are ephemeral, but Khaled helped focus world attention on the Palestinian struggle begun more than 20 years

After the 1949 armistice between Israel and the Arabs, almost two-thirds of a million Palestinians fled from Israeli-occupied territory. Some 70 per cent of them went to the West Bank, then part of Jordan, and the Gaza Strip, under Egyptian control; the rest took refuge in neighbouring territories including Transjordan, Lebanon and Syria, with smaller numbers going to Egypt and Iraq. There were Arab blockades against Israel and attacks by Palestinian *fedayeen*; from 1955 the Arabs were supplied with Soviet weapons – notably Egypt, under General Nasser (1918–70), which saw itself as leading Arab efforts to liberate the Palestinians. These developments led to the Sinai War of 1956, when Israel seized Sinai and Gaza, then the Six Day War of 1967, involving both Egypt and Iraq, which ended in Israel's capture of the Golan Heights and the recapture of Sinai.

As the Americans continued to support Israel with money and weapons, Palestinian militancy increased. Palestinian enclaves took root in Syria, Iraq, Lebanon, South Yemen and Algeria. Both Iraq and Syria were controlled by Ba'ath Party regimes based on a revolutionary, pan-Arabist ideology, and both countries licensed the establishment of Arab terrorist organizations to prosecute the Palestinian struggle. The Baghdad-based terrorist group was run by one Sabri al-Banna (1937–2002), whose family had been one of the richest in Palestine before their orchards were seized by the Israelis. Under the *nom de guerre* Abu Nidal, he launched numerous deadly attacks, also targeting the PLO leadership, and worked alongside the secret services of various Arab nations. Fatah, the group that had taken control of the PLO under Arafat, was at first busy with its own terrorist agenda, launching the terrorist organization Black September. Most shocking was their attack at the 1972 Munich Olympics, when Black September terrorists scaled the perimeter fence and then, sub-machine guns blazing, killed two Israeli athletes instantly and slaughtered nine more taken hostage. The group was involved in hijacking and political assassinations before and after the worldwide reverberations from this. Later, though, the PLO played down terrorism in favour of politics.

Lebanon was another major flashpoint in a conflict of hideous complexity. For a time it was seen as the epicentre of Middle East terrorism, owing to the presence of large Palestinian refugee camps and of the PLO leader Yasser Arafat. The Palestinians fought the Lebanese in the late 1960s; Israeli raids started in the 1970s.

earlier with the founding of the Israeli state. Ever since that day, known across the Arab world as 'the 1948 disaster', the Palestinians had enjoyed the support of other Arab nations. This despite the fact that each of these nations tried to use the Palestinian issue to advance its own political interests. Yasser Arafat (b.1929), who took the leadership of the Palestinian umbrella organization, the PLO, some two decades later, was wary of allowing the Palestinian cause to become too closely identified with other Arab interests in general and with single Arab states in particular.

1988

Explosion over Lockerbie

21 December 1988. The US navy battle cruiser *Vincennes* shot down an Iranian airliner over the Persian Gulf in July 1988, killing all 290 people on board. The Americans voiced deep regret; they had mistaken the plane for an F-14 fighter; warnings were ignored. Then comes Lockerbie. At first investigators concentrate on an Iranian revenge theory; later, the focus shifts to Libya, with bombing raids launched on Tripoli and Benghazi.

08:15 **21 December.** Passenger check-in opens at Luqa airport on the island of Malta for Air Malta Flight KM180, bound for Frankfurt. Christmas is coming, so the mad rush of the high season is long past, but the airport is busy again with people trying to get home for the winter break. While checked-in baggage for KM180 was being loaded into containers, to be stowed safely in the plane's hold, an unidentified brown Samsonite suitcase may somehow have been slipped into the system, evading security in spite of Malta's stringent safety procedures, which include computer cross-checks and sniffer dogs. There is no record of an unaccompanied suitcase loaded on the plane.

16:53 On the assumption that it has been transferred at Frankfurt to the Pan Am feeder flight PA103A to London, the brown

suitcase heads on to join Pan Am Flight PA103 to New York. At Heathrow baggage in transit is handled at a separate building called the interline shed, located within the terminal complex. The suitcase is packed into a container by an airport worker, then placed in the port side forward cargo bay of the Boeing 747. As the flight begins to board, a substantial majority of the passengers – 189 out of the 243 people coming aboard – are US nationals heading home for the holidays. Accompanying them on this flight are 16 crew members.

18:25 Flight PA103 takes off and swings north towards Scotland, where it will turn west and fly on to New York. Everything seems normal as the passengers settle in for their five-hour journey. But down in the baggage hold, an ordinary-looking Toshiba radio-cassette player is packed in the brown suitcase among an unexceptional collection

of clothing. Inside the casing of the player is an electronic timer, linked to a detonator and a charge of Semtex plastic explosive, counting off pre-programmed seconds.

19:03 The bomb goes off, blowing a ragged hole in the fuselage. The plane breaks up and plummets from 9,500 m (31,000 feet). In the small Scottish town of Lockerbie, it is early evening and there are traces of rain on the streets. Suddenly a terrible hail of body parts, burst luggage and metallic fragments crashes down into its quiet evening routines. Aviation fuel from the tanks bursts into flame, igniting buildings; smaller fires are everywhere. Debris is strewn far and wide across surrounding countryside. Eleven people who live here die along with all 259 who were travelling in the aircraft – a total of 270 innocent lives wiped out.

Dawn **22 December**. A huge search begins by Scottish police investigators, lasting many months and extending over 1,360 square km (845 square miles). Tens of thousands of items are recovered and taken to a hangar in Longtown for sifting by accident investigators; part of the fuselage is painstakingly reconstructed at Farnborough in southern England. Eleven years later, two Libyans are charged: Abdel Baset Ali Mohamed Al-Megrahi, who had links to Libyan intelligence, is found guilty in 2001 and jailed for 20 years, Al Amin Khalifa Fhimah is acquitted. President Gaddafi of Libya offers $2.7 billion (£1.7 billion) to compensate victims' families in 2002, seeking an end to UN sanctions. Yet many questions remain, from weaknesses in the prosecution case to the true motives of the bombers.

Above left: A huge crater marks the site of the Lockerbie crash amid scenes of devastation.

Above right: A memorial to the 270 people who died in the Lockerbie disaster.

The country spiralled into civil war in the 1970s – a bloody conflict between leftist Arab militias and Christian Phalangists. The Palestinian Liberation Army then marched in with Syrian support, battling first against Christians, then against Muslims and Syrians. Israeli bombing raids increased sharply; an Israeli attack on a Palestinian refugee camp in 1974, followed by suspected complicity in the Lebanese Christian massacres at Sabra and Chatila camps in 1982, caused widespread Arab revulsion and led to a new upsurge of Palestinian support. In the same year the Americans arrived as peacekeepers, ushering in a new round of diplomatic shootings, car-bombings and hostage-taking. Arafat was exiled to Tunis in 1983; two years later terrorists from the Palestine Liberation Front hijacked a cruise-ship, *Achille Lauro*, to put the squeeze on Israel.

By that time another Middle Eastern minefield had opened up. The rise of Ayatollah Khomeini (1900–89) and his Islamic fundamentalist regime in Iran set the USA on a collision course with the Muslim world – an enmity based as much on religion as politics. In late 1979 almost 100 US embassy staff were taken hostage in Teheran in a bid to force the return of the Shah to face trial; then the US embassy was stormed in Pakistan. In 1980 a bold attempt to rescue the US hostages ended in disaster with a mid-air crash; soon after the SAS stormed the Iranian embassy in London and shot down the terrorists who had taken it over. The US hostages in Teheran were released in early 1981 after 444 days of captivity. However, the shady circumstances of their liberation were to erupt five years later in the 'Irangate' scandal, when it emerged that $30 million in profits from a secret arms-for-hostages deal with Iran had been diverted to help 'Contra' rebels in Nicaragua fight the left-wing Sandinista government.

So began the remorseless escalation of anti-USA hostility through the Middle East and Far East, continuing throughout the 1980s and 1990s and culminating in the emergence of Al-Qa'eda and its leader, Osama bin Laden (b.1957) – a wealthy Saudi of messianic pretensions – as the new figure of Western terrorist nightmares. In September 2001 four US domestic passenger jets were hijacked by Al-Qa'eda terrorists who had infiltrated the USA with ease and even taken flying lessons there. The hijackers flew two of the planes straight into the Twin Towers of Manhattan's World Trade Center. Those lofty symbols of US economic confidence were razed to the ground; some 3,000 people died in the fiery collapse. Another plane was used to hit the Pentagon in a separate suicidal assault, this time on the citadel of US military might. Within a month the US and its allies embarked on the destruction of the Taliban regime in Afghanistan, raining down cruise missiles on its cities and the Al-Qa'eda training camps based there; then came war on Iraq.

In its terrible way the destruction of the Twin Towers was a kind of terrorist apotheosis, exceeding the wildest dreams of those who hate the USA most. For the USA, it marked a turning point. And yet, as the nation emerges from its 'successful' war with Iraq it is getting harder to distinguish the concept of a 'just war' from that of terrorism. As the 'rules of engagement' blur, both are gradually coming to resemble different facets of a common madness, fatally entwined.

Terrorism has flourished across the world in many places – in the Indian subcontinent, from Kashmir to Sri Lanka, and other parts of Asia; in Africa, where several states have been torn apart by brutal civil wars, fuelled by a poisonous cocktail of tribal hostility and economic rapacity. Also in Latin America, where guerrillas such as the Shining Path or the Tupamaros resorted to methods of great savagery against the peasants they affected to champion. Besides, terrorism does not only come from abroad. Britain discovered this long ago; for the USA the realization came when the Oklahoma bomb went off in 1995, killing 168 people. It was planted by a 27-year-old American, Timothy McVeigh, said by the government to have been a member of a 'right-wing militia', by others to have sought revenge for the Waco massacre two years earlier. McVeigh saw himself as a hero. But in the new madness of war, there are precious few of them left.

The apocalyptic destruction of Manhattan's Twin Towers in 2001 launched the USA on a policy of direct confrontation with terrorists.

INDEX

ACKNOWLEDGEMENTS

Richard Bradley would like to thank Jane Root and the team at BBC Worldwide for commissioning the TV series and for their excitement about the idea of a history project that was deliberately international from the outset. Adam Kemp and Neil MacDonald at the BBC have shown unstinting enthusiasm for the project, and Susan Werbe at the History Channel has supported us from across the Atlantic. Most of all I would like to thank the team at Lion Television, regrettably too numerous to mention by name: an outstanding team of researchers, directors and producers who have shown remarkable commitment and resourcefulness and wrestled with the ambition of this idea, and against the odds brought it to successful fruition.

PICTURE CREDITS